Fables for the Patriarchs

Fables for the Patriarchs

Gender Politics in Tang Discourse

Jowen R. Tung

ROWMAN & LITTLEFIELD PUBLISHERS, INC.
Lanham • Boulder • New York • Oxford

ROWMAN & LITTLEFIELD PUBLISHERS, INC.

Published in the United States of America
by Rowman & Littlefield Publishers, Inc.
4720 Boston Way, Lanham, Maryland 20706
http://www.rowmanlittlefield.com

12 Hid's Copse Road
Cumnor Hill, Oxford OX2 9JJ, England

British Library Cataloguing in Publication Information Available

Library of Congress Cataloging-in-Publication Data

Tung, Jowen R.
　Fables for the patriarchs : gender politics in Tang discourse / Jowen R. Tung.
　　p.　　cm.
　Includes bibliographical references (p.　　) and index.
　ISBN 0-8476-9512-3 (alk. paper). — ISBN 0-8476-9513-1 (pbk. : alk. paper)
　　1. Women—China—Social conditions.　2. Sex role—China—History.
3. Patriarchy—China—History.　4. China—Social conditions—221 B.C–960
A.D.　5. China—Civilization—221 B.C–960 A.D.　I. Title.
HQ1767.T86　2000
305.3′0951—dc21　　　　　　　　　　　　　　　　　　　　99-16335
　　　　　　　　　　　　　　　　　　　　　　　　　　　　　　CIP
Printed in the United States of America

⊗ ™ The paper used in this publication meets the minimum requirements of
American National Standard for Information Sciences—Permanence of Paper for
Printed Library Materials, ANSI Z39.48–1992.

for my female ancestors:
unnamed heroes of pain
brave women with bound feet
shapers of a great tradition
who have perished
in an irrevocable past

Contents

Preface   xi

Acknowledgments   xv

INTRODUCTION: The Tang Paradoxes   1
    Emergence of a New Ethics   4
    From the Periphery to the Center   10
    The Inflation of Words and the Rise of the Literati   13
    Transfigurations and Use of Buddhism   14
    Earthly Heaven of Religious Taoism   17
    Representations of Tang Women   19

PART ONE: Imperial Discourse and Its Discontent

CHAPTER 1: The Dragon's Ministers   25
    Configuration of the Palace   26
    The Minister-Concubine Complex   30
    The Use of History   40
    Among Themselves   42

CHAPTER 2: Fate of the Imperial Daughters   45
    The Emperor's Knife   46
    Desires as Transference   47
    Princesses Canonized   49
    Pawns to the Barbarians   50
    The Chastisement   53

CHAPTER 3: Monument without Inscription:
The Case of Wu Zhao   57
    Cruelty   59
    The Use of Omens and Sutra   61
    Passions   64

Monument without Inscription   67
The Erasure of History   69

CHAPTER 4: Sacrificial Lamb: The Case of Yang Yuhuan   **73**
The Sacrifice   76
The Woman   77
The Mythical Body   78

PART TWO: Internal Split of the Imperial Subjects

CHAPTER 5: The Making and Unmaking of Confucian Wives   **83**
Women According to Legal Codes   86
Fragmentation, Abstraction, and Desexualization: Women According to
  Historians   88
Survival Handbooks: A Metaphysics for Women   91
The Battlefield of Home   94
The Radical Virtue of Jealousy   97

CHAPTER 6: Problematics of Male Desires   **101**
Dilemma of the Desirable Literati   103
Inner Split of Male Desires   106
Loneliness of the Literati   108

CHAPTER 7: Icons of Flesh   **113**
A High Drama at the High Tang   114
Unequal Transaction of Words   115
Inscriptions on the Body   117
Freedom from the Periphery   120

PART THREE: Self-Representation of the Tang

CHAPTER 8: Logic of the Unconscious   **125**
I. Logic of the Tang Narrative   125
II. Submission of the Feminine   132

CHAPTER 9: Desire against Decorum   **143**
Explanation of a Jealousy   143
A Courtesan's Desire   145
A Further Split of the Text   146

CHAPTER 10: In Feminine Voice   **151**
Boudoir Lament of the Literati   151
An Allegorical Beauty   153
The Supreme Object of Desire   155
Writing for the Silenced   158
A Double Absence   163

Mythical Solitude   165
Coda: Return of the Voyeur   166

CHAPTER 11: Literati in Love: The Case of Li Shangyin   **169**

PART FOUR: Resurrected Voices

CHAPTER 12: The Shaping of Female Tradition   **179**
Conditions of the Female Tradition   180
The Eating of Books   182
The Anti-Sun Myth of the Moon   185
Gaze of the Bronze Mirror   187
A Counter Dialectic   192
La Femme Écriture   194

CHAPTER 13: Against Boudoir Lament   **199**
Political Allegory of the Feminine   199
In Masculine Voice   202
A Woman Alone: Against Boudoir Lament   205
Death of a Courtesan   210

Epilogue   **215**

Notes   **219**

Glossary   **245**

Index   **249**

About the Author   **255**

Preface

As we turn a new page in the magnificent history of human civilization, one thing at least remains certain: with all the trafficking of postcolonial discourse, the East remains dominated, both in its physical outlook and its unconscious, by the West. For both the colonized and the colonizers, although apparently for very different reasons, speaking across cultural boundaries is understood as a necessity—for the colonized, it is in fact an inescapable fate. Applying the ever-evolving Western theories to one's tradition has thus become normative in the practice of cultural critique for non-Western intellectuals. Writing from Hong Kong, the just-healing scar of a model colony, exemplary in its ingrained servitude coupled with a partial loss of memories, this necessity is felt with a painful urgency. This is a predicament I must come to terms with: in order to engage in a cross-cultural dialogue, however confined it may be, I borrow not just the richness of Western discourse, but its now invincible language of structured precision.

For every woman who has learned the injustice that her female ancestors had endured, the injustice that continues to shape the destiny of her contemporaries, feminism does not carry with it a cultural boundary. Here, the predicament becomes strength. At a time when feminism is suffering from internal quarrels, when this last movement of human emancipation stands in unhappy contradiction with the postmodernist climate, a critique of one of the world's most ancient patriarchies might yet infuse it with recharged vitality and remind us of the original goals of this far from completed project. By a strange decree, the deprived and the dispossessed now converge. Both China and feminism are moving belatedly in the quickly evolving modern world; because of this belatedness, their agendas of the search for subjectivity are threatened to be rendered outmoded in the general milieu of radical indeterminacy. When feminism and China converge at this historical juncture, however, the imminent crisis of contemporary cultures is exposed under fresh insight, demanding careful reconsideration of modernity and its premises.

As an effort to join the ongoing feminist critique of patriarchal mechanisms, this study offers a viable strategy for a rethinking of Chinese traditions. Of the predominant feminist pursuits, the present thesis's immediate concern is with the following: an analysis of the patriarchal mechanisms of oppression; a critique of the masculinizing progress of civilization; the building of a female tradition; and a critique of the dualism of masculinity versus femininity that damages both genders. Envisioning an emancipation of women through which men will also be liberated is an integral part of feminism that has not been sufficiently understood. In the light of the Chinese cultural construct, this vision is particularly important and provides the grounding for a significant part of my argument. Such a vision renders feminist cultural critique relevant to all, thereby lifting it out of the ghetto it is prone to be ascribed to.

While the transformation of sexual configurations in recent decades presents women and men with the possibility of liberating themselves from congealed gender definitions, an inequity between the sexes persists. After two centuries of struggles that bear important records of women's rage and courage, that break new ground for future generations, feminism nevertheless has been co-opted into the self-regenerating apparatus of the patriarchal system and inadvertently has become one of its many embellishments in this age of emancipation. With a grave sense of alarm, we come to realize that after all the vigorous critiques and cries of anger, patriarchy stands intact. And as patriarchy moves all too quickly into this postmodernist/postcolonial stage, it threatens to make feminism, a collective movement of the belated sex, obsolete.

It is with an acute awareness of this encroaching impasse that I turn to Tang China (618–907), an epoch to which modern Chinese often turn with a sense of nostalgia. An era considered the epitome of imperial China, the Tang's gender politics has important cultural implications and deserves careful examination. As perpetrators and alleged beneficiaries of patriarchal laws, Tang elite dominated the cultural scene and were responsible for delineating the shape of the Tang heritage. Precisely because of this, their psychological complexities under the shadow of the despotic machine are enlightening for a feminist critique of the era.

My concern for such cultural critique springs from a general despair among modern Chinese intellectuals, who since the nineteenth century have oscillated between self-hate and self-aggrandization in the face of an eloquent Western civilization. Seeking salvation from the wisdom of the West, they try to arrive at a diagnosis of a culture forced to accept the truth of its debility in its disastrous confrontation with the West. An excruciating introspection comes to characterize their writings, in which an ancient civilization is put under severe scrutiny. In a struggle to "modernize the traditional," Western values from science to democracy are hailed as absolute, while from realism to romanticism, from modernism to postmodernism, Western trends are swallowed without adequate reflection, which results in an ill consumption. In an urgent pursuit of cultural transformation, individual enlightenment is superseded by national demands, and the burden of an ailing state weighs heavily on its people. Driven by a sense of belatedness and swept along by the changing West, China moves along the high road of progress with its logic of the masculine, continuing, even heroically, with its historical downfall.

As the feminists' full-fledged attack has brought patriarchal politics under fire, it dawns on us that a civilization that builds itself upon the alienation of half of its population suffers inevitably a grave sickness. Without claiming that the oppression of women contributes to China's cultural crisis (although this was precisely the proposition of many late Qing and Republican intellectuals), I wish somehow to find the relation between such oppression and the decline of Chinese cultural vitality through investigating the historical positioning of women. For this purpose, I have chosen the rethinking and rewriting of the Tang through a feminist reading of its sociopolitical and literary discourses. My purpose is threefold. First, to present the problematics of ethical codification and its damaging effect on both genders. Second, to bring insight into sexuality as defined by the state and its profound influence on the shaping of Chinese cultures. Third, to search for a female consciousness in the belief that Tang women were apprehensive about the patriarchal constitution of meanings and power. To deconstruct patriarchal politics by exposing its desires and frustrations, to search for a female tradition by surfacing the unconscious, and to question gender politics that eradicate both male and female subjectivity are the goals toward which this work steadily steers.

Aside from witnessing the sole woman emperor in Chinese history, the Tang is considered an era in which women exhibited brilliant vitality. However, it was inevitable that Tang women were equally bound up in gender ideologies as well as in the intricate play between repression and resistance. This countermovement is unraveled through a careful reading of various discourses, which include imperial memorials, official histories, legal and ethical codes, social documents such as tombstone inscriptions and contracts from Dunhuang, literary writings such as narratives and poetry, and miscellaneous records. These various texts expose the desire and its discontent suffered by both the subjects and the objects, as they struggled against the machinery of power and the deployment of sexuality. How this struggle between power and resistance reached for a delicate balance in the relatively liberal Tang is scrutinized.

In an empire that built itself partly upon the objectification of women to keep the male "sane," partly upon the ethics that positioned each squarely in a strictly defined social hierarchy, all fell into a prescribed position. While women were stationed in the household and were defined by suffocating domesticity, men were equally caught up in a state politics that subsumed them under the hovering shadow of the monarch, exacting from them not only loyalty, but intellectual servitude and sexual restraint. The latter entails a peculiar condition: the canons enforcing female subjection were in fact drawn by a certain group of men who had themselves lost control of the self. Caught in the nets of the despotic state and invested in the despot's overcoding machine, their desires suffered inexplicable constraints beyond normal understanding.

* * *

The fables at the beginning of some chapters are my own creations, most of them drawn from concepts pertinent to the chapter. As the title of this book suggests, these fables are for the patriarchs (and is not every man a patriarch of his home?) who fashioned (and ironically fell victim to) an injustice that spanned more than two millennia. By addressing the fables to them, rather than to my female ancestors, I try to expose the wounds they dealt to themselves with their double-edged knives, a most wretched plight. An invitation is thus extended for a self-searching reflection from their male descendants. These parables, as intensified abstraction and lyrical reverberation of the analytical sections, open up the space and are my attempt at breaking away from a discourse weighed down by the logic of the masculine, the logos without the body.

Although my debt to Western theories is immense, I have relegated them to the references as a way of avoiding subjugating this study of an ancient empire under the modern instrument of the West. It is also one gesture of the implicitly colonized to disguise her plight. I would like to acknowledge here my debts to the late Foucault, whose theory on the field of discourse and power has changed the scenery of modern scholarship and given shape to this study. The deconstructionist move throughout the book is inspired by Derrida, whose influence on me goes back a long way. Of the many feminists to whom my allegiance is passionate, I am especially indebted to the French feminists, chief among them Luce Irigaray, whose acute understanding of woman's position in relation to language shatters all self-delusions and makes our efforts all the more vital.

This study is dedicated to my female ancestors, whose strength and agony pass down to me like an engulfing river, and force me to write, to envision them into being, so as to amend for a waste, a collective sacrifice the scope of which is not to be measured.

Acknowledgments

It is now time to give thanks. During my long years of odyssey in the States, many have shown generosity for one away from her natural habitat, and there are moments and people that will always stay with me. For people at the State University at Albany and at Cornell University, their significance in shaping my future course is well recognized.

During the process of thinking through as well as writing the dissertation from which the present book developed, I was supported by many whose judgment and breadth of knowledge are beyond the confines of my still-formative scholarship at Columbia University. To Professor Paul Rouzer whose meticulous comments charted me to a sound course, I am greatly indebted. Professor Bob Hymes's range of interests sustained this study, and the many excited conversations with him further chiseled and led to its fruition. Professor Haruo Shirane, whose support at the critical stage of my study is fondly remembered, has opened up to me the perspective of Japanese Heian women who are worthy of comparison to Tang women. Professor David Wang, whose perspective of a modern Chinese intellectual was indispensable for readjusting my approaches, brought the original manuscript to a far more succinct form.

In my deeply inspired years in New York, I wish to thank faithful friends Kanja Lee, Hazune Takagana, Hsiao Yongqiang and Wong Bohua, Yu Minling, Hsu Xianglin, and David Kamen and Hengding—together we ventured through a great city without coming out empty-handed. To Yang Hsien-ching I owe a special thanks for his unwavering patience. It was he who brought me to the States; to complete the journey, however, I must put up my own efforts. I also wish to thank Yu Xingzhong for sharing with me complex feelings for a tradition with which we engaged in an ambivalent agon, and for bringing China home to me together with Liang Zhiping and many Chinese dissidents, chief among them Su Wei, who made my first journey to China unforgettable.

In the Division of Humanities at Hong Kong University of Science and Technology, I am tremendously lucky to be surrounded by affectionate friends such as Huishu Lee, Yip Kam-ming, Wong Xinyang, Angelina Yee, Karl Kao, Flora Fu, and Taksing Kam, who have all helped me in their generous ways and made the academic environment enjoyable. For students in my graduate seminars, I thank them for thinking through the issues with me with their young, lively minds.

I cannot thank Arif Dirlik enough for, out of sheer kindness, bringing this book to light. If not for him, the manuscript would still be lying in the dust. It was he who reminded me of its existence and the significance I once attached to it, and encouraged me through the final revisions with reassuring words.

I was supported by a grant from Chiang Ching-kuo Cultural Foundation during 1991–1992, which took me on a trip to China that was long due. Professor Pauline Yu brought me to Columbia University, which supported me without fail throughout the years. For the years 1995 and 1996, I received a Direct Allocation Grant from Hong Kong University of Science and Technology, which sponsored my further research and revision of the book.

Most importantly, I wish to thank my anonymous reader for her unreserved endorsement, my editors Susan McEachern and Karen Johnson for their warm support, and Jane McGarry for her meticulous efforts at copyediting the manuscript.

In the city of New York, I was blessed with the companionship of Virginia Hardman, a noble guardian and kindred spirit, whose invincible presence and courage made my American experience profoundly endearing. Both in my final years in the States and back in Asia, I had the rare fortune of having Shi Zuocheng as my dear philosopher, who reveals to me a sphere beyond the bondage of language and a feminism that questions the direction of human civilization. With him, a spiritual home is located; as we were neighbors in a foreign city on the boisterous Broadway, the idea of a shifting home is understood not without a sense of gratitude.

It is to my devoted brothers and sister and my loving parents that I wish to express the deepest gratitude. Long years of waiting and disappointment did not erode their trust in a wayward, undeserving sibling and daughter, and the self-sacrificing love from my parents constitutes the most solid, unchanging part of my life. All my books are inherently dedicated to them, for, as the gypsies say, life is for returning undeletable debts.

Introduction

The Tang Paradoxes

In a rare document, a Japanese monk named Ennin recounts his travel through the Tang empire between the years 838 and 847, as he observed the people and customs of an empire that was the vibrant center of all of Asia.[1] In episodes that are often altogether absent from regular Tang documents, Ennin presents unflattering images of the empire. Descriptions of the shrewd or miserly sides of the folks, widespread famine caused by locusts, and hair-raising imperial cruelty alternate with tales of stunning events and monotonous routines. A crude picture of the Tang empire unfolded as the monk went deep into the land considered the second home of Buddhism. With the refreshing perspective of a foreigner, Ennin's observations reveal realities that are at times more telling than the sum of official Tang discourse.

The Japanese monk's traumatic pilgrimage ended abruptly during Emperor Wuzong's (840-846) relentless proscription of Buddhism; Ennin fled China with his companions, leaving behind thousands of distraught monks and nuns who were forced to return to mundane order, with the properties and slaves of monasteries confiscated and numerous Buddhist icons lying in ruins. The massive doses of secularization were part of the manifestation of the empire's growing hostility toward foreign influence, which gained momentum after the An Lushan rebellion and reached its peak around the year 800. The purge of Buddhism was wrought with political and economic rationales and embodied a more fundamental change of cultural milieu.

Ennin's pilgrimage and its disastrous end are symbolic of the glory and demise of the Tang; witnessed by a foreign monk, this historical necessity is brought close to us with tangible details. As we begin our examination of the era, the diary serves as an apt warning that there are as many facets of an era as there are perspectives. The particularly palpable anecdotes documented here show how deceived we can be if we rely solely on texts written by Tang subjects, who somehow were not free to present their times from a sobering distance, when their personal destinies were deeply bound up with the fate of a despotic empire whose overcontrolling machine encompassed all desires and frustrated attempts at closer scrutiny.

1

Tang woodblock print of a Buddhist *dhârani* wheel talisman.

From *Zhongguo gu banhua.*

In the second scroll of the diary, Ennin describes his ecstasy at entering Mt. Wutai, the legendary holy land for Buddhist devotees.

> Before entering the cloister we saw toward the northwest the central terrace, and, bowing to the ground, we worshipped it. This then is the region of Monjushiri. . . . On looking at the [five summits] from afar, our tears flowed involuntarily. The trees and strange flowers are unlike those anywhere else, and it is a most unusual region.[2]

This tearful description echoes one of Ennin's letters, composed in the early days of his pilgrimage, which requested official credentials to "wander and beg as destiny permits":

> We monks . . . have come from afar to this benevolent land with our hearts set on sacred places and our spirits rejoicing in the pilgrimage. It is said that Mt. [Wutai] and some other places are the source of the teaching and the places where the great saints have manifested themselves. . . . We monks have admired these glorious places, and having chanced to meet with this happy destiny, have by good fortune come to this holy land. Now we wish to go to these places to fulfill our long-cherished hopes.[3]

This humble tone reminds us that at its zenith, Tang China was the center of a cosmopolitan civilization, emitting a brilliance that attracted people from all over Asia. With its many sanctuaries, illustrious masters, and famous sites of pilgrimage, the Tang stood like a magnet, alluring monks who traveled long distances to seek wisdom and blessing from it. It was also an economic center, with all sorts of commodities trafficked in prosperous cities, drawing merchants from all over. On the streets of the capital Chang'an walked Turks, Uighurs, Tibetans, Koreans, Persians, Arabs, Indians, and people from Khotan, Kucha, and Kashmir. Their foreign customs, music, and exotic goods contributed to a boisterous atmosphere and were woven into the rich textile of Tang culture. The empire was indeed the destination of not only Buddhist but cultural pilgrimages, when scholars from Japan and Korea came to learn the Chinese rites and characters, among other inventions, that would cast lasting influence on their national cultures.

Yet as the diary unfolds and as Ennin moved to the capital Chang'an, an ignoble Tang emerged to expose its irrational mechanism of bureaucracy with its absurd and frustrating obstacles, and at the center of everything, a brutal monarch. In an episode that seems to come straight out of Kafka's parables, Ennin records the fatal whim of Emperor Wuzong amid the building of an ostentatious Taoist terrace.

> The Emperor . . . ordered the two armies to build a terrace of the immortals in the Palace 150 feet high. It was started in the Tenth Moon, and each day he had three thousand legionaries of the Left and Right Armies of Inspired Strategy transport earth to build it. The Emperor earnestly desired to have it constructed quickly, and there were daily edicts urging on the construction. The General Supervisors of the two armies held sticks and oversaw [the work]. When the Emperor went to inspect it . . .

[he] told them, "We do not want you to hold sticks. . . . You yourselves should be carrying earth." . . . Later the Emperor went again to the place . . . and drew a bow and for no reason shot one of the General Supervisors, which was a most unprincipled act.[4]

This unusual account, together with Wuzong's annihilation of Buddhism, embodies the anticlimax of Ennin's pilgrimage. With an increasingly debilitated Tang empire, the central government gave way to the autonomous military regions; chaos broke out with incessant upheavals, and the empire fell into an abyss of blood and double treason. The following was recounted by Ennin during the Liu Congjian rebellion.

> The soldiers, fearing [the Imperial wrath], seized the herdsmen and farmers of the border region and sent them to the capital, claiming that they were captured rebels. The Emperor gave ceremonial swords, and right in the streets [the prisoners] were cut into three pieces. . . . The slaughtered corpses constantly littered the roads, while their blood flowed forth and soaked the ground, turning it into mud. Spectators filled the roads, and the Emperor from time to time came to see, and there was a great profusion of banners and spears.[5]

This, then, is what the holy land had come to; the sacred sites for which the pilgrim toiled and labored were shattered to pieces and the gold of Buddhist icons melted to cast sacrilegious coins. This grand self-dismantling provides an indispensable channel for us to gain insight into the Tang, revealing as it were an inverted darkness that sheds foreboding light on our study. It is not accidental that the present study of the golden era in Chinese history should open with such disheartening accounts from a disillusioned foreigner, for the Tang stands with all its complexities and dark secrets, luring us into its labyrinth of victory and defeat. As such, it promises gratification and at the same time delivers inevitable frustrations, its truth buried deep within layers of paradoxes. A foreigner's diary, then, serves as a luminous mirror for this feminist reading of a great empire of the patriarchs, both the foreigner and the woman gazing at the empire as perpetual outsiders, fated pilgrims.

EMERGENCE OF A NEW ETHICS

The Han empire (206 B.C.–220 A.D.), which embodied the twin peaks of Chinese civilization together with the Tang, was the first empire that brought China to long years of unified prosperity. With its centralized material brilliance and expanding territory, the Han coerced literati into composing flashy rhymed prose, the representative literary genre of the time, that vents itself in praising the lustrous palaces, lush imperial gardens, and gallant hunts with excessive embellishment, exhibiting at the same time the sexual self-constraint of the ministers in the face of a sexually monopolizing monarch. Moral advice steals into the prose with subdued, ambiguous tone, pointing both to an ossified literary convention and the subservient character of the courtiers, and the moral admonishment is absorbed into flattery in an underhanded way. One could stress that the rhymed prose, together with the eclipse of the courtiers' autonomy, was contemporaneous with the birth of the authoritarian state. Never before had literature served the Son of Heaven with such humble submission; with this exercise, the relation between the all-encompassing state and the literati entered a new phase.

Half a millennium later, after a long period of division and the lavish liberation of individual energies in the Six Dynasties (317–589), a powerful Tang empire emerged to bring the literati again under its wings. This time, although the proliferation of literary writings forbade overt political utilization of any one genre, in the stylized prose one can detect a pervasive anxiety fermenting under the overarching power of the state, and a great portion of the literati's energy was spent on entering officialdom and, subsequently, on serving the empire. In *Quan Tang wen* (The complete collection of Tang prose composition), amid numerous elaborate memorials composed to persuade, dissuade, or plead to the emperor and discussions on state affairs written for civil service examinations, are many letters addressed to friends and acquaintances that offered mutual comfort as one took leave of the capital after failing the state examinations, or upon being banished to mortally harmful regions. The fate of each individual clearly lay in the hands of the state, and with an acute awareness of this plight, Tang literati expressed bitterness, resignation, or compliance variously, each according to his temperament and, more importantly, his changing fortunes.

Han Yu, a famous essayist and the foremost guardian of orthodoxy who proposed a return to traditional Confucianism, bid farewell in such a letter to Li Yuan upon the latter's return to his hermitage.

> These are Yuan's words: "I know what people call a great man. . . . He is one who sits in the court, works with the ministers, and assists the Son of Heaven in giving out commands. . . . His robe flows in the air, his long sleeves concealed, his face powdered white and his eyebrows jade black. He lives in his mansion in leisure, and is jealous of those favored by the lord and full of self-conceit; he competes with other beauties and vies for his lord's patronage. A great man being appreciated by the Son of Heaven— it is for those who aim at the mundane world. I do not escape from it out of resentment; rather, I am fated not to attain it."[6]

The prevalent epochal consciousness is presented here in a nutshell. Continuing with the tradition of Han court poets, the Tang literati's existence to a large extent was defined against the will of the state. This condition is further manifested in Han Yu's political theory, which registers a regression to the later Confucian Xunzi and deviates considerably from Mencius, Han's professed prototype, in its unconditional acceptance of the supremacy of the monarch.[7]

Han places the lord and the courtiers in a binary opposition, with the ruler managing people's livelihoods and the ministers receiving reverently his teachings. In his famous "Yuan Tao" (The origin of the Tao), Han states:

> Hence the lord is one who gives order. The minister is one who transmits the law of the lord to the people. The people are those who present corns, rice, silk and make vessels and commerce and serve those above.

Failing their assigned missions, the lord then "fails as the lord," while the ministers and the people, according to Han's indictment, are to be executed. The asymmetrical verdicts expose Han's betrayal of Mencius's original challenge of the despot's weight over the people, while his definitions of the ministers' and the people's separate roles place them in absolute passivity. Writing in the early stages of Tang's decline, Han represents the voice of the orthodox, steeped in total surrender to the despotic state.

The challenge to such a subservient mentality came from the sacrilegious Liu Zongyuan, who questions the metaphysical basis of the rule of the Son of Heaven, rendering the much-revered concept of heaven's mandate obsolete. By advocating the conception of ministers as the independent vessels of Tao, Liu reverses Han's submission and returns to the original Confucian proposition of the serving of the state as the moral burden of an intellectual.[8] However, Liu's tormented life in a treacherous district versus Han's escalating reputation attests to the prevalent moral climate of the time. This carefully packaged submissive frame of mind is a far cry from the nonconformist mentality of the iconoclastic Six Dynasties, separated from the Tang by the short-lived Sui Dynasty (581–617). Characterized by a taste for spontaneity, a horror of conventions, and contempt for rites, the troubled period of division marked by political apathy provided fertile ground for the cultivation of independence of mind, for a kind of aestheticism that manifested itself not only in poetry and landscape paintings, but also in exuberant individualities. While the strongly sinicized northern empires of the Western Wei (535–57) and Northern Zhou (557–81) provided Sui and Tang with political, social, ethnic, and cultural foundations, and the reunion of North and South China was prepared during the whole of the sixth century by the exchange of merchandise and ideas, these continuities between the aristocratic Sui and Tang and the divided Six Dynasties should be juxtaposed to a drastic shift in consciousness.

The different mentalities between the two periods can be observed through comparing a classic presentation of the Six Dynasties, *Shishuo xinyu* (New words from the contemporary), by Liu Yiqing, with *Da Tang xinyu* (New words from the great Tang), a private history by Liu Su, which is modeled after the earlier work. Famous for its flamboyant rebels and poet hermits, the Six Dynasties appears in Liu Yiqing's work as an era that appreciated individuality with a vision bordering on the metaphysical. By contrast, with its principle of categorization, the Tang text exemplifies a different sensibility in which an emphasis on political and ethical merit takes precedence, replacing the earlier text's aesthetic appreciation of individuality as manifest by unusual male physical beauty or sheer eccentricity. A didactic tendency shaped by a court-centered mentality dominates in the later work; the majority of recorded individuals are bureaucrats engaged in state affairs, and the multiplicity of character types in the earlier text, together with its daring defiance of decorum, disappears.

Although the Tang historian Liu Zhiji's original *Shi tong* (The generalities on history), with its recharged historiography emphasizing factual precision, appeared on the scene, in terms of the structuring of official histories, the Tang remained trapped in the dynastic historiography carved out by the Later Han historian Ban Gu's *Han Shu* (The Han history). Ban's seminal work constitutes a significant deviation from the nonprescriptive conception of human lives proposed by the great historian Sima Qian of the Former Han. Sima Qian's masterpiece, *Shi ji* (The book of history), lays down the foundation of Chinese historiography, in which brave assassins with an acute sense of honor and folks of all walks in life appear on the same historical stage with kings and noblemen. By contrast, both in its principle of categorization and its ideology, the dynastic history fashioned by Ban Gu focuses on court events and activities, with each individual positioned squarely within imperial order. In histories of previous dynasties compiled by Tang historians, and in Tang official histories compiled in the Five Dynasties (907–960) (*Jiu Tang shu,* Old Tang history) and in the Song (960–1279) (*Xing Tang shu,* New Tang history), imperial hierarchy is strictly followed.[9] As a consequence, a state-sanctioned moral conception dominated official presentations of the Tang.

Delimited by an agenda fraught with imperial ideologies, the images we have of Tang subjects from both private and official historical documents are thus at a far remove from images of prominent figures in the Six Dynasties, who guarded vehemently their self-definitions against the orthodox. They also deviate from characters presented by Sima Qian, whose love for action and freedom from perceived values present us with a time alive with diverse possibilities. The turbulent social structures of the pre-Han era, epitomized by the Warring States (403–221 B.C.), may explain the juxtaposition of diverse character types from the assassins and merchants to the courtier-fools in *The Book of History,* which in itself stands against the mentality of contemporary court poets preoccupied with composing rhymed prose. The rigorous compartmentalization and the predominant ethical-political themes of the Tang texts, however, are clearly underlain as much by transformed social circumstances as by overarching state ideologies. With the founding of a powerful empire that quickly set out to expand its territory and build itself through reorganized bureaucracies, a jealously guarded sense of hierarchy moved in.

This image of the Tang fails to correspond with the general impression of the era as marked by lush creativity and extravagant inclusiveness, whose absorption of foreign cultures and customs was extensive. One senses a discrepancy between the identification of the epoch with an open-mindedness that gave imagination and the most audacious drives free rein, and its presentation in historical discourse as overdetermined by political hierarchy. It is in literary writings, rather, especially in narrative and poetry together with other miscellaneous notes, that the Tang which evokes until now a profound cultural nostalgia presents itself more forcefully.

The vivid figures of Taoist and Buddhist cults, the hermits who appear in the histories as rare counterexamples to the state-oriented elite, are joined in more private modes of discourse by magicians, witches, esoteric entertainers, women of varied talents and characters, cunning criminals, self-made warriors, and resourceful entrepreneurs. Furthermore, the basic contour of Tang cultures drawn by these private records reveals for us some major concerns of people living in medieval China, which are of a different character than those ordained by imperial ideologies imbued with Confucian morals. What comes to the fore in popular consciousness is an obsession with financial and political success, which converged on the obsession with the state examinations. In major cities such as Chang'an, Luoyang (the eastern capital), and Yangzhou (a prosperous southern city of commerce), the high concentration of pompous mansions and the display of endless silk, beguiling entertainers, and gallant horses constantly stimulated the senses. In miscellaneous writings, wealth with its grandiose display often reached mysterious dimensions and was intensely admired by urban folks. The purchase of official posts further created affiliations between wealth and political glory, and while merchants with astonishing resources intimidated members of royalty, high officials ventured to join the business venue.

The unprecedented prestige of the old clans who embodied the noble heritage from the Six Dynasties also rendered "names" associated with social status and refinement keenly coveted. In the marriage market where women were trafficked together with household heritage and family properties, these old clans (including the Wang, Lu, Zheng, Cui, and Li clans of various regions) posed a strong attraction to the gentry, overriding even the desirability of the royal Li clan. Wealth, nobility, and political glory: these then were prominent obsessions in the aristocratic Tang. When cumbersome moral pursuits and the defiant bent lost their Archimedean point, the imperial subjects turned and invested their energies in pursuing the most visible goals at hand.

Apart from the material and the political, general concerns at the time included the Taoist quest for immortality; the irony of history; the erratic doings of fate (which typically involved the downfall of the powerful and the ascent of the outcasts in the archetypal overnight glory brought by the examinations); language as belles lettres (another interest tied in with the phenomenal weight placed on the examinations); knowledge of others and of the self; anthropomorphism; and the fate of deserted women. These obsessions, which appear repeatedly in Tang miscellaneous writings, provide a basis for an understanding of its sociocultural milieu, counterbalancing the hegemonious ideology in imperial discourse and court-centered private histories.

*   *   *

In a more schematic framework, five things stand out in the sociocultural climate of Tang China. First, the Tartar blood of the imperial Li clan and its affiliation with the tribes at the borders provided the ground for the integration of intersecting foreign cultures. Tang emperors enjoyed the unique status as the Heavenly Khan (*Tian kehan*), the highest chief ordained collectively by the nomads, with the right to oversee affairs among the tribes. At its heyday, the Tang was an empire with colonies scattered around its expanding kingdom. This political privilege contributed to its sociocultural makeup and influenced the formation of an unusual site of dynamic cultural cohesion.

Second, the entrenchment of the civil service examinations and a contagious admiration for belles lettres gave rise to the literati elite. The pursuit of wealth and glory converged in the general populace's invested interest in the examinations, which points further to a collective surrender of intellectual autonomy to the calculated give-and-take of the state. Through an invincible design, the state solicited learned men to its service, until it became the sole channel for intellectual self-fulfillment, while ambitions and anxieties began to gnaw at scholars, who directed much energy toward passing the exams. Intertwined with this weight placed upon the examinations was the Confucian mission of correcting the world through performance as public vessels, serving the Son of Heaven who was ordained by Heaven's mandate.[10] This moral burden is apparent in the prose compositions, where painstaking efforts at acquiring the Confucian classics without material or political rewards in sight are repeatedly stated. However, it was clear that what the examinations promised had insidiously redefined the Confucian mores.

Third, the craze for Buddhism, and its Chinese transformations, culminated in the creation of Zen Buddhism. Preaching the renunciation of the worldly, Buddhism enjoyed an enthusiastic following throughout the turbulent Six Dynasties and continued well into the Tang, when solemn ceremonies such as the moving of the bones of Sakyamuni brought mass hysteria, as gentle folks squandered their possessions and burned their arms and hair in religious rapture. Such irrational faith in a foreign idol was severely criticized by Han Yu, vanguard of "original" Confucian values, as the empire closed in on itself at the turn of the ninth century. The true resistance to and transformation of Buddhist renunciation, however, were to be realized in the invention of Zen (*Chan* in Chinese), which infused not only a transfigured insight into Buddhism, but a new sense of aesthetics.

Fourth, state-sanctioned Taoism enjoyed unprecedented imperial patronage. With its elaborate rituals and its cult of immortals echoing the state bureaucratic structure, religious Taoism made an essential contribution to the heterogeneous climate of the era, providing its lush rituals and folklore to the already rich sociocultural tapestry of the Tang. As Ennin's account manifests, Taoism was in constant battle with Buddhism, with abbots of both orders summoned to engage themselves in prolonged debate in front of the despot. A mundane Taoism against the unworldly Buddhism—it was perhaps inevitable that their coexistence would end in the dramatic crash of the destruction of Buddhism in an empire overflowing with earthly desires.

In each of these phenomena, women played a particular role. Famed for its liberated female energies, the Tang witnessed a spectrum of shrewd wives, cunning witches, spoiled princesses, versatile courtesans, and wayward Taoist priestesses. The spectacular outburst of wifely jealousy further testifies to a female consciousness unbound by regulating ethics. The high value of the old clans' daughters in the marriage market and the ascension of the woman emperor Wu Zhao certainly infused heightened confidence in Tang women. A comparison of the handbooks for Confucian wives written separately during the Han and the Tang further shows the later era's lapse of control in terms of women's domesticity and wifely virtues.

However, there is a curious discrepancy among the images of women presented in different discourses, and their self-presentations in poetry further depart from the general image of noninhibition. To fully understand this discrepancy, we must consider the inner split of female selves and the dangerous separation of the ideal women perceived in male desires from the much more complex existence of flesh-and-blood women. As the empire moved to its final stage, its grip on women tightened, and its strength and weakness posed an inverted symmetry with the rise and fall of female vitality. As we extrapolate various texts, the truth of Tang women becomes increasingly blurred, and the myth of its liberated women requires careful reconsideration.

All the phenomena above are entangled with degrees of complexities, and inherent in them are intriguing paradoxes that force us to rethink their cultural significance. As an effort toward structuring a feminist cultural critique within the context of traditional China, this study begins by unraveling these paradoxes to arrive at a more profound understanding of the Tang. In the process, some of the era's long-standing myths may be dispelled, and the most glorious period of our past is revealed to us with all its pathos and inherent contradictions.

FROM THE PERIPHERY TO THE CENTER

The aristocratic Li clan, with Tartar blood on its maternal side and steeped in tribal customs and heritage inherited from the non-Chinese Northern Dynasties (420–589), had a taste for military affairs, and its members were talented with horse breeding and archery. The gallant first emperors and their general-ministers who fought bravely in the battles demonstrated rare physical vigor. With the characteristic confidence of the strong, the royal members opened the gate for foreign influences and daring customs. The later era's criticism of its lack of propriety reveals precisely how far China has regressed from the less inhibited Tang.[11] In the capitals of Chang'an and Luoyang, an explosion of energies extended invitations to foreigners and their diverse ambitions, and memories of the era refer to the many foreign merchants and versatile entertainers who roamed the streets and wine shops of great cities. The empire had a comprehensive appetite for foreign cultures: from religions to music and dance, from exotic fashion to funky hairdos, the fusion of cultures resulted in a sumptuous fruition of art and literature, at the center of which was the fervent crowning of Buddhism, a decidedly foreign religion.

Receiving foreign guests. Mural painting in Prince Zhang Huai's tomb.

From *Li Xian mu Li Chongrun mu bihua.*

The strategic moves toward its tribal neighbors and the internalization of foreign influences were the font of the empire's inspirations, which flourished into its cultural achievements. However, the strategic alliance Emperor Taizong and his father Li Yuan, founder of the Tang, established with the Turks and the Uighur, at various times; the large population of tribal immigrants at the borders; the high number of generals recruited from the tribes, together with the state's military strategy of employing tribal troops to fight its losing battles since the high Tang—all these proved fatal for an increasingly weakened empire.[12]

The turning point of the dynasty, the years 755–63 of the An Lushan rebellion, was the culmination of the accumulated retributions for the above operations. Doted on by Emperor Xuanzong (712–756) for his disarming charm as an overweight "barbarian," the sinicized general An Lushan became covetous of the imperial dominion and led his *fanzhen* troops stationed at the border into the capital, driving Xuanzong to a nightmarish flight and finally to his abdication. After An Lushan's rebellion, from which the Tang never truly recovered, a profoundly altered climate in every domain emerged, which was marked by a proliferation of regional autonomy. Historically, this signaled the changes to come that would constitute the gradual transition from medieval China to modern times in East Asia.[13] In terms of military reconfiguration, posts at the borders and the imperial commissioners in command of military regions (*jiedushi*) gained threatening autonomy. The process of decentralization continued to disrupt the state, and in the end it was these burgeoning military regions with self-appointed generals that robbed the state of its control over the provinces and finally brought the Tang its downfall.[14]

Ironically and perhaps inevitably, these nomads with much to offer to the empire were exactly the same forces that weakened it, exemplified by the Uighur and Tibet's continuous intrusions at the borders and, more immediately, An Lushan's invasion and occupation of the capital. When the barbarians (as they were called by the empire) turned truly barbarous, the delicate tension between antagonism and integration broke, and the absorption of the Other became fatal. This provided the historical background for the cultural movement to return to the sources of Chinese antiquity, spearheaded by Liu Zongyuan and Han Yu's "ancient style" movement and Han Yu's call for a return to original Confucianism, and culminated in Wuzong's destruction of Buddhism. In an incessant dialectic, China was ready to withdraw and turn in upon itself after two centuries of foreign influences, shunning influences from the periphery that had come threateningly close.

The movement from the marginal to the central was completed and brought to its peak by Wu Zhao, the self-styled woman emperor who took over the empire for more than a decade, establishing her own dynasty of Zhou (690–705) and thus disrupting the continuity of patriarchal empires. For a woman, the absolute Other, to ascend to the throne in a society that did not encompass the existence of an heiress, an absolutism sustained by the practice of concubinage that ensured the mechanism of the patriline—when a woman achieved sovereignty in such a patriarchal order, it necessarily constituted the ultimate reversal from the periphery to the center. With this, the Tang's incorporation of foreign customs, its absorption and transformation of others, together with its tolerance of the expansion of female energies, had reached the paradoxical point of the nadir.

Such violent moves of the Other would ultimately be obliterated, in the same manner as the dispersal of the Buddhist communities and the attack and massacre of Arab and Persian merchants in the attempt to drive foreign elements out of the now diffident center.[15] The center came back to reclaim its legitimacy, and the dialectic of power, both of gender and of race, exacted countless victims on both sides.

The Tang's inward turn, contemporaneous with the closure of the silk road to central Asia, now occupied by the Tibetans and the Arabs, had profound consequences for the history of Chinese civilization. With the loss of territories west of the Yumen Pass since 790, the Chinese land's relations since the Han with central Asia, together with cultural stimulation from the Muslim world and India, were severed. The empire would from now on lose its many colonies in the northeast and the south, along with its cultural ambitions, and adopt a radically transformed worldview.[16]

THE INFLATION OF WORDS AND THE RISE OF THE LITERATI

Annually, young men from all over the empire flooded to Chang'an, crowding the numerous hotels with their zithers, their heavy boxes of books, and their unrealized ambitions. There were students fresh to the great city with high hopes for success, and scholars whose minds were shadowed by repeated failures of the state examinations, the center of all these vibrant activities. Established in the Sui, implemented and refined in the Tang under the reigns of Gaozong (649–683) and Zetian (Wu Zhao), and stabilized under Xuanzong, the examinations were instrumental in the rise of the literati as a new class.[17] Through the examinations system, canonical expertise, competence in politics, and literary expressions were exchanged for bureaucratic positions, and the new meritocrats were presented with the opportunity of serving the imperial personage, thereby answering their Confucian calling.

The examinations, however, had the inherent danger of buying out the literati, for whom civil careers meant, in realistic terms, financial security and personal fulfillment. When ambitious men of letters were enlisted by the despot, it soon became apparent that not all bureaucrats were beyond temptation, and many were in danger of losing their intellectual independence, against which cultural rebels in the Six Dynasties had been vigilant. With obsessive accounts of the examinations recorded in various writings, their imprint on scholars' consciousness is evident. As such, the examinations cast a great shadow on the historical character of Chinese intellectuals. This constitutes one of the greatest paradoxes in Chinese cultures: the system that brought immediate success to the literati and uplifted them socially was at the same time a mechanism that exacted a subservient mentality from them and would finally fashion the debilitated minds of modern Chinese intellectuals.[18] In their glorification is their bitter end—this is one harsh lesson we learn from history.

The popularity of the *jinshi* examination (which as time progressed placed more stress on literary skills) over the *mingjing* examination (oriented toward testing canonical knowledge) illustrates the era's admiration for poetic brilliance. With its growing significance and the activities surrounding the examination—the circulation of writings among established ministers; romantic liaisons and lyrical exchanges with courtesans—an inflation of language was in effect, when the value of belles lettres became virtually identified with that of material goods or, more ideally, political careers.[19] The inflation of language was not an isolated instance, but a function of the transformation of social structures and the eventual disfranchisement of the great clans.

This change of social configurations had a serious effect on women, for the inflation of the literati's value, together with rapid commercialization and urbanization, as well as the expansion and localization of learning in the Song Dynasty, contributed to the increasing worth of the literati and, subsequently, the deflation of women. In contrast to the appreciation of the great clans' daughters in the Tang marriage market and their high prices, the dowry soared in the Song. On the one hand, a handsome dowry elucidated the transaction of patrilineal property through a daughter and served as a testimony to her value for her birth family. On the other hand, it testified to the daughter's devaluation in the increased need for interconnections among the gentry circle, who sought out promising young men through the transaction of daughters as exchange gifts.[20]

Placed in the climate of the neo-Confucian prescription for self-control, and with the widening practice of foot binding, the devaluation of brides seems to be the true meaning of the escalating dowry. With this, the historical consequences of the inflation of words that contributed to the increasing worth of the elite are fully delivered. Women were progressively degraded as the empire became an intricate machine, epitomized by the glorification of words and the calculated exchange between talents and power, submission and rewards. Paradoxically, when the society of men clicked together in the accelerated mechanism of power, women suffered a fated fall.[21] We are reminded here of the original historical fall of women in Engel's theory, which was contemporaneous with the possession of private property. That the masculine drive toward progress often spells a progressive downfall for women is an apprehension essential for feminist cultural critique. Ultimately, the idea of progress itself requires thorough redefinition.

TRANSFIGURATIONS AND USE OF BUDDHISM

Theoretically, a religion as ascetic and otherworldly as Buddhism is a direct counterpoint to the sensuous Tang, to which the flamboyant Taoism seems a more logical match. Nonetheless, fervent faith in Buddhism continued during the era, and with the propagandistic purpose of Wu Zhao, it was granted precedence over Taoism during her reign. Although in the narratives, the protagonists are often initiated into the illusiveness of life through sudden enlightenment, it was rather a secularized Buddhism with its preaching of metempsychosis that elicited faith from the gentle folks. Moreover, as commoners sought Buddhist temples as a convenient retreat and support for easy livelihood in turbulent times, less-than-pious monks and nuns were a widely criticized phenomenon, and Buddhism was put in the position of serving as a sham for the flocks who could not fend for themselves otherwise.

The Buddhist influence on the literati's lifestyle, on the poetic rhyme schemes developed during the Southern Dynasties and entrenched in the Tang, and its infusion of the popular mind with the concepts of karma and transmigration, are evidence of the extent to which this Indian religion influenced Tang cultures. Yet its more philosophical concept of *sunyata,* emptiness, although often serving a mitigating function for the aged and disillusioned, did not prevail in public sentiments as much as the more ingrained popular teaching of retribution. Thus the essentially negative character of Buddhism fell short of shaping the popular consciousness, and sensuous enjoyment continued to reign in populated cities.

There are layers of problematics involved in a study of the roles of Buddhism, and it is not my intention to discuss them at length here. Fundamentally opposed to the native tradition of moral acceptance of social-ethical obligations, the Buddhist teaching of renunciation must undergo essential transformations to ensure a prolonged following. To this end, the transformation achieved by Zen Buddhism is gradual and absolute. In the cultural combustion of the Tang, the Zen sect's vision, together with fervent translations and hermeneutics of Buddhist sutras, constitutes its chief philosophical achievement, filling in for the virtual vacuum left by the speculative quiescence of orthodox Confucianism—that is, until the ancient style movement and the call for ideological cleansing settled in.[22]

By rendering everyday life part of the esoteric practice and the only way to sudden enlightenment, Zen Buddhism rescues mundane life from total denial. Furthermore, by providing a rationale for domestic meditation, the severance of ethical ties becomes less of a necessity, which is an essential move for Buddhism's sinicization. Zen's transfiguration of Buddhism further entails locating a mysterious vision through which nature, unlike the human world, is understood with its absence of a sense of purpose. This intuitive experience reinvents Chinese aesthetics, and the religion that forbids the world is metamorphosed into an occult with an aesthetic vision of a distilled nature, with life perceived as a transient moment in which the absence of the will to power marks an emptiness not without its share of ecstasy. The Buddhist annihilation of life is thus transformed into an aesthetic perception of existence; in this transformation, the move from denial to affirmation is unmistakable.[23]

Deeply indebted to philosophical Taoism, the invention of Zen was a curious antidote to the cultural climate of the time, when language took center stage and was admired almost fetishistically. The Sixth Patriarch and the builder of the sect, Hui Neng (638–713), was allegedly an illiterate, or at least that's what the *Liuzu*

tanjing (Platform sutra of the Sixth Patriarch) proposes. In the midst of the celebration of embellished words, an illiterate monk came up with a drastically different concept and deemed language superfluous to an essential understanding of the
Ultimate Truth.[24] Styling its objective as seeing Buddha in one's own nature, Zen
Buddhism emphasizes meditation without depending on the external instruments
of the scriptures or conceptual thinking. An emphasis on intuitive wisdom (*prajna*)
and enlightenment without the burden of words or learned discussions thus comes
to characterize the sect as a separate transmission outside the scriptures. This emphasis on independence from language created an alternative in an era overfilled with
verbal icons and can be considered its healing antithesis. The secularization of
world-denying Buddhism, together with this emptying out of words in Zen, thus
constitute part of the Buddhist paradox in the Tang.[25]

In its most daring move, Zen Buddhism threatens to annihilate the Buddha.

> If you want to have the right understanding, you must not be deceived by others. You
> should kill everything that you meet internally or externally. If you meet Buddha, kill
> Buddha. If you meet the Patriarchs, kill the Patriarchs. . . . Then you can gain your
> emancipation.[26]

With this, the weight of all icons is removed, with only the monotonous existence
of daily lives to deliver us. The replacement of words with physical abuse such as
a knock on the head in the exchange of dialogue between the master and the dis-
ciple is Zen's radical departure from realities, when physical pain is translated into
spiritual emancipation and becomes the immediate channel toward the inexplicable First Principle. In this method holds the most profound teaching of Zen: physical agony amid silence creates a vacuum in the illusion of life and constitutes its
negativity.[27] With this, the abandonment of language is complete, and in an era of
overflowing materialism, a radical antithesis conjures up a self-correctness. Zen
Buddhism hence presents a profound dialectic of the self in the Tang and should
be understood as its philosophical cleansing. It is perhaps in this capacity for a complete reversal of self-definition that the Tang can be called a truly great era.

The relationship between Buddhism and Tang women was equally intricate. For
many intractable women, retreating to a Buddhist convent was a statement of
avowed chastity and a drastic means to reject marriage. The large population of
Buddhist nuns in the Tang, discounting those who entered the order out of sheer
expedience, attests to a need for this religious retreat.[28] Providing a safe haven for
women escaping from marriage or those deprived of means to sustain themselves,
Buddhism also provided a spiritual retreat for wives who sought solace in its teaching of the denial of the sensory. Judging from evidence gathered from numerous
funerary inscriptions, many gentry wives were devoted Buddhists, and the sect's
renunciation of sensual enjoyment, together with its doctrine of celibacy, helped
to strengthen a desexualized consciousness mandatory for the well-being of sexually superseded wives.[29]

Considering that one common depository for women entertainers had been the Buddhist convents, a practice exercised by both imperial and gentry patriarchs alike, this function of the erasure of female sexuality was in closest affinity with the original Buddhist dogma. The dividing line between these women's sensuous identities and their forced celibate existence was so filmy and drawn so suddenly, the transition from sexual objects to desexualized nuns so drastic, that the populace's resistance to these consort-nuns' religious identity, evidenced by the many poems alluding to their secretly amorous hearts, was at the same time a conceited fancy and a sympathetic apprehension. Considering the large number of imperial consorts, aged courtesans, and concubines on whom this bitter end was imposed, we can imagine a collective female desire, stifled to safeguard masculine sexual monopoly, looming large in the temples of confinement.[30]

Ironically, when Buddhism underwent a secularizing process and absorbed mundane lives into its practice, it was women who were made to shoulder its original teachings of renunciation to cleanse themselves of desires that were denied legitimacy. The self-serving character of such a utilization of Buddhism constitutes another Tang reversal/paradox that juggles, rather cunningly one must say, between appeasing and erasing separately the desires of opposing genders.

EARTHLY HEAVEN OF RELIGIOUS TAOISM

While claiming Laozi as its source of inspiration, the very character of religious Taoism is in actuality a contradiction to philosophical Taoism. While one proposes a letting go of willful adherence, the other professes an obstinate clutching onto life. The quest for immortality on earth through internal and external alchemy, together with the myth of immortal hermits traveling through human abodes, created the image of a Taoist heaven that existed alongside the carnal world. The paradox of Taoism thus lies basically in its conflation of the transcendent with the secular. The confusion of Taoist heaven with the human abodes, when many were led to the path of immortality through chance encounters with the immortals, created the illusion of the nearness of eternal life. And immortals, the center of Taoist mythology, retained human shapes in their transcendence, rendering immortality a continuation of sensory existence and a sublimation of earthly prosperity.[31]

Yet ironically, the dream of immortality had led many to a speedy death from the consumption of a Taoist elixir, which was extracted by alchemy from mercury, gold, and various minerals. The most prominent among the victims were the emperors Muzong, Wuzong, and possibly Xianzong, who inherited the throne from their far more competent fathers after the high Tang.[32] Among the gentry, laments for the untimely deaths caused by dangerous consumption are found in many funeral inscriptions. Such biting irony embodies the most salient contradiction of the empire, which is not untainted with an insidious dark humor.

In direct contrast to Buddhism, the flamboyant attire and practice of Taoism gave certain leeway to female sexuality. The conventionalized naming of courtesans as goddesses (*shennü*), together with the ambiguous identity of Taoist priestesses who sometimes served the social function of courtesans (as in the case of Li Ye and Yu Xuanji, two leading women poets of the era) further shore up the conflation of the identity of women who picked up priestesshood as a protecting veil, and courtesans who acted both as prostitute and entertainer. This phenomenon is offset against the domestication of supernatural women in Tang narratives, where the Taoist belief of an earthly paradise is mirrored by the taming of mythical women into objects of satiable human desires. This demonstrative lust of the mind among the literati was concurrent with a cult whose transcendental blueprint is intricately tied in with earthly motivations, whose lust for life had induced a self-deluding yearning for immortality on earth.[33]

To achieve this earthly immortality, sex is conceived as one essential method, and the copulation of man and woman is perceived as the universal dance of *yin* and *yang,* while each union is sanctified by heaven. By imitating the cosmic mating of heaven and earth, sex is made the solution to the problems of health and salvation. However, emulation of nature here leads to an audaciously unnatural practice, in which *coitus reservatus,* the withholding of ejaculation to retain male *yang* energy, is used to tap female energy for self-enrichment. Male practitioners are instructed to have intercourse with various women, and virgins, especially young girls with certain features, are ranked as the best partners for *shuangxiu* (paired practices). In blatant terms, women are called the "stove" within which man brews his elixir of immortality, and it is instructed that the secret of sexual enrichment be withheld from women.

Originated from *The Book of Changes* perception that all lives spring from sexual intercourse between woman and man, and inspired by Laozi's concept of the necessity of curtailing desires, Chinese sexual yoga focused on the containment of desires and male energy in the pre-Qin and Han eras. This sexology and its practice reached a climax in the Six Dynasties and continued its influence in the Sui and Tang, producing various sexual texts that emphasize *coitus reservatus* as a means to guarantee male indulgence in sexual excess.[34] With this new development, the original meaning of Chinese sexology was transformed into its opposite, which might have been an inevitable move in the general expansion of concubinage and overflowed sensuality among the aristocratic circle and the rising literati.

Like the consumption of drugs, such deviant sexual exercises caused the early deaths of many gentlemen, whose wills proved to be inadequate to sustain the tremendous self-restraint required. In the populated harems of the patriarchs, the invention of such sexual practice was understood as expedient, exposing the inherent threat of an irrational polygamous practice by which a man's sexual capacity was dangerously tried. As such, Taoist sexual yoga exposes the irrationality of concubinage, and its proposition is a futile attempt at reversing threatening female desires into a collective instrument for male longevity. This attempt constitutes the most self-defeating aspect of Tang social life. At the core of its inner contradiction stands the absurdity of the institution of polygamous households.

REPRESENTATIONS OF TANG WOMEN

We have seen how women were affected by and got tangled up in various paradoxical phenomena of the Tang. Just as the principal cultural manifestations of the era bear some sort of ironic twist, the truth of Tang women is also marked by inherent contradictions. As stated above, a slippage between the visual presentations of Tang women and their self-representations in verse is apparent.[35] The immediate visual images we have of Tang women are their plump figures dressed in audacious, low-cut outfits or in man's wear of foreign styles, agile palace women riding on horseback or playing polo, lethargic court entertainers playing foreign instruments, or miniature figurines of charming entertainers. Most of the women we see in the extant Tang art works and funeral figurines seem self-content in their leisure and confident in their actions. That these women, most of whom are entertainers and imperial consorts with the sole purpose of pleasing, should appear so unanimously complaisant, is of no surprise. A good number of them—the figurines and maidens on the wall paintings of royal tombs—indeed serve as the perpetual companions for the dead.

By contrast, the images of Tang women in their own lyrics are disconcertingly marred by a sense of inertia, a quiet anxiety that borders on melancholia. Writing in the mode of boudoir lament invented by the literati since the Han folk songs, Tang women express discontent in the enclosing space of the inner chamber, and seldom do they describe the spring outings when peonies were in full bloom, or the gala events of major Buddhist sermons, the two common occasions that brought them out in the public. The persistent inward turning of the gaze on their sorrow over the prospect of abandonment or over a transience that will soon deprive them of their beauty, more than anything else characterizes their poetry that has passed down to us.

This contradiction between visual images and literary self-representations should caution us to a more careful study of Tang women, when their inner landscape and imposed masks confront each other and demand equal attention, simultaneously questioning and interlocking with each's credibility. Basically we are dealing with an era celebrated by luxurious edifices, audacious costumes, banquets overflowing with exotic music and dance, and flamboyant sensitivity, even sensuality; an era marked by an insatiable appetite for brilliant poetry as well as the fervent following of mundane religions. We experience a dazzling show of an explosion of vitality and a spillover of desires, in which female desires dashed forth with rare vigor, all the time under the overarching will of the patriarchs. It is in such an epoch that we find the women of our subject, and unearthing their consciousness, as the above contradictions have elucidated, is not an easy task.

Detail of *Lady Guoguo's Spring Outing*, Emperor Huizong's copy of an 8th century painting by Zhang Xuan.

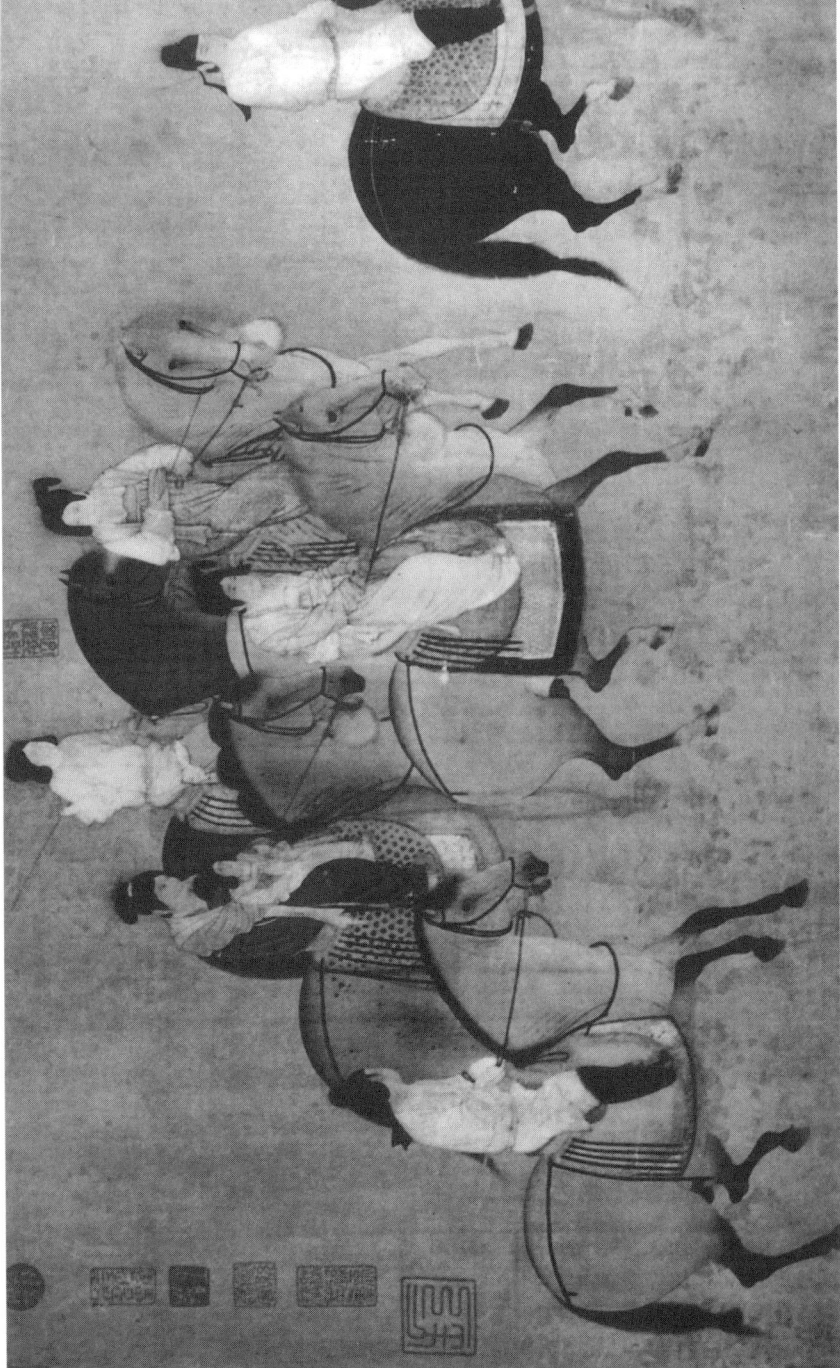

From *Liaoning bowuguan canghua*, pl. 8.

Companions for the dead: a pair of dancing figurines. From a Tang tomb in Beimangshan, Henan, Luoyang.

From *Tangdai Diaosu xuanji,* pl. 32.

Revered by many as the epitome of imperial China, the Tang, as I try to show, is not without its ambiguities. The entrenchment of the examinations system is the harbinger of a prolonged practice that placed the elite in the pigeonhole of an overpowering institution, within which their struggle for perseverance was morally exacting. Modern criticism of the subservient character of Chinese intellectuals finds its more immediate origin in the establishment of state examinations, which imprisoned the gentry class in an invisible mental cell. From a more fundamental perspective of cultural critique, the weight placed on the examinations, the expanding bureaucracy, and the phenomenon of the worship of literary embellishment might have endowed the manmade world with a self-blinding pomposity. When a person's value was weighed against the embellished words he created and against his ethical-political merits based upon the state's verdict, the circular motion of cultural mechanism was marked by a circumscribed self-manifestation, as human civilization turned its back on nature and the latter's absence of an obstinate will to power.

One radical assessment of the Tang can hence be formulated thus: by building an all-encompassing state, and through an unprecedented obsession with words as well as the institutionalization of linguistic creations, the Tang contributed greatly toward the Chinese civilization, while simultaneously moving it further along the road of the inventions of tyrannical systems, arbitrary categorizations, and the entrenchment of a highly sophisticated language, casting subsequently the inherent danger of the instrumentalization of human lives.[36] It is perhaps from this perspective that we can best understand a cultural discontent with post-Tang dynasties expressed by modern Chinese, while the seeds for the failings of later eras, very likely, were sown in the greatness of the Tang itself.[37]

Part One

Imperial Discourse and Its Discontent

Chapter 1

The Dragon's Ministers

On the Back of a Fast Horse

A horse who could run a thousand miles in the twinkling of an eye was presented to the emperor new to his throne. At first the emperor pondered: "What would I do with a horse that could run a thousand miles when the best of my retinue's could only run five hundred? This will leave me all alone on that fast animal, with all my servants lagging far behind. Really, what use do I have for a horse that outruns all of my people?" Nevertheless, the ministers persuaded the emperor to submit himself to the gallant horse. Assisted by his servants, the emperor mounted the tall horse, and after some beatings, the handsome animal sprang to its feet and galloped away from the imperial stable, through the palace courtyard and over the imposing palace gate. Before the pale emperor could give any order, it had already carried him into the magnificent city with shining pavements of gold and splendid mansions on the endless streets.

The horse galloped too fast for the emperor to enjoy the brilliance of his empire, and before long he found himself in the depth of the country, where the myriad peasants worked on barren land to provide for the infinite expenditure of the court, and still other myriad were weaving silk to be tailored into ever widening robes of noble men and women. Face after face, his dazed people passed by the emperor's eyes like tumbling seaweeds, and the emperor in his yellow robe was carried thus through his vast empire. The speed of the magnificent horse was such that however hard the emperor might try, he could not comprehend any of the strange scenery his people or his empire had to present to him. In truth he could barely hold on to the horse, who was deaf to all the royal orders delivered at him that were quickly dispersed in the swiftly blowing wind.

A day in the capital started with the solemn drumming issued forth from the imperial city. At dawn, successions of beatings of heavy drumming sounded the breaking daylight, and as the drumming traversed the span of Chang'an, city gates opened one by one, and the various iron, silk, saddle, medicine, diviner, pawn, and wine shops started another day of business, following the rhythm of the regulating drums. As the drumming began from the imperial palace, the order of everyday life, together with a sense of temporal progression, was thus under the control of the Son of Heaven, who had the empire under his disposal. Following imperial drums, all the official street drums sounded loud, until three thousand beatings were completed, and the whole capital woke up to a new day.[1]

The bureaucrats, whose official quarters lay south of the palace, woke up before daybreak to prepare themselves under torchlight. Mounting on horseback, they lined up by the gates, waiting to attend morning court session. At the court, after the ministers had entered solemnly according to each's rank, the monarch stepped up to his throne, fans opened to reveal his dragon's countenance amid the misty smoke emitted from the incense burners.[2] Various poets have borne witness to the brilliant procession of the ministers and the dignified court scene, either as participants or as envious observers. With each beat, the heavy drumming from the palace penetrated all corners of the capital; in like manner, the imperial presence penetrated deep into the scholars' consciousness.

The following memorial testifies the extent to which the temptation of officialdom was detrimental to the ambitious among imperial subjects: "The state opens up wide the gate to officialdom, and the gentlefolk all abandon various professions to vie for it vehemently. Now one peasant's land is to feed hundreds."[3] What was this career that drove the whole empire into abandoning proper occupations to enter its narrow gate? What had been sacrificed, besides the farm lands left unplowed by those who dreamed of political glory?

CONFIGURATION OF THE PALACE

In the magnificent imperial palace, it was with the thousands of palace women and eunuchs, together with palace guards and sometimes the crown prince, that the Tang emperors resided. At night, when the court receded and ministers retreated to their homesteads, the emperor was left alone with his favorite consorts and chamber servants in the closely guarded palace. Severe laws were installed to forbid any trespassing, especially where the monarch and his palace women resided. As jealously guarded imperial possessions, palace ladies were forbidden to converse with outsiders, and those found delivering letters or packages to them without permission were punished with the sentence of strangling.[4] Physically and emotionally kept in the closest vicinity of the monarch, the eunuchs and, not infrequently, imperial women also proved to be liable to stage a bloody coup. With decreasing royal strength in the late Tang, eunuchs endowed with military power took over control, and the master/slave hierarchy was inverted.

The monarchs were hence balanced dangerously on the complex maneuvers of court politics. Threatening were the powerful courtiers and in-laws who maneuvered to satiate their private ambitions, manipulating the monarch to disastrous ends; and treacherous was the bitter competition among palace women whose feuds could continue for generations. The tragic turn of events in the late Tang, which saw a series of emperors installed and terminated by militarily powerful eunuchs, manifests the perilous potential of the castrated, victims and compensatory benefi-

Emperor Taizong in detail of *The Imperial Sedan Chair*, handscroll, attributed to Yan Liben.

From *Gugong bowuyaun canghua,* pl. 3.

ciaries of the encompassing imperial phallus. One case in point is Emperor Wen-zong (827–840), who after the bloody coup of the powerful eunuch Qiu Shiliang often fell into a fit of soliloquy with wild eyes, and no one dared approach him.[5]

Thus the monarchs fell victims to their coveted throne; the founder of the dynasty, Li Yuan, was forced to offer it to his resourceful second son Li Shimin, who won his kingdom by killing two siblings in a tightly woven fight and became the most illustrious of all Tang rulers, Taizong. This self-made monarch himself made a remarkably pathetic scene when facing the vital decision of naming an heir apparent that would guarantee a smooth transition. Possessing the bounty empire was indeed a precarious thing, and the untimely death and imprisonment of many a crown prince or contender for the throne were direct results of violent political intrigue.

In this manner, uncertainty lurked perpetually beneath the power of the Son of Heaven, so revered and unrightfully envied. In a farcical episode in the late Tang, the joint intrigue of a diviner and a dyer gathered a force of hundreds of gangsters who broke into the palace and succeeded in what they set out to accomplish: to sit on the throne and enjoy meals together.[6] For a monarch who was provided with limited and often falsified information, whose friends and enemies confused him with equally faithful oaths, acting on impulse had serious consequences. Standing at the meeting point of men and Heaven, the highest and the shakiest ground, the sovereign often found himself alone not only in time of crisis, but also in the absolutism of his power. For a sensitive ruler, the terrifying power over life and death sometimes left him with haunting remorse.[7]

According to traditional Chinese political ideals, ministers acted as forces of rationality, providing a necessary check and balance of propriety. Both the relation between the ruler and his courtiers and the way the latter functioned administratively and ideologically were consolidated from the Han empire onward, and however turbulent the political climate, however unworthy the sovereign, ministers were bound by the moral principle of loyalty. Through the ingenious works of the Han scholar Dong Zhongshu, the complex process of the infusion of Legalism into Confucianism was completed, rendering the Legalist code of the ministers' absolute subordination intrinsic to Confucian doctrine. After this fusion, the ethic of political fidelity gradually shaped the gentlemen's definitions of their roles, and their moral right over a tyrant was not often entertained, leaving Mencius's belief in the precedence of the people over the state and the king obsolete. This had the effect of registering courtiers as unconditional servants to imperial families, and as the despots became increasingly authoritarian with the decreasing power of the chief ministers since the Ming (1368–1644), courtiers suffered humiliation under an autocrat who fell far from the ideal of a sage king.[8]

A complex deep in ministers' consciousness was epitomized in an early text, *Lisao* (Encountering sorrow) by Qu Yuan, a high minister and reverent poet of the Chu in the Warring States. In this major cultural text, the lyrical self alternates between presenting a rending plea to the king Huai of Chu and moving defiantly into the mythical sphere in search of an ideal mate symbolic of his political ideal.[9] From early on, tensions between the calling of heaven's mandate and that of political fidelity constituted an inner split for a minister of principle, as he struggled between faithfulness toward himself and toward the sovereign. With the consolidation of the civil service examinations in the Tang, literati were further bought out by promises of a political future and moved ever away from the intellectual independence of the gentlemen *shi* in the times of Confucius and Mencius.

At the level of institutionalized ethics, the implementation of ethical codes in the *Li ji* (Book of rites) had a definitive effect on the shaping of Chinese tradition since the book's canonization in the Han. In imperial discourse, much energy was spent on invigorating these codes to ensure a smooth following. Periodically, ambassadors of customs, *fengsu shi,* were sent to provinces with the mission of directing the morals of local people by transforming their less than civilized practices. This consolidation of ideology through political reinforcement has significant bearing on our study of the bureaucrats: having gained access to power through the use of eloquent words, they now used that same eloquence to insinuate ideologies into people's consciousness. That the literati themselves were also caught up in the overcoding machine of ethics deserves our close attention here.

If the Son of Heaven, from a somber perspective, was in essence a solitary figure fending off impending rebellion from all fronts, other calamities awaited the courtiers. Low-ranking officials and ministers of the highest standing alike could be humiliated, exiled, and sentenced to death at the sovereign's changing whim, and an insignificant event might lead to total erasure of the minister's lifelong devotion. The courtiers' vulnerability is most vivid in their fear of being exiled to uninhabitable regions, where crude habitat had exacted the lives of many of their worthy colleagues. The aged high minister and celebrated calligrapher Chu Suiliang, when exiled by Emperor Gaozong for protesting against the installation of Empress Wu, pleaded for pardon. This much-treasured chief minister of Taizong (father of Gaozong) begged with pathos for permission to return; Chu's request was denied, and he died shortly after. Such examples of a reversal of fate for a minister whose devotion should have promised him a glorious retirement abound in Tang history, and a reading of official records quickly makes clear that only when a minister was dead and buried was he saved from the threat of sudden downfall.

This statement, however, is to be qualified by posthumous action or punishments. The practice of bestowing a posthumous name for the dead (*shihao*) that functioned as the state's final verdict on a man demonstrates the pervasive use of language as an instrument to scrutinize the subjects' worth. Sometimes the debate over a posthumous name is amusing for us to read, but it was anxiety-ridden for the dead's kin.[10] Besides the conferral of a posthumous name, the despot had other ways of demonstrating his superior judgment, such as granting royal kinsmen and ministers the honor to share his final resting place. The configuration of Tang emperors' imposing burial mounds, especially that of Taizong, is a telescopic version of that of the palace, reflecting each's status with varying size and height of the earth covering their remains.[11]

The nonfinality of the imperial verdict, echoed in the open-ended fate of ministers, has more gruesome aspects. The death of Wei Zheng, Taizong's high minister celebrated for his unusual courage, was received as a blow by the monarch; yet suspicion of Wei's alliance with two illicit ministers gave Taizong second thoughts, and a monument installed on behalf of Wei was destroyed. Although the monument was resurrected later after the disastrous war with Korea, the marriage between Wei's son and one of the princesses fell through, marking the beginning of the decline of Wei's clan, as the historians note.[12]

More horrendous was the vindictive punishment by exhumation, which involved actual lashing of the dead and snatching of funeral gifts bestowed by previous sovereigns.[13] Such violence was typical of ongoing court intrigues that continued across generations of imperial clans, in-laws, and bureaucrats, with different cliques pursuing each other relentlessly, vying for the monarch's patronage. When the glory a man had enjoyed at his burial was snatched away through public posthumous humiliation, the erratic will of the despot was unmistakably manifested. Except for the changing opinions of historians, such was the final downfall that could befall a minister who had served the great empire well.

The purpose here is to direct our attention to the bureaucrats' endurance of a harsh political contract, when their predecessors shared the historical responsibility of its drafting. The significance of this community in the context of our study lies in its indispensable function in the reinforcement of ethical codes, in the compilation and modification of Tang legal codes, and in the applications of these codes in their memorials and juridical duties as local magistrates. Interacting with a willful monarch without irrefutably consolidated administrative channels for checks and balances, when the right of final verdict lay with the despot, a courtier's anxiety resided not simply in the shakiness of his career, but also in the maintenance of order within the state, which was achieved partially through an imposition of legal codes, and partially through teachings of ethical values, chief among them loyalty and filial piety. When the persuasion of moral teachings was the basis of Confucian calls for a political career as an answer to heaven's mandate, and when the lord-minister relationship constituted one of the essential ethical pairs, the irony of the ministers' roles lay in the fact that they were both perpetrators and victims of the ethical values they so adhered to. An analysis and identification of ministers' vulnerable positions in the imperial configuration enables us to reconsider their unquestioned acceptance and implementation of social stratification—when they exacted similar conformity from others, in particular women and slaves who were assigned a circumscribed space.[14]

THE MINISTER-CONCUBINE COMPLEX

The three pairs of elementary ethical relations, emperor-minister, father-son, and husband-wife, were the invention of the Legalist Han Fei and later incorporated by Dong Zhongshu into his political ethics.[15] These metaphorically analogous pairs formed the basis of the traditional ethical hierarchy and were frequently conjured up in Tang official discourse. In a peculiar twist of irony, a parallel presents itself between the status of a courtier and that of a wife, a parallel that was taken to surprising dimensions. The hierarchical and (to a lesser degree) complementary relations in these ethical pairings have deep-rooted manifestations in Chinese culture, and in this feminist critique, how the parallel of the ministers' role to that of women affected the courtiers' conception of the second sex and of themselves requires careful reexamination.

In the *I Ching* (Book of changes), the first two hexagrams, *qian*, the Creative, and *kun*, the Receptive, are symbols of the principles *yang* and *yin*, presented respectively by heaven and earth in the natural sphere. Applied to human affairs, the principle of this complementary relationship is reflected in the relation between father and son, man and wife, ruler and minister. Tang ministers were certainly familiar with such codifications, and one courtier commented to Emperor Gaozong at the sign of an alarming earthquake: "The heaven is *yang*, and the earth, *yin*. *Yang* is the image of the ruler, *yin*, that of the minister. It befits a ruler to move, and a minister to keep still." He thereby identified the earthquake as an ill omen and urged that Gaozong be watchful.[16]

The dualism of *yin* and *yang*, however complementary in its essential opposition, has a clearly defined hierarchic structure, as the Receptive is defined by the attribute of devotion in relation to the Creative. When the Receptive is activated and led by the Creative, beneficial effects would issue forth; when it struggles against the Creative, it becomes evil and constitutes threat. The emphatically defined aspect of the Receptive is perseverance, and its image, as against that of the Creative which is a dragon, is a mare roaming over the vast expanse of the earth. It is further stated in the commentary that "the mare combines the strength and swiftness of the horse with the gentleness and devotion of a cow."[17]

Applied to the analogy of lord and minister, the images of dragon and mare match well with the traditional symbols assigned to the pair. Dragon is the received totem representing the Son of Heaven; as a revered icon, the dragon appeared on the monarch's robes and on imperial edifices, and euphemisms like "the dragon's countenance" and "brushing against the dragon's scales" appeared frequently in imperial discourse. Employed in the sphere of public service, a common metaphor is the horse, and a horse that can withstand long journeys, or a fast horse, is dearly treasured. In the *Zhenguan zhengyao* (Essentials of Zhenguan politics), the story of the Han emperor Wendi's rejection of the offer of a fast horse (a horse that could speed a thousand miles) was brought up in a discussion between Taizong and his courtiers. Wendi was praised for his decision, for such a marvelous horse is a luxury violating the doctrine of frugality. But Wendi had a rational, rather than moral, reason for his rejection: "What could I do with it when the best of my retinue's horses run with the speed of only five hundred miles?" In ruling his empire, the despot was dependent upon his faithful servant-courtiers for their administrative skills and moral guidance. On this symbolic level, it is awkward for Wendi to reject the magical horse—yet it is also enlightening. Such a magnificent horse of a minister who exceeded all others' capacities will take him to uncharted spheres, and for an empire that rests itself on stability, extreme talents are undesirable. On this note, the confines placed on the ministers can be further deciphered.

Allegorically, the irrational organization of the empire itself *is* the magic horse upon which the emperor loses himself. In this regard, the absurd situation of an emperor riding on his horse the speed of which exceeded everyone else brings us back to the latent solitude of a monarch and his alienation from abiding courtiers and presents a perfect symbol of the impossible position of the despot.

The analogy of ruler and minister with the principle of *yin* and *yang* in the *Book of Changes* does not stop at the first two hexagrams; it runs throughout in more central and accommodating ways. Each hexagram is composed of six lines, with the broken (- -, *yin*) and unbroken (—, *yang*) lines as its two basic elements. As the lines move upward, changing situations are deciphered based on the different character and position of each line. In the structuring of the hexagrams, the places occupied by the lines have specific roles according to their relative elevation, differentiated as superior and inferior. In principle, of the four active places in the middle of a hexagram, the fifth place (below the top place) is that of the ruler, and the fourth, that of the minister. In some situations the fourth place may represent the wife, and the fifth that of the husband; or the wife will occupy the second place, also a place for local officials. The two central lines, in the second and the fifth places, which stand in the correct relationship of official to ruler, son to father, and wife to husband, are the most important in the general framework of correspondence in the lines. In the official-ruler analogy, a strong official (a firm line of *yang*) corresponding to a yielding ruler (a weak line of *yin*) often creates a favorable result. This is very much in line with the Taoist concept of a nonstriving ruler. However, as regards the relationship of holding together between two adjacent lines of different characters, the fourth and the fifth lines are of primary importance, and here it is more favorable for a yielding minister to hold together with a strong ruler, for reverence becomes important in such close proximity.[18] Thus the hierarchy of the Creative and the Receptive holds through in the analogy of ruler and ministers, and by virtue of their close vicinity to the emperor, the ministers must remain tied to the yielding virtue of the feminine.

Such ideal combinations of the masculine and the feminine principles in the hexagrams are mere abstractions, and they remain to be realized in real-life situations. Although the nuances of and variations on the characters of each line in different elevations are as stated above, the previous speech on the earthquake demonstrates that it is the analogy of heaven and earth, of *yin* and *yang,* that prevailed in the courtiers' interpretation of their symbolic standing with the ruler. That the ruler would act according to the *yin* principle, yielding and consenting, could only be a pious wish; verbally, the courtiers were instructed to refer to themselves as *yin,* the yielding servant, or worse, as the concubine.

We have now arrived at an important psychological complex prevalent in the minister's consciousness, namely, the minister-concubine complex, a further complication from the demand of absolute loyalty. Tracing the genealogy of this psychological trait is in order here, and again it is to Qu Yuan's *Encountering Sorrow* that we must turn. In the text, the poet rendered himself effeminate with fragrant adornments, symbols of his virtues, and alluded to himself as one of many royal consorts competing for the king's favor. The romanticized metaphors Qu used to describe his relationship with the king further placed the self in a compromised position and exposed a dilemma at the core of this verse, which sets the tone for future poets caught in the same plight. The literary conceit of minister-consort coined by Qu Yuan, virtually the first known poet of the Chinese lyrical tradition, became predominant in the writings (and readings) of political allegories that present a courtier's bemoaned separation from his sovereign, in which the feminization of the courtier is a telling sign of the by now entrenched binary opposition between the lord and the courtier, rendered analogues to that of *yin* and *yang*.[19]

After a display of military might in the eighth year of the much-celebrated Zhenguan period under the reign of Taizong, an assembly of tribal leaders gathered before the high-spirited retired emperor Gaozu (618–626) and Taizong in the No-End Palace. Having summoned a dance from a Turkish khan and a poem recital by a chief from the southern tribe, Gaozu laughed and congratulated himself and his gallant son: "The northern and the southern tribes all united in one family— such a thing has never been since antiquity." Upon this, Taizong toasted for the father-emperor's longevity:

> "Now with the blessings of your highness, the time is peaceful and the year prosperous, while those with hairs untied and jackets opened on the left have all become your minister-concubines. . . ." Gaozu was immensely delighted; all the courtiers shouted, "Long live the emperors," and the celebration lasted till the end of the night.[20]

The phrase *minister-concubine* in imperial discourse is a general denominator for imperial servants, a usage derived from the two groups' corresponding roles of serving. In the present usage, the word *concubine* is absorbed into the leader of the term, as is often the case with such coined phrases. Well grounded in socio-ideological basis, the two words merge into one another, sharing each other's connotation, fashioning a common name for servility.

At times, the identification of the minister with the concubine is carried further into an ambiguous dimension not without some sexual charge. At the court of the charismatic Taizong, devoted ministers often enjoyed heartfelt appreciation from the monarch, which exposes ironically the approximation of the identity of a minister with that of a concubine and its curious consequences.

> Taizong was good at calligraphy in the style of Wang Xizhi, and was especially good at the dry flying brushes. Once when a banquet was given at the Xuanwu Gate to min-

isters above the third rank, the emperor took the brush to produce flying brushes and bestowed them on the courtiers. Made bold by the wine, the ministers vied to grab it from his hand; Liu Mi ascended the imperial seat, extended his hand, and got it. The ministers all presented: "Mi has ascended the imperial bed—his crime deserves death, please see him to the law." Taizong laughed: "Of old we heard of a concubine who declined imperial carriage, today we see a minister ascending imperial bed."[21]

In the parallel structure Taizong had chosen to use, the consort Ban famous for her declining of a Han emperor's invitation for a pleasure ride is juxtaposed to Liu Mi, who presumed to transgress into the imperial seat, often referred to as the imperial bed for its sumptuous size. With a none too subtle sexual hint in the playful atmosphere of a banquet when certain rules were abandoned, the courtier who climbed on the monarch's bed was made to counter a famously chaste consort in a word play. Through the principle of juxtaposition and replacement, Taizong's parallel sentences render Liu and Ban interchangeable—their social-linguistic correspondence is carried further into the proximity of sexual identity via the imperial bed. Taizong's joke is not innocent, and it reflects the kind of light conversations circulated in the palace at more casual, telling moments.

This may be the closest we can come concerning explicit sexual identification of a minister with a concubine, although other episodes spell out implicit court politics with equal poignancy. At another intoxicating banquet, Taizong complained about Wei Zheng's refusal to give consent when he failed to heed Wei's advice, and he suggested with a lofty naiveté:

> "Why not consent first, and restate the matter afterwards?" Zheng replied: ". . . If I consent in your highness's presence and then represent the case, it is 'complain after retreating'—surely this could not have been the will of Ji and Qi who had served the sage-kings Yao and Shun?" The emperor laughed heartily and said: "This is exactly why people hold that Wei Zheng is proud and insolent, yet I simply feel that he is enamoring." Zheng bowed and apologized: "Your majesty guided me to talk, therefore I presume to admonish; if your majesty does not accept my advice, how would I dare to offend the dragons' scalps time and again?"[22]

At another moment, Taizong solicited criticism of his royal self and, having received only flattery from the courtiers, he cast out his own verdict on the men with a cutting straightforwardness only the despot was privileged to deliver. Of Chu Suiliang he judged thus:

> Chu is upright, honest, and erudite; he comes close to me with all sincerity, like a flying bird perching on one, and naturally I cherish and love him.[23]

In both instances, Taizong's descriptions of the high ministers have attributes more commonly associated with the feminine. The phrase "a bird perching on one," *feiniao yiren*, is often used to describe a gentle woman (sometimes a child)

Calligraphy by Chu Suiliang. Detail from mourning for the emperor Taizong.

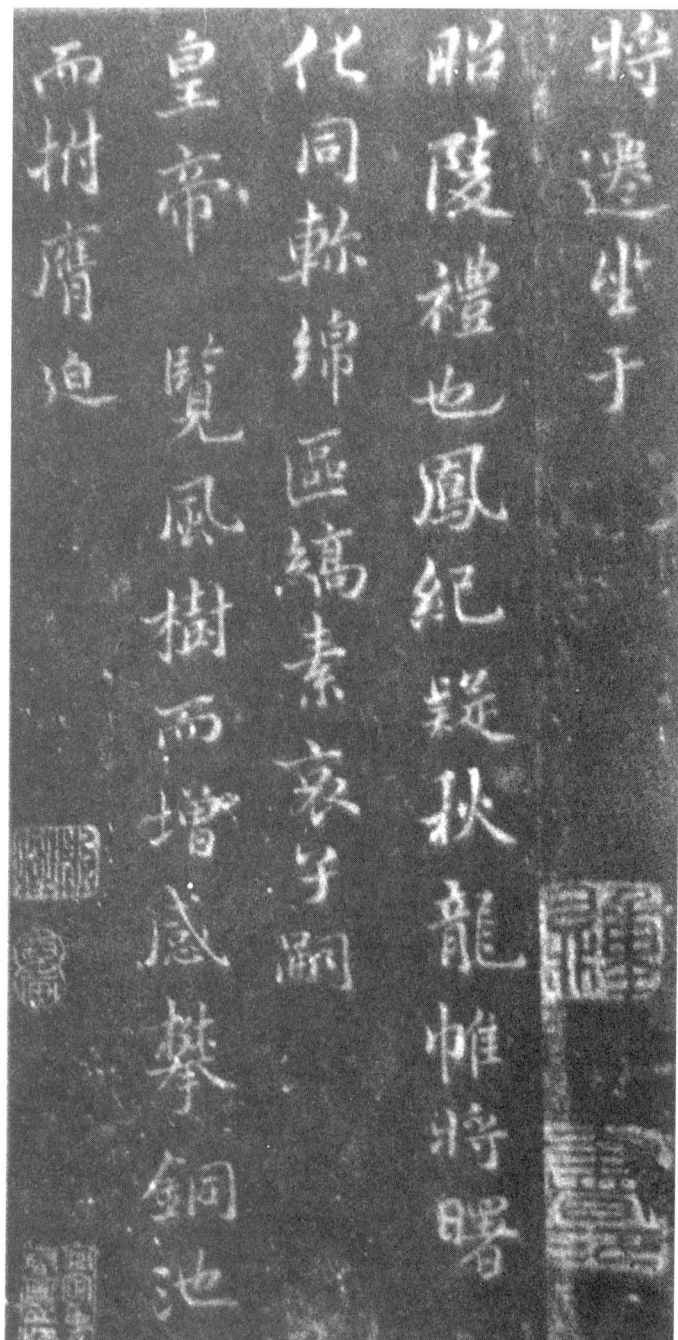

而䏌膺迫皇帝覽鳳樹而增感攀銅池化同鮌綿區縞素哀子嗣船陵禮也鳳紀疑秋龍帷將曙將遷坐于

From Chu Suiliang shitie xingshu.

who makes herself dissolve into her man in a fetching way. "Enamoring," *fumei*, is more commonly used to describe the physical charm of a woman, an attraction with an undertone of softness, of a pleasing, bewitching kind.[24] One need not be reminded that Wei Zheng's appearance "did not exceed the average, and he was always courageous and wise; whenever he remonstrated with offending words, even if the emperor was furious, his looks remained unchanged."[25] Chu Suiliang, equally upright and later a victim of his unwavering principle, was one of the prominent figures in Tang calligraphy, an art form considered the manifestation of one's upright personality. Certainly the two men did not warrant descriptions that rendered them effeminate, however well intended, and it appears that only a self-assured ruler could produce such patronizing remarks. Starting from Emperor Xuanzong, Tang emperors moved closer to their eunuch-servants, distancing themselves from ministers proper, and such intimate tones of speech all but disappeared.

The ministers' role had another dimension that moved them to closer proximity with concubines, defined as providers of pleasures. In the aesthetic climate of the Tang, poetic compositions, calligraphy, and paintings were celebrated and circulated widely at the court, while the emperors and their ministers shared a remarkable craving for belles lettres. During banquets, poetry recital was common; in court sessions too, obsession with poetry sometimes led to disorder while courtiers cited recent compositions to each other.[26] This love of embellished words led to an assortment of talented men of letters in the Academy of Literature (*hanlin yuan*), whose duties included providing advice, giving lectures, serving on imperial journeys, and attending private banquets in his majesty's presence.[27] The spectrum of their services hence crossed from advising on state affairs to providing private pleasures through linguistic entertainment for the despot; in this respect, their role was partially identified with that of the courtesans.

The four leading calligraphers of the Tang, Liu Gongquan, Yan Zhenqing, Chu Suiliang, and Yu Shinan, had all been important ministers at the court. Wang Wei, a chief minister, was both a leading poet and an established painter; and Li Bo, the much admired genius, had been recruited by Xuanzong as a court poet. At its best, the Tang court was populated by men of rare talents, serving the empire both administratively and artistically, creating a vibrant cultural scene. It was in this epochal atmosphere that Yan Liben, a court painter sharing a high reputation in Chinese art history with his brother Lide, was summoned to paint the colorful fish swimming in the pond that Taizong and his scholars were enjoying. The painting master Yan Liben, a senior secretary in his own right, at once arrived at the scene, running and sweating:

> He kneeled by the pond and brushed on pigments, glancing at the distant guests; his shame was beyond words. Back home, he warned his son: "I am known for my artistry, so am subjected to the task of a lowly servant—there is no greater insult. Take heed and don't practice this small skill."[28]

The shame Yan felt speaks directly to the plight of those who were compelled to create upon royal summons. At boisterous imperial banquets, this shame was keenly felt by the artist who became the victim of his art, who succumbed to a prostitution of his art. This shame must have lurked beneath the general merrymaking at the court, and it brings to the fore the intrinsic frustrations of a minister-concubine.

The degrading employment of one's artistic talents was not the worst fate for a man of ambition; nor were servant and concubine the only metaphors for ministers. In a telling moment, and at a strictly symbolic level, two ministers read a poem by Li Shangyin, entitled "Palace Entertainers," and interpreted the dancers' alluring dance as an ironic allusion to the bitter struggle between courtiers. Although these were Song ministers conversing in their bureau, it spells out an anxiety shared by bureaucrats in different dynasties. That they saw themselves in these dancers, among the lowest ranks of palace women, is an eloquent manifestation of the minister-concubine complex; as such, it reveals the courtiers' apprehension of their fundamental subservience in relation to the monarch.[29]

* * *

Chengui (The track for ministers), compiled under Wu Zhao, starts with these words:

> To the ruler, ministers are like the arms and legs carrying the head, the ears and eyes employed by the mind. When combined together by a necessity, they form into one body; after having obtained each other, they begin to function. Therefore a minister serving the ruler is comparable to a son serving the father; although father and son are the closest of kin, theirs is yet less than the intimate fusion into one body of ruler and ministers.[30]

In this metaphor of body, the intimate relation between ruler and courtiers becomes physical. The coordination between various parts is mandatory, and the many ministers that constitute the ruler's body are important for its welfare. Paradoxically, the ministers' bodies, metaphorically those of the emperor, were sometimes mutilated with the intention of serving the ruler better.

By this I am referring to the eunuchs, who constituted the populated Bureau of Inner Service. More than three thousand eunuchs, at the peak, together with thousands of palace women, formed the largest population in the inner palace, and if we imagine the existence of thousands of castrates in the forbidden city, where the monarch's was theoretically the only "legal" phallus, the irrationality of imperial sexuality presents itself with a grotesque arrogance. Originally servants of low ranks, eunuchs were later placed in charge of the palace army and were given increasingly high ranks after Xuanzong; by the late Tang, they wielded their power to interfere with state affairs. Physically impaired to prevent them from violating the emperor's sexual monopoly, eunuchs were despised as "the leftovers of castration," and their political aggressions were associated with their physical

Eunuchs, detail of a mural in Li Chongrun's tomb.

From *Li Xian mu Li Chongrun mu bihua*.

deformity, as if the two were inherently connected. Often in earnest memorials against the despot's intimacy with these bureaucrat-servants, they were deemed "little men" by indignant ministers.[31]

At the fringe of bureaucrats' communities, the existence of these castrates created a peculiar problem in the minister-concubine analogy and exposed the sexualized imperial politics in its extreme. Bereft of manhood, eunuchs were defined by abnormality in social consciousness, and their official name, *zhongren* (neuter person), has all the connotations of its synonyms, from neuter to asexual to sterile. As desexualized beings tailored for imperial service, they came closest to the definition of concubines as nonthreatening creatures and yet were simultaneously at the furthest remove from it by reason of their sexual deformity. These men, tamed physically, were not without ambitions. Appearing first as self-debasing servants, they gained strength as the rulers, disarmed by their low profile, moved dangerously close to them. In the end, they transformed themselves from the despised handicapped to usurpers and bloody rebels. That things pushed to the extreme would turn into its opposite with catastrophic consequences, we have already been adequately warned by the *Book of Changes*.

* * *

As figurative concubines, ministers too may have lost their manhood in part, with the embarrassment of this loaded situation transferred from physical deprivation to psychological repression. As men with pride in their learning and high self-expectations, in the changing rules of the game ministers continued to guard vehemently their places above actual concubinage. The following episodes may elucidate the sort of humiliation they were forced to come to terms with. When Li Jing, the prominent general who had brought the empire great victories, arrived with his retinue at an official guest house, the local clerks removed the palace women who were already resting themselves there to accommodate Li. This infuriated Taizong tremendously; having the clerks put into prison, he proclaimed: "How could the control of power and glory be in the hands of Jing?" The steadfast Wei Zheng advised: "Jing and others are your highness' arm-ministers; the palace women are slaves to sweep the floor for the empress" and remonstrated that the county clerks be released; Taizong gave in and consented.[32]

The despot suffered an intrinsic anxiety: as the supreme patriarch, he must protect his kin against the administrators who remained outsiders but with considerable authority—although much, if not all, of that authority was granted by him and could be retrieved in an instant. The offense to his palace women and offspring was taken personally, and the territorial consciousness pointed both to the monarch's expanded ego and his intention to keep his courtiers at bay. It is at such moments that the ministers are seen as standing outside and against the imperial palace with the disdainful monarch at its center.

The following event symbolizes well the courtiers' position. In the reign of Emperor Muzong (820–824), the court sessions became increasingly scattered and started increasingly late; one day, the ministers stood waiting outside the Zihuan Gate, and hours went by without the imperial summons. The ministers, wearied by their rigid posture under the sun, began to falter. This humiliation led to an obstinate remonstration, as Liu Xichu went inside the court and knocked his head against the dragon's stairs until blood covered his forehead; the heavy beating of his head was heard by his anxious colleagues waiting outside.[33] This dramatic episode exposes vividly the ministers' alienation from the haughty Son of Heaven as well as the ultimate inequity between them.

Standing outside the imperial gate and acting as the bridge between the despot and his subjects, the courtiers were trapped by the necessity of protecting the monarch and his subjects from each other. In an eloquent memorial to Muzong, the monarch's generous gifts to entertainers were said to be subtracted from the slow, painful accumulation of "the oil and blood of the living souls" (*shengling gaoxue*) and should not be squandered thus. In another biting dialogue between Liu Rengui and Di Renjie, Wu Zhao's high ministers, Liu professed that the building of extravagant constructions should be concealed within the palace, so as "not to hurt the feelings of the gentlefolks."[34] These statements instruct us on the perilous position of the ministers, and the still more vulnerable condition of the commoners. Standing between the monarch and the gravely deprived folks, courtiers with higher self-regard shouldered the Confucian moral burden with considerable pathos. The continuous battles over sustaining their dignity as proper ministers, hence, sometimes bordered on the tragic.

The contempt for courtiers was blatant in the reigns of the capricious Zhongzong (705–710) and Ruizong (710–712). To their great delight, Zhongzong and Empress Wei watched the farce they staged as the palace women and ministers played the role of peddlers and merchants, slandering each other with vulgarity. The tasteless drama placed palace maids and high ministers on equal footing, and the minister-concubines moved perhaps never closer to their figurative Others.[35] At worse moments, high-ranking ministers, all talented men of letters, shuddered in utter silence in the presence of an enraged despot. In the court of Emperor X'uanzong (846–859), we are told, the atmosphere alternated according to the well-controlled tempo of the monarch, and in the high minister Linhu Tao's own words: "In my ten years of political career, at the Yanyin court, my back was covered with sweat even in the coldest winter."[36] In such a forbidding climate, it took a man of rare courage to oppose the monarch's will and guide it sternly to the path of propriety. That many were sacrificed thus was amply recorded, and victims of clashes between one's moral principles and a willful despot were well remembered.

THE USE OF HISTORY

The use of language embodied a significant facet of the courtiers' career, and when poetic talent received the highest admiration in the Tang, supremacy in verse became the inherent site of power struggles. When X'uanzong's poetic composition was compared to the famed poet and critic Shen Yue, by a minister, X'uanzong remarked indignantly: "Comparing me to a courtier—is this appropriate?" The unfortunate man was soon exiled to a distant post.[37]

The editing of history constituted another site of power struggles, in which imperial authority received considerable checks and balances. The concern Taizong showed for the records of his daily conduct was refreshing. Forcing Fang Xuanling to submit the records kept by the historians, Taizong comforted the courtiers by stating his intention of not giving them reasons to state his vices.[38] This evokes the suspicion that the most effective weapon against royal vices was the writing of histories. Eloquent speech had served the courtiers well in favorable circumstances, but for far-reaching effects and the ultimate resource to curtail the monarch, the writing of history became essential for scholars who had weathered the insult and punishment from a despot. The use (and misuse) of history indeed becomes transparent in official Tang histories.

Of the two hundred chapters in the *Old Tang History,* twenty are devoted to the emperors, thirty to various cultural, political, and natural codes and systems ranging from rites to astronomy, and at the center of this voluminous work, over one hundred chapters are devoted to ministers, which constitute the bulk of the compilation.[39] While its latter half was compiled after the demise of the Tang, it was based on the extensive materials left by Tang historians. In historiography similar to the Six Dynasties histories compiled by Tang historians, the *Old Tang History* presents the Tang consciousness in its structure, in which ministers stand out as indispensable forces that create history.[40] Although the arrangement of ministers' biographies follows the transitions from ruler to ruler, these biographies serve mainly to unfold the lives and characters of illustrious ministers. By contrast, the annals paint rather sketchy pictures of the monarchs, whose more complex images are to be pieced together through reading the biographies of their ministers.[41] The *Shilu,* virtual accounts of independent monarchs, follows the events of each reign and does not present the despot with telling details. The glorifying space assigned to the courtiers thus attests to a self-perpetuating mechanism of the scholar-minister's clique, and the critique on past rulers presents the ministers' ultimate control over the final verdict.[42]

The problem of editing and the power of discourse are complex issues and demand more careful study than we are allowed here. Suffice it to say that a power struggle between the despot and historians was blatant, as deliberations on the process of historical compilation were presented repeatedly throughout the era. Liu Zhiji, author of the illustrious *Generalities of History,* resigned on account of the large number of scholars and consequently opposing opinions involved in the compilation of Tang history. By contrast, a joint memorial from the imperial Grand Secretariat (*zhongshu sheng*) and imperial Chancellery (*menxia sheng*) points out distortions of historical records and suggests collaboration between the chief minister, the history department, and their bureaus.[43]

The struggle among courtiers over the charge of history is further exposed in the confusing verdict on certain ministers, for violent clashes between cliques have undoubtedly colored the description of events and of individuals involved. The decision to appoint historians to be in charge of the compilation of history hence had serious consequences, and here the subjective character of history is fully exposed.

The monarch's interference in the actual process of writing further reveals the power struggle in the control of history. In a discussion between Gaozong and his courtiers, the monarch remonstrates on the unfaithful transmission of Taizong's illustrious deeds into Wei Zheng's biography, rendering the ruler's benevolence the result of Wei's advice.[44] This complaint reveals in full scale the underhanded mechanism of history and the intrigue of the courtiers. Obviously, the ultimate power of words stood with the ministers, as they gained control over the presentations of their contemporaries and their lords. Shattering the minister-concubine complex, they often emerge in these records as upright men of principle who chastised those of opposing minds.

AMONG THEMSELVES

A good portion of the *Complete Collection of Tang Prose Composition* consists of memorials drafted by the courtiers, which are imbued with flowery rhetoric and stiff moralities. Their concerns remain basically one-dimensional, centering on the ideal of sagely ruling, the necessity to observe propriety and frugality, and the urgent need to guard against the little men. The last point, however, may be more complicated, for the little men are also good with words, and the confusion between them and the gentlemen could be disastrous.

Herein lies the ministers' dilemma, whose metaphorical position is identified with a concubine. It is basically a contradiction. As a concubine, a courtier should make himself intimate with the emperor; yet as a gentleman, he avoided letting himself be on intimate terms with others, a manner associated commonly with the lesser men, as was the judgment of Confucius. In a memorial from Wei Zheng, a section is devoted to this matter of discriminating carefully between the gentlemen and the illicit. It reads:

> One treats the gentleman with respect, and thus remains distant [from him]; one treats the little man lightly, and is hence intimate [with him]. When intimate, exchange of words is profuse; when distant, feelings cannot be well channeled.[45]

Caught in a double bind of intimacy and intrigue against that of respect and distance, the relation between the despot and his courtiers reminds us of the ideal relation between conjugal couples as one defined by mutual respect, rather than affection. The aversion from intimacy in ethical considerations seems consistent.

The usual spite for the in-laws and eunuchs who had climbed high through women and lowly services for imperial members was intertwined with a social consciousness that tended to treat marginalized people with suspicion. Because of the gentlemen's aversion to socially deprived groups, in their consciousness, women and eunuchs were often associated with a propensity for unnatural behavior.[46] It is therefore important that women should be suspicious and ask what those men really mean when they talk about the "little men," when women had been placed at close proximity to them. Only when one has been subjugated under a painfully biased gaze can one realize fully the illusive logic behind it.

We must reconsider the judgment, on women and on others alike, made by courtiers who were themselves immersed in an ideology shaped by Confucian-Legalist ethics of unconditional loyalty, and question the basis of their assumptions.[47] This precaution is mandatory exactly because of the ministers' own contradictory positions, which actually made their efforts to differentiate themselves from the little men (and women by analogy) excruciatingly frustrating. What creates problems for this moral cleansing is the difficulty to clean from within, when courtiers embodied the principle of *yin,* together with women, and shared the role of servants with concubines. Prescribed by an inner contradiction, the various analogous roles of ministers affected inevitably their self-definitions as well as their judgment of others. To name another a little man is thus dangerous, when one is implicitly a concubine in the terminology of imperial discourse.

*   *   *

Since the consolidation of the Han empire, maintaining order through imposing ethical codification had been one major measure of social repression. With neither an autonomous administrative system nor the rule of law, the preaching of adherence to one's social and ethical positions took precedence in governing. *Tang lü shuyi* (Tang legal codes), the earliest extant Chinese legal document on which later legal codes were based, presents in transparency a rigid hierarchical stratification that dictates meticulously classified degrees of punishments for members of different ethical and political statures for the same offenses, including that of murder. A legal system constituted largely by penal law, collaborating with the complex functions of the rites, was essentially the way imperial China commanded order. In a society where each was bound to the other by scrupulously classified obligations, even the sovereign was morally bound to Heaven and to his people, as was presented to him repeatedly.[48]

Seeking to curtail the floating energies of willful monarchs, potential usurpers, and dissatisfied commoners, ministers also worked vigorously to restrain women, situated at the lowest level of the ethical configuration. In the following chapters, we see how imperial discourse contains the overflowing desires of the spoiled princesses and their ultimate model, Wu Zhao, as well as imperial consorts who could cost the monarch his empire. In various memorials and edicts, in urgent dissuasions and historical records, indefatigable ministers strove to steer rulers to pro-

priety and women to their proper places. As I state above, the courtiers' conception of women should be considered in the light of their own status at the court.
Clearly, they did not speak from a vacuum but were implicated in a relentless imperial politics in which they played, with all sincerity and great expectations, a rather
vulnerable part.

Chapter 2

Fate of the Imperial Daughters

Daughter of the Yellow Emperor

In the manner of the sage kings, the Yellow Emperor did not let his daughter inherit his mighty sword. He did not as much as give her the beauty rightful to princesses. That is why Draught walked alone in the wilderness with her bald head; the fires lit by her loneliness burned down forests and farm fields, and people chased her away like a deadly disease. In her green robe blown big by the wind, Draught could not return to heaven and unite with her powerful father and brothers. Exiled to the human world, she carried within herself a vengeful fire, estranged from love.

Her fate is archetypal. Starting from her, all the fathers' daughters will suffer the same fate without end. Look, the daughter of the Yellow Emperor and her devoted maid form a solitary troop. They walk by the country roads and climb up the mountains, blowing the horn loud and shrill, her broken flag hits against their broken foreheads, and they laugh harshly.

Like a bald soprano, Draught appears in the open field. Her sleeves are blown by the hot wind, her maid as fierce as herself. Standing on the hill, her voice rises high, and her terrifying songs make poor folks' eyes fill with tears. Appearing in the desolate field against the desolate sky, Draught poises like a precise signal, an unwanted stranger, an insatiable hunger artist.

As royal daughters, Tang princesses shared with all daughters of the empire one destiny, the destiny of an outsider. As tokens of social value and natural stimulants, women were exchanged through a reciprocity of power, and marriages, especially in the Tang when old aristocratic clans exerted intense attractions, constituted the basic form of gift exchange, with women being the most precious gifts. The exchange of women placed their oppression within social systems, and women were exchanged for political favors and religious blessings, sent as tribute and kept as pawn, and bought and sold on the same footing as fine horses. Tang princesses' trafficking by their patriarchs was but the most salient facet of the traffic in women, and the most complete conversion of female lives into marriage alliances. In the traffic of women into the hands of political allies of different racial makeup, the marriage system was prominent in the political process of state making, in the maintenance of access to political resources, in the building of alliances, and in the consolidation of aristocrats into a closed strata.[1]

THE EMPEROR'S KNIFE

In the biographies of the royal princesses in *New Tang History* is this short entry on Princess Danyang, daughter of Gaozu and sister of Taizong.

> Princess Danyang was married to Xue Wanche, who was particularly dull-witted, and the princess, ashamed, would not share seats with him for several months. When Taizong learned of this, he laughed and had wine prepared, and had his brothers-in-law, together with Wanche, summoned to the court. . . . As they played dice, Taizong made his knife a forfeit and, intentionally losing the game, he unfastened his knife and bestowed it upon Wanche. The princess was pleased and let Wanche ride with her home on the same carriage.[2]

Xue Wanche, as we learn from other parts of Tang official history, had made decisive contributions to the founding of the Tang, winning important battles over the northern tribes and demonstrating rare bravery on the battlefield. It was not without ample reason that Danyang was married to such a man of military might and poor intelligence, and Taizong's attention showed his stake in this marriage.

Tang princesses were known for their haughtiness and flamboyant appetites for men and luxuries. There is a record-high remarriage rate among them compared with other dynasties, which demonstrates a disregard for the code of chastity adhered to by women of later eras. According to the historians, the gentry, preferring to unite through matrimonial ties with prestigious clans, shunned proposals from royalty to avoid their notorious daughters, known to make poor Confucian wives.[3] It was not unusual for husbands to be treated with contempt by their royal wives, sometimes cuckolded and humiliated openly. To tame their spoiled sisters and daughters, the monarchs admonished or, as in Danyang's case, designed clever expedients.

The bestowal of a knife worn on Taizong's waist to a belittled husband was enough to change the princess's heart—a knife, a sexually charged token, was exchanged between the monarch and the husband; a symbolic transference was enacted, and Xue regained his legitimacy as a husband with recharged vitality. This episode reveals the psychology of a princess who understood her place in the imperial configuration. A continuity between her imperial identity and her present role was to be sought by turning her glance back to the palace—together with the palace women, the princess oriented herself toward the patriarch's will. With the encompassing royal desire, the knife of an emperor, the "alter phallus," had a special significance, and here its transmission to Xue made him metaphorically potent.

Danyang rode home with her husband content; however, the course of history is treacherous. As a military man, Xue had the reputation of either triumphing victoriously or suffering disastrous defeat. So it was with his alliance with the rebellious Princess Gaoyang and her husband Fang Yiai in a plot against the newly enthroned Gaozong. The plot was discovered and Xue was executed among the clique.[4] The alliance of the three in-laws in this rebellion exposed the ambitions of the *fuma,* the princesses' husbands, who were later prevented from associating with important courtiers and from visiting the prime ministers' houses.[5]

The bestowal of the emperor's knife, then, imbued with symbolic meaning, may in turn solicit unwanted ambitions. The story of Xue Wanche spells out the complex conditions involved in the delicate position of the princesses: standing at the threshold of the palace, they could be fatally jealous of their brothers' privileges. The phenomenal power of Princess Taiping (daughter of Wu Zhao) and Princess Anle (daughter of Empress Wei) manifested the will of ambitious Tang princesses covetous of the throne itself.

DESIRES AS TRANSFERENCE

The concept that the Tang signaled a moment of liberation for women in Chinese imperial history is partially borne out by the illustrious princesses who enjoyed political and sexual freedom denied their female posterity. The many memorials against their daring conduct present a persistent attempt to curb these women, who, favored by a unique historical occasion, indulged themselves in sensuous excess.

After having donned the mask of a Taoist priestess to shun a marriage proposal from Tibet, the Princess Taiping danced before her doting parents Gaozong and Empress Wu in a purple robe with jade belt, worn by military officials, suggesting thus the absence of a *fuma;* and Gaozong soon handpicked a husband for her.[6] Taiping's contempt for courtiers was explicit; she thought them narrow and pathetic and bribed them with handsome gold and silks to sway their opinions on state affairs. The scholars did not prove themselves beyond bribery, and Taiping's influence was extraordinary. The historians took pains to record that after her failed coup against Xuanzong, the treasure in her possession took three years to count.

The daring desire of Taiping and its precedence over others was not an isolated instance. Princess Anle had an adulterous relationship with Wu Yanxiu, a member of the empress's clan.[7] Full of splendor, Anle gathered many lords and influential ministers under her wing. Together with Taiping and five other princesses, she had her own official administration, and its posts were sold to "merchants and butchers."[8] The material indulgence of Anle was of stunning magnitude:

Since the princess started to make feathered skirts, noble ministers and the rich followed suit, and the feathers of all rare birds and strange beasts in the south were exhausted.[9]

Anle's elder sister, Princess Changning, was extravagant in her craving for architectural brilliance; at both capitals, she had expensive halls built adjacent to a lofty terrace and magnificent temples, with an athletic field attached to them.[10]

Equally extravagant was the princesses' sexual drive, and the keeping of *mianshou* (male concubines) was practiced among the more daring. Under the leadership of Empresses Wu and Wei, female desires were allowed daring expression.[11] Below is a quick listing of the princesses whose will was expressed through extravagant sexuality. The compulsive Princess Xiangyang, who often disguised herself to roam the streets, kept several lovers; she was later imprisoned by Emperor Muzong, her lovers all exiled or executed. Princess Gaoguo, after the death of her second husband, kept several officials for her private enjoyment. Princess Gaoyang had an illicit affair with a monk and introduced two women for her husband's pleasure. Such liberal sexuality also presented itself in jealousy, the counterpart of a liberated consciousness. Princess Yicheng, jealous of her husband's concubine, cut off the woman's ears and nose and the man's hair. Punished for this transgression, she was soon reinstated.

The material abundance and extra lovers enjoyed by the princesses notwithstanding, one must not romanticize their existence. The officials' fear of having a princess forced upon them indicates that, privileged to satisfy their wildest wishes, these women were not welcomed by the orthodox. Caught between instincts and an ethics that demanded female servility, they received punishment time and again that testified to this tension. Except for rare exceptions, the princesses, deprived of worthy careers, were left with the inviting option of squandering away energy in vain endeavors, allowing unfocused desires to define their mode of being.

In the chapters on ill omens in official history, imperial women with a propensity for particular luxuries are cited as "clothes devils."[12] Compared with the much more expansive chapters on their male siblings, the only chapter on these imperial sisters is extremely succinct, leaving most of their lives obscure. What gets written down in this economical rendition, then, provides an insight into the politics of historical editing. The historians' unspoken intentions and will to persuade are revealed in the scarce details. It is not accidental that princesses of licentious desires, pious princesses, and rebels are recorded with relatively extensive details. The editing of history is never innocent. Images of the vainglorious princesses were put up as targets for scorn and horror that epitomized direct opposition to perseverance, a virtue of the feminine principle. Placed next to their pious sisters, these women gained their entrance to history—and this is the irony—as negative examples.

A comparison of biographies of imperial children shows that it was the daughters who suffer criticism for excessiveness. Among the sons, Prince Chengqian was the only one criticized for irrational extravagance, including his indulgence in a boy lover. Perhaps the historians were busy with political struggles that engulfed these lords; perhaps material indulgence was not conceived to be as dangerous in men as it was in women. The material indulgence of the princesses was deemed licentious and posed inherent threats: the association of excessive female desires with immorality is obvious here.

Sensual excess and political ambitions are interconnected in the historian's judgment; that unchecked female vigor will lead to a rebellious frame of mind is inherent in their historiography. Yet in Tang princesses, a reversal may be in effect: it is through the vainglorious exhibition of estates and riches that the princesses channeled anxieties over a delimited status. In an underhanded way, obsession with wealth worked as a psychological transference, when desires put on costumes to disguise the unspeakable. In this sense, the grandiose conduct of the princesses should be understood as no less than a transformation of the political ambitions that were denied them.

In rare cases, this transference exposed its hidden nature, and the imperial sisters moved toward their goals with determination. They pitted their wills against that of the patriarchs who offered them unprecedented freedom and, in the end, must suffer the sisters' drive for self-glorification and their insatiable thirst for the throne. Compared with imperial daughters, the princes, implicated in political intrigues, were constantly plagued by a fear that fills their biographies with anxiety and pathos. Their sisters, by contrast, were less compelled to involve themselves with such intrigues; but when the more ambitious decided to join in, they were often portrayed as relentless, moving without the fear so often smelled in their male siblings. The imbedded ideology seems to be that fearlessness, counterpart of ambition, is another form of female vice, identified with sensual excessiveness.

PRINCESSES CANONIZED

The royal Li clan had halfheartedly employed the propaganda that professed Li Er, the legendary founder of the sect and the great Taoist philosopher, as their ancestor and ordained Taoism the state religion. Amid dynastic enthusiasm, a number of princesses were lifted into holy orders and acquired the rank of priestess, residing in the splendid belvederes in and around the capitals, with the mission of procuring blessings for their royal relatives.[13]

The number of Taoist princess-priestesses who took holy orders (about a dozen recorded), compared with that of the princes (none recorded), shows how this was an alternative mainly for the princesses. Along with the practice of marrying princesses to the barbarians, it manifests their identity as outsiders. The many lords and princes, burdened by the duty of ensuring a descent line, were without the alternative of a religious life, and the ethical duty of procuring spiritual blessings for their seniors fell naturally on women. This explains well the feminine outlook of Taoist adepts in the imperial circle. Yet from evidence gathered in discourses other than imperial, and in light of the unique freedom enjoyed by Tang priestesses, the entering of holy orders may not have been always ethically or religiously oriented. The many poems alluding to these royal priestesses' liberated sexuality in their extravagant belvederes suggest that to become a capeline meant sexual independence, sublime splendor, and in the case of Princess Yuzhen, lush attention and posthumous fame. Considering the high status of Buddhism and its nunneries that housed the many palace women of deceased monarchs, the absence of Buddhist nuns in the princesses' biographies also speaks to the particular nature of this choice.

In Tang poetry, Taoist capelines are celebrated for their mystic existence, shrouded in the magical atmosphere of mist and bell chants. In the resplendent belvederes, no one knew what pleasures they had accorded themselves: this was one of the thematic obsessions of the poets, and it points to a general suspicion of their celibacy.[14] This particular condition presses us to rethink the initial hypothesis that priesteshood was another existence of alienation. By virtue of the belvederes' geographical position, nearby the capital, the priestesses were not entirely secluded. Physically (and mentally) removed from the palace, they nevertheless maintained a bond with the imperial family, praying for their families' welfare as filial daughters, while in the meantime enjoying a liberal mode of life.

The building of Yuzhen's belvedere was a gala event in the capital and was sternly criticized for its indulgence that might bring harm, defeating its purpose.[15] Without disappointing others, Yuzhen achieved rare religious intensity: she pleaded to forswear her title and fief to be independent of an imperial pension. Paradoxically, this move away from the status of princess made her a prominent figure in the records of history. In the many poems composed on her belvedere, Yuzhen haunts the scene in an enchanting aura. There were no predefined qualities for a princess in ethical codes, but piety, both religious and ethical, marked the more recognized ones besides the negative examples of the licentious.

That the austere existence of a Buddhist nun was not an alternative available to Tang princesses is culturally telling.[16] Compared with the many lords and ladies who entered the Buddhist order in the Japanese Heian period (794–1068), when such a choice marked the enlightenment of the earthly as illusion, the choice of the more flamboyant life of a capeline suggests not only that the Li clan preferred self-celebrating luster even in matters religious, but also that this decision was, more than anything else, a way for these royal women to be the architects of their own existence. Whether this choice led to an exuberant career, a liberated life without the burden of a husband, or a lonely seclusion, it belonged to their separate destiny and is left out of the domain of official histories.

PAWNS TO THE BARBARIANS

The "Biographies of the Princesses" in *New Tang History* ends with this eulogy:

> Women dwell inside their husbands' houses; even for noble ladies, historians are left
> out and could not know their lives. In addition, after the upheavals at the reigns of

Emperors Xi and Zhao, documents were destroyed, with only their birth and death dates remained; those that are lost hence are left unrecorded.[17]

A double exclusion can be detected here: It is not that the historians were left out of the princesses' lives, which were shut "within," but rather, the princesses stood outside of history. The historians excused themselves by explaining the inaccessibility of these women, a unique statement in their encompassing project. The princesses were exiled from history, and this is nowhere more clearly manifested than in the *Old Tang History,* where their biographies simply do not exist.

This condition of outsidedness is conspicuous in these royal daughters' forced departures from the empire to a foreign land.[18] As a token of exchange, a princess was of the highest value when sent to the barbarians as a peace envoy–bride. As the ministers feared being exiled, the single fate that most haunted the princesses was marriage to the nomads. One famous victim of such a marriage is Wang Qiang, an imperial consort given to the Tartar by a reluctant Han emperor. Her lyrics upon leaving were inspirational for women poets of later dynasties, who shuddered with the thought of her fate. The symbol of woman as outsider, when manifested in this exile from home and civilization (from the perspective of the empire, that is), acquired a tragic dimension to women of keen imaginations. By an apprehensive instinct, dynastic women internalized the fate of Wang Qian as intrinsically their own.

The significance of a princess given to the barbarians is twofold. Ideally and from the perspective of the Tang, she acted as an ambassador from a higher culture to assert influence over the uncultivated tribes, at the same time securing peaceful borders. The reluctance of the Tang to give real blood royal and the nomad's resentment at being given a makeshift princess make clear the subtle politics involved, with the transmission/transfusion of blood and fear of contamination all part of this intense deal.[19] At the diplomatic level, the princess acted as a pawn between two potential enemies and served as a fragile covenant of peace.

Marriages to the tribes acquired different meanings as history unfolded.[20] At the time of the illustrious Taizong, the marriage of Princess Wencheng to Tibet was an event the Tang could be proud of. Ashamed in the face of the dignified display of the empire's rites and wealth, the Tibetan king treated Wencheng with reverence and requested education from the Tang, thus fulfilling the ideal meaning of this political marriage.

As the empire suffered a slow demise, princesses were forced to endure situations beyond the control of their patriarchs. Princess Jincheng, who was married to a Tibetan king in the reign of Zhongzong, asked messengers from home for the *Classic of Poetry, Spring and Autumn Annals,* and the *Book of Rites* after a prolonged turbulent period between the two countries. The court's reaction is helpful for an insight into its foreign policies. One minister argued that to "endow [the enemies] with the books and equip them with military strategies will enhance their treachery, and is not in our interest." Another proposed that the classics contained the ethics of loyalty and propriety and would cultivate the Tibetans for the empire's own good.[21]

The argument against exposes a fundamental attitude of the empire, characterized by a guarded distrust of the tribes. The debate was decisive for Jincheng's delicate position: compelled to pass the test of her value as a Tang princess in an already hostile land, she stood at the mercy of her father. Her plea was granted, and Jincheng's task was completed—if only temporarily.[22] The plight Jincheng suffered during the years of prolonged war between the Tang and Tibet—starting a few years after her marriage and lasting until her last days—can only be imagined.[23]

The turbulent career of Princess Taihe exemplifies the fate that may befall a princess married to the "barbarians" when they turned truly barbarous. When Taihe returned from her disastrous mission to the Uighurs of twenty-two years, ministers and the palace army of four hundred soldiers were gathered in an elaborate ceremony.

> Weeping, Taihe retreated to the Guangshun Gate to change and take off her jeweled headgear. She waited for the emperor Wuzong's verdict, submitting that she had failed her mission. Wuzong sent agents to console her, and Taihe put her headgear back and entered. All the ministers congratulated the Son of Heaven. . . . When the princess arrived, Xuancheng and seven other princesses did not come to welcome her; Wuzong was angered and ordered their pension silks be retrieved to compensate for the offense.[24]

The solemn welcome for Taihe who had failed her mission is a perfect example of the politics of sacrifice and compensation. Again, what is left out in Taihe's biography is intriguing.

When rebellions and epidemic broke out among the Uighur people two years before Taihe's return, a period of chaos began. A new khan installed himself, and a debate was held at the court over the issue of aid. Li Deyu presented:

> Now the Uighur confederacy is in ruins, and the whereabout of Princess Taihe is unknown. If messengers were not sent to investigate, the barbarians will think that we marry our princesses to them because they are not cherished—this both betrays the princess and hurts the tribe's feelings.[25]

Agents were hence sent to search for Taihe, carrying with them additional diplomatic missions. Meanwhile, the new khan kidnapped Taihe and crossed the desert to the border, there forcing her to request aid and recognition from the Tang. The court hinted in a mild letter that Taihe be returned to the Tang. In the following months, the khan and his horsemen posed an immediate threat at the border and finally invaded. During the next winter, Wuzong sent Taihe winter garments with a letter enclosed:

> Our past sovereigns severed attachment and married you to the tribe to bring peace to the state, believing that the Uighurs would stand by it. Now its conduct is improper—every time you, my aunt, turn your horse to the south, could you not fear the brave souls of

Gaozu and Taizong? Invading the border, could you have forsaken the love of the retired emperor and empress? As their national mother, you should rule over them; should they disobey, they are discarding our marital tie, and hereafter may not use you as an excuse.

The diplomatic tone of this letter shows the delicacy of the matter, as a weakened state tried to threaten the khan, while the princess who belonged neither to her fatherland nor to the country of which she was the queen mother was made to take the blame for this violent breach of contract.

In the following spring, during a survey of the battlefield, a dozen carpeted chariots with servants in Chinese costumes were detected, and Taihe was located. The troops launched a swift attack at night, procured the princess, and Taihe was escorted back to the capital. The cooperation of royalty in showing moral support for this retrieved princess was mandatory. Again the emphasis was on female piety: that the princesses were punished for failing to appear at the ceremony seemed the most important facet in this national disaster for the historians, and it was praised as the manifestation of a moral rule.[26]

As a political pawn, a kidnapped princess surely bruised the imperial pride, as the changing politics put both the princess and her father state in a difficult situation. The abducted Taihe loomed large at the border, the imperial chicken came home to roost, and the two alternately timid and stiff-faced letters from the court exposed its anguish. With Taihe, the meaning of the token bride suffered a reversal; it was not the tribes, but the great empire, that was tied down by its daughter who wandered at its border like an open wound.

There will be more princess tokens until the end of the Tang, but with an altered meaning. The marriage of Princess Pingyuan to the son of a member of the rebels was clearly beyond Emperor Zhaozong's (888–904) control, as he submitted: "If this is not done, I shall have no place for myself."[27] The princess as token now had more immediate but less exchange value, and still less political significance, as the empire approached its end, and the necessity of binding a powerful son-in-law for royal interests became too urgent to retain any subtlety.

THE CHASTISEMENT

The difference between female virtues upheld in the princesses' biographies and those in "Lienü zhuan" (Biographies of exemplary women) in Tang official histories is considerable. The mildly chaste princesses, praised for their piety and frugal styles, together with their flamboyant sisters, create a sharp contrast to civilian women of self-demolishing virtues appearing at the end of the histories, divided from their imperial sisters by a social stratification represented by the sheer weight of these bulky volumes. While these gentry women died in jealous protection of their sexual integrity or their husbands' lives, the exercise of marital piety was not the princesses' trait. Their principal objects of piety were the imperial family, in particular the monarch; by contrast, their plebeian husbands were not nearly as closely respected, nor was chastity.

However, ethical demands were tightening on them after the subsidence of the wave of female revolutions championed by Wu Zhao. The princesses' administrations were terminated after Empress Wei's defeat; Xuanzong continued the surge of suppression by ordering palace women from consorts down to raise silkworms and to learn the art of embroidery, the quintessential feminine labor. Since Kaiyuan, the princesses' pension was sometimes not enough to maintain the cost of their carriages and costumes; the *fuma* too were barred from real posts.[28]

The changing rules of conduct were explicitly manifested in several incidents. Princess Yan'an was rebuked by the frugal Emperor Wenzong (827–840) for wearing an extravagantly wide robe to a palace banquet. An edict was issued:

> The princess came to the palace transgressing the dress code; a wife submits herself to her husband, to whom her faults will be traced. [The *fuma* Dou] Wan is to be stripped of two months' pension.[29]

This verdict had the effect of placing Yan'an under her spouse's guidance, thus stripping her autonomy. The insult was meant to teach her her place, both in the dress code and in the conjugal relationship. The identification of female desires with impropriety was the historian's verdict on the licentious princesses; here in the sovereign's edict, a similar ideology was in effect, and female excess was contained in a nutshell by making women submit to their husbands' authority.

X'uanzong, who was responsible for arousing the princesses' anxiety over their own conduct, issued the following edict:

> Husbands and wives are the beginning of rites and propriety. All widowed princesses with sons are forbidden to a second marriage.[30]

A new code of chastity was thus established. With the decentralization of the state's power, princesses were to show more concern for their in-laws, while their husbands acquired authority over them, exacting a bond both in life and in death. These royal women now moved closer to their civilian sisters when the patriarch surrendered the symbolic authority of his knife to the ever-threatening son-in-law. As the Li clan was losing its grip, its daughters, dispersed into gentry families, must adhere to a relentless codification from which they had hitherto escaped.

The fate of the imperial daughters, as I try to show, was no less treacherous than that of the ministers, with whose pens their images were cast. It quickly dawns on us that in this empire, manifestations of one's subjectivity were often costly. The one essential feminist question—"What does it mean to be a daughter?"—is answered not without bitterness in the case of these imperial daughters, who were caught in impossible situations imposed by their fathers, and whose lives were often converted into marriage alliances. Suffice it to say that the transactions remained crucial, and these royal women continued to serve as important commodities for their fathers whose concern for them was hopelessly confused with that of the interests of the state. The law of the father gained momentum, ironically, as the Tang suffered its gradual downfall, and its daring daughters were instructed to take a radically altered self-definition.[31]

Chapter 3

Monument without Inscription:

The Case of Wu Zhao

The Woman Emperor

Once there was a woman who coveted the throne, and she kept it a sternest secret. How was it possible for a woman to proclaim herself emperor in a kingdom that placed women at the lowest of the social strata? Because of this impossible situation, and because of her fierce will, the woman became terrifying. Many lives were surrendered and much blood was shed, until finally she ascended the throne. Moving against the thick stream of blood toward the dragon's seat that at long last was hers, her magnificent robe, her jade tablet, and her pitch-black hair had blood all over them.

The woman emperor ruled for several decades. In the palace courtyard she installed a bronze urn for people to cast complaints into, and a giant bell was molded to celebrate her reign. She changed the colors of court banners and robes, coined new names for official bureaus, and built an outlandish sacrificial hall. Thus she brought prosperity and talents to the state, as well as the bone of Buddha all the way from India.

After her death, a blank monument of stone was erected. Standing in defiance of language, the monument says nothing about the glory, the crime, or the miracle of a woman emperor. Did the woman rule as a man or as a woman? What can something as contradictory as a woman-emperor be? Was the grand human sacrifice that sustained her power worthwhile after all? On these, the stone remains absolutely silent. Was the blankness of the monument a mistake, or was it ordained by Her Majesty? No one could decide on the matter, and the will of the woman emperor remained unknown.

In Emperor Gaozong's reign, Chen Shuozhen, a peasant woman, proclaimed herself emperor and made her brother-in-law chief minister. Her troop of over ten thousand men overtook the Mu district, and it was rumored that the troop was transported by a spirit. Chen was defeated by a gallant governor; within a month her followers surrendered, and Chen was executed.[1] This short-lived revolt of a self-styled woman emperor is an apt prelude to the career of the much more resourceful Wu Zhao.

57

Monument without Inscription. On the Spirits Road of Wu Zetian's Mound Qian, Xi'an.

Photo courtesy of Jowen Tung, 1991.

In a custom that the Tang inherited from the Sui, after the death of their lords, imperial consorts were sent to either Buddhist temples or Taoist belvederes to spend their remaining days—essentially a transformed observance of burial sacrifice.[2] It was thus in Ganye Buddhist Convent that Li Zhi, Taizong's ninth son and his heir, found a despondent Wu Zhao, consort of his deceased father. This episode is essential for a study of Wu, for it was from austere confinement and sexual deprivation that a determined Wu Zhao reemerged. Sharing between father and son was not rare in the palace; without ethical bonds with their lords, concubines and maids were not infrequently exchanged among covetous fathers and sons, and in the inner palace where power and sexuality were identified with one another, ethical restraint played a rather feeble role.[3]

The characters of the father and son were of drastic opposite poles: the self-conscious Taizong, vigilant against female troubles and preferring virtuous consorts, was the model of an ideal monarch, whereas Gaozong, who was enthroned partially because of his exuberant observance of filial piety, was not forgiven for having provided the channel for female usurpation and had since borne the contempt of historians for his incompetence at shaking off female influence.[4] The unprecedented ordination of a woman emperor should be explained both by the Tang's liberal climate, which provided women space for self-realization, and the characters of those involved. The physically and mentally weak Gaozong contrasted vividly with a strong-willed Wu Zhao, and when Wu realized that her ability far exceeded those surrounding her, it was inevitable that this ambitious empress would move forward to claim what she deserved.

During the consolidation of the Tang, Princess Pingyang fought gallantly for her father Gaozu, contributing to the founding of the empire; Empress Zhangsun of Taizong was exemplary in her unassuming assistance in managing state affairs and in directing Taizong back on the track. Steeped in nomadic customs, these imperial women loomed large in both social and political arenas, unintimidated by their male counterparts. Wu Zhao stood thus at the focal point of the culmination of female consciousness in the Tang, with these stately women as her worthy predecessors; although desiring more for herself and stretching the boundary much further, she would fight a much more violent battle.

CRUELTY

To talk about Wu Zhao, we cannot avoid the extreme violence shrouding her career as she rose high against the patriarchal will. The copious blood shed to realize the ambition of a woman unique in history warns us against the dialectic of oppression. Precisely because of a patriarchal system that stood obstinate against female transgression, Wu staged a fight horrifying in its vindictive drive. Traditional presentations of Wu Zhao are hence clouded by her stupendous cruelty and present her as the epitome of feminine vileness, citing the (fabricated) murders of infant and sons that blew her vices to inhuman proportions.[5]

The particularly cruel inventions with which Wu disposed of her female rivals should be discredited for their fictitious quality.[6] Official histories, adapting anecdotes in private writings, point to her cruelty as the historical cause for Wu's preference for Luoyang, where she took refuge from a palace haunted by her victims.[7] Such logic belongs to an entrenched presumption of female cruelty in the inner palace, a place subject to public curiosity, where prolonged confinement and jealousy had eaten away these women's proper perspectives. The socially deprived often feed on each other in an intense struggle for mobility, and this sealed female existence produced a mystifying aura surrounding the back palace, providing sumptuous food for insipid fancy.

As with much of Wu's cruelty, the best strategy is not to whitewash her from the many alleged murders but to guard against a discourse that, through manipulative overtones (*and* manipulation of truths) was eager to sentence Wu for her one fundamental crime of usurpation. The inadequacy of official histories attests to a basic prejudice of imperial discourse, which renders the reconstructing of history, especially that of a woman emperor, essential. This rewriting of history, however, is undermined by a serious deficiency: due to the complex and prolonged collaborations among hostile historians, some truths may never be fully recovered.

While the death of the crown prince Li Hong, Wu Zhao's first son, had been caused, as argued more forcefully by modern scholars, by consumption, the death of her second son Li Xian is less easily removed from the list of Wu's alleged crimes.[8] With Wu Zhao, the myth of motherhood is betrayed, a betrayal that is exactly what official discourse holds against her and where she seemed particularly morally obtuse. Following the tradition of imperial power struggles, Wu had done no more, and possibly less (if Xian was but an illicit son forced upon her) than her male counterparts, yet its implications and reception were radically different. Wu Zhao's demystification of motherhood proves that like the patriarchs', women's ambitions are not to be deprived on account of her demanding young. The surprising weapon Wu Zhao had in store against the existing order was thus the persecution of her own flesh and blood, the bond with whom lies particularly heavy with women.[9] With an intrepid Wu Zhao, this bond was overruled, when motherhood as a controlling mechanism governing the milk-givers lost its power of persuasion.

The extreme case of Wu Zhao makes an extreme example of female ambition. To remove the unyielding blood royal and hostile ministers, executions and exiles were in effect for years. To contain dissatisfactions at the court, Wu's grip tightened under the instrument of cruel officials, who effected a virtual rule of horror. Practically all who had stood in her way were terminated by a vengeful woman emperor, sometimes in perverse manner.[10] This less than civilized behavior supports Wu's vicious reputation, and it is here that we must confront the truth of a monumental female cruelty, which stands at the core of Wu Zhao's early image as a monarch.

To comprehend the necessity of Wu's drastic measures, we must put into context a patriarchy that had never witnessed a woman emperor and had instinctively put on a tough resistance; her fight against it, likewise, turned ferocious. To create the precondition for the ordination of a woman emperor, the weight of patriline bore down on the male clans mercilessly, and the biographies of Tang princes are very much blood-stained records of this woman's revolution. As heirs of the Li patriline, these princes—together with their guardians, the devout ministers—became its very victims.

Here, the two-edged knife of patriarchy cut deep when one of its exiled determined to move to the center, and the movement from the margin to the core, by virtue of its sheer magnitude, created a storm of similar dimensions as the counter-move from the existing order. The difficult problem of Wu Zhao's brutality should be understood in light of the necessary evil that accompanied the revolutionary move from an outcast, which exacted a high price from the ancient machine of patriarchy.

THE USE OF OMENS AND SUTRA

Preceding Wu's ordination, side by side with military upheavals and relentless persecutions were numerous edicts for grand pardons and bestowal of meals that were issued to ensure healing. As these operations elucidate, it was through the daring application of symbolic discourse along with the manipulation of political tools that Wu Zhao succeeded in ascending to power. Following the swift defeat of the revolting Li clan, Wu created a dozen new Chinese characters for prominent concepts, including that for the term *human,* in which the notion of birth by one (woman) is dominant. This echoed Wu's efforts to grant an equal mortuary mourning period for one's mother, extending it from the original one year to three years. Wu also created a character for her first name, *Zhao,* depicting two heavenly bodies, the sun and the moon, circulating over heaven—another bold move at the symbolic level to claim heaven's mandate. Wu's very name became the manifestation of a heaven resplendent with light. Without actually naming herself the Daughter of Heaven, Wu had in effect claimed more—she was heaven itself, with the two brightest planets overarching it, giving out unobstructed light. Such willful inscription of meaning into one's name is unprecedented: it bespeaks Wu's ingenious imagination as well as her apprehension of the importance of language as social symbol. Thus Wu circumvented the system of meaning, prominent in the mechanism of power. If Wu's creation of these characters was ideologically oriented, it has the archaeological function of causing manuscripts written in her time to be identifiable through characters that have become tokens of her reign.

Preparing for her ordination, ten Buddhist monks, headed by her lover Xue Huaiyi, presented Wu with the Chinese translation of the *Mahamegha Sutra* (The Great Cloud Sutra, *Dayun jing*) together with its commentary, professing that it contained the sacred manifestation of her ascension as a woman ruler. In an episode in the sutra, the Buddha prophesies to a *devi* called Vimalaprabha that in future metempsychosis she is to incarnate as a woman sovereign, bringing blessings to the myriad. From there she would continue the transformation of the *samadhi,* until she reaches Buddhahood.

When you abandon this aspect of a Devi, you shall reign over the territory of a country with the body of a woman and you shall obtain a quarter of the places governed
by a Cakravartin king; you shall obtain great sovereignty. . . . you will teach and convert the cities and the villages which depend on you, men and women, great and small.
. . . Then you will in reality be a Bodhisattva who will show and receive a female body
in order to convert beings.[11]

The woman [as your future samadhi], having received the true power, will subdue the
world. . . . there will be none who will resist or oppose her. . . . she will hoist marvelous flags and parasols of many-colored cloth and everywhere she will make acts of
veneration with the wonderful perfume of sandalwood. . . . in a future generation,
when incalculable *kalpas* have passed, this queen will be able to be a Buddha . . . connoisseur of the world, unsurpassed lord . . . master of gods and men, awakened and
honored by the world.[12]

The sutra was received with delight by Wu, who had long patronized Buddhism,
and the veneration of the sutra was a prelude to her ordination. Knowing that
orthodox Confucianism offered no leeway for a woman monarch, Wu turned to a
Buddhism that, although equally discriminating, was not as absolute. Through pro-
pagandist employment of the sacred text and its commentary, which identified her
with the bodhisattva, Wu Zhao sought consent from believers and from the large
assemblies in Buddhist temples. In the commentary, the sacrificial *Mingtang* (Bright
Hall) was presented as the Magic City of which Sakyamuni spoke in a parable in
the *Saddharmapundarika* (The lotus of the true law). In this manner, the hall was
made a soteriological symbol where Wu conducted the *Pancavarsika* ceremonies
befitting her identity as a bodhisattva, and two of the most important political-sacral
tokens employed by Wu, the sacrificial hall and the sutra, thus concurred.[13]

The prophecy about the *devi* as future queen, however, was intended as an expedience in a greater design, as transformation into a female body was only transitory
in a grand cycle completed with the achievement of Buddhahood. In this sense,
the queen, albeit glorified, was herself but a transient form that awaited the highest existence defined by Buddhahood. In the text, the female body was regarded as
a negativity; as Buddha explained, "it is an instrumental body and not a real female
body. . . the body of a Bodhisattva Mahasattva which in this *samadhi* is free and can
use all sorts of expedients as suits him: in spite of having the features of a woman,
there is no sensual attachment or amorous ties in her heart, *she is not impure.*"[14] The
female body as contaminated yet nonetheless *not itself* in the great transmigration
was stressed in this discussion, and Wu Zhao as the queen-bodhisattva, however
celebrated and omnipotent, was inherently denigrated by the nature of her gender.

A similar twist of irony can also be discerned in Wu's name: the character for
heaven/sky has another meaning of emptiness, imbued with the Buddhist teaching of the world as illusion. Interpreted in this context, the self-glorifying character is undermined by a sense of ultimate futility, which defeats Wu Zhao's political purpose. In this reading, the Buddhist principle that Wu Zhao had utilized well
turned against her unexpectedly.

For Wu Zhao's purpose, however, the goal justified the means, however flawed. An apprehension of the function of ideological mechanisms had urged her to adopt these religious-political tokens, and by adopting a new concept of sovereignty—namely, the sacral-political identity of Wu Zhao as bodhisattva (or as Cakravartin of the Golden Wheel, with whom she was also identified)—a new order was installed. If the sutra was steeped in masculine ideology, Wu applied what was useful for her immediate purposes. A bold manipulation of discourse was the true significance of these various propaganda, and for her audacious end, no means were spared. In a society where all things had a prescribed position and received meaning, where rites and rituals were regulated by painful details, where superstition had the power of persuasion on minds that believed in preternatural destiny, and where names provided indelible definitions of an entire life, Wu, in her lavish manner, used these cultural signs well, bypassing other undermining assumptions.

A few months after the presentation of the sutra, requests for Wu to ascend the throne came from all sides, and Wu's son Li Dan, the token emperor, requested to be granted Wu's surname, replacing that of the father. After this show of enthusiasm, followed by more auspicious omens of phoenixes and red peacocks, Wu Zhao finally ordained herself emperor and changed the dynasty's name to Zhou, following the dynasty (12th century–771 B.C.) that had established the system of rites and decorum with decisive influence on the future course of Chinese civilization. The year was 690.

* * *

Clearly, Wu was well-versed in the give and take of court politics, in the delicate balance of punishment and compensation. Thus she managed to sustain her authority by using the gesture of generosity alongside the equally prominent rule of terror. Even the *Old Tang History,* after condemning her for exercising hair-rending cruelty, submits that Wu after all was good at correcting herself.[15] The Song historian Sima Guang in his carefully manipulative masterpiece states that her knowledge of governing and her art of deploying talents were unusual, and in conversations between Wu and her courtiers, an assured ruler well equipped with canonical knowledge presented herself. Intelligent and charismatic, Wu enacted a resurgence of the reassured interactions between the monarch and courtiers that once were characteristic of Taizong's court.

Wu Zhao's most prominent gesture of compensations may be the elaborate expansion of both the civil service examinations and the bureaucratic staff. Under Wu, the administrative bureaus expanded tremendously, and in her effort to recruit talent, the court exam was established with examination candidates interviewed by the sovereign herself. Recruiting the socially less-prominent scholars to balance incumbent ministers and the aristocratic clans, Wu utilized to the extreme a calculated imperial generosity, lavishing posts and ranks on the examinations-recruited literati with whose interests her personal concerns coincided.[16] When Wu's prominent minister Di Renjie was asked to recommend a "good man" to serve the empire, Di replied: "Perhaps the literati are base, and your highness wishes to obtain a special talent to manage the state?" To this Wu replied: "You have spoken for my heart."[17] Sharing with royal members a contempt for literati whose rise and fall depended on their whims, Wu's overt enthusiasm in obtaining talent was underlain by political considerations, and the scholars became her strategic instruments.[18]

In *The Track for Ministers* compiled under her order, Wu laid out clearly defined rules of conduct for her ministers, in which the relation between ministers and sovereign as the coordinated function of one body was emphatically stated. By focusing on the body metaphor, Wu bypassed the traditional analogy of father and son based on male monarchs and produced a more intimate fusion of emperors and courtiers. This handbook is a counterpart to *Models for the Emperors,* produced by Taizong for his heir; while Taizong had found it necessary to teach his offspring examples of good governing, a mother-empress in the process of consolidating herself as the despot deemed it more urgent to present to her courtiers binding rules of conduct. Like her new character for *minister,* coined with a *one* on top of the character *loyalty,* the handbook places emphasis on the concept of political fidelity.

The courtiers had served Wu Zhao through the reign of terror, some holding on to their principles in the most trying hours. Wu had come to appreciate these indefatigable men, although her resourceful responses to their remonstrations often demonstrate an ability to either contain or bypass their exacting morals. The fact that Chen Zi'ang, a respected poet of the early Tang, served at Wu's court faithfully is significant for a reassessment of her career. That this fact has not been adequately acknowledged is a telltale sign of the selective process of historical editing.

A woman on the throne, a *yin* occupying the place of *yang,* is considered an aversion; according to the *Book of Changes,* this entails a disastrous situation, as the first half of Wu's reign had proved. Yet the continuation of this usurpation proved itself beneficial, and the fear and revolt against Wu's rule, once receded, seemed unwarranted. Wu had used confidently the imperial pronoun *zhen,* a nongendered self-reference, and the courtiers had addressed her as *bixia,* "Your Highness," without difficulty. The hierarchy of *yin* and *yang* was not inverted—rather, it was a female occupying a male position. It turned out that all could, after all, be very well under the rule of a woman monarch. In one anecdote, a palace woman advised Wu to cut the number of her male consorts, so as not to have herself overcome by masculine energy: "Then women will gain more strength until we topple the masculine power. Such is my wish."[19] This ambition for a complete reversal of gender powers, as we know only too well, was not realized.

PASSIONS

At the year 696, the symbol of Wu's reign, the Bright Hall, was burned to the ground by Xue Huaiyi (her monk lover) in a fit of jealousy. Adepts of Taoist and Buddhist sects had long been welcome guests at the Tang court; under the circumstances, a monk became the convenient disguise for a mother-empress's lover. Perhaps nothing could have been more absurd than a monk-concubine; in this strange fusion of identities, an intriguing paradox manifests itself. Buddhist monks and nuns of superhuman crafts had been obsessions of folk imagination. When commoners joined the Buddhist order as cover-up, religious codes were transgressed, causing the drafting of several edicts in the Tang to effect the expelling of unorthodox practitioners. The massive removal of such an unpious population speaks for an intrinsic confusion within the sect, which provided a safe haven for both the desperate and the devious.[20] And through an insidious inversion, monks, theoretically sexually repressed, became in the unconscious the figure of sexual potency. Xue's disguise hence had some underhanded cultural meaning behind it, when the supposedly celibate was transformed into the licentious.

For consorts who were forced into Buddhist convents, an opposite inversion was at work, when the object of desire became an emblem of its denial. The joggling of imperial desires between the feminine and the masculine was indeed full of intrigue, as they moved in opposite directions in shaping the sexual definitions of their partners. With the woman emperor in the making, some new rules of the game must be invented, and Wu's expedience is by any standard sacrilegious. Herein lies an unequal parallel: the concubine-nuns were made to safeguard the deceased emperors' sexual supremacy, while the mother-empress's sexuality was legitimized by enlisting a monk in disguise. The absurd existence of monk-consorts, eunuchs, and consort-nuns raises questions about imperial sexual politics, when so much manipulation and transference were involved to maneuver the machine of imperial sexual intrigue.

One special request from a courtier had made explicit the transgressive nature of Xue's role. When the mother-empress made Xue oversee some palace construction, it was suggested that he be castrated, so that the inner palace would not be offended.[21] This request pointed to Xue's peril, and the threat of castration was imminent. Whether or not the courtier intended to defeat Wu's purpose is not certain, yet it seems improbable that he could be ignorant of Xue's true function. This request exposed the precarious condition of a mother-empress's desire, and its danger of being annihilated in a single stroke.

A man of untamed temperament, Xue preferred to reside with his gang in the monastery where he was ordained abbot. Unlike Wu's later consorts, Xue retained a loud masculinity that proclaimed itself in fighting and trouble-seeking. An impudent man, Xue's missions to the frontier and his architectural knowledge had made him more than a plaything. Although others had risen, over time, to supplant him, Xue's resentment against going to the palace to observe his duty suggested some deeper discontent, rendering Wu Zhao a rather unappreciated patron-lover.[22] The sovereign in her sixties most probably made a less than pleasing bed partner, and here sexual inequality is at its crudest. While she herself had served an aging Taizong in her youthful splendor, the monarch in her senility had picked for herself a concubine who did not disguise a bitterness about his role.

When continued resentment and uncivilized behavior at his monastery finally wearied Wu Zhao (now the emperor Zetian), Xue was beaten to death by Wu's order. Her new lovers, the Zhang brothers, rose to the stage with an entirely different self-definition. The change from Xue to the brothers marked the consolidation of both Wu's reign and her sexual freedom as an emperor proper. In a rare, outspoken episode, a courtier suggested that the willingness to serve her highness sexually had reached an appalling self-exposition, indeed vulgarity. He cited a courtier who claimed his son to be white with pleasing hair, and a guard leader who boasted that his sexual endowment exceeded that of Xue Huaiyi and who "had wished to present himself to serve Your Highness." The monarch's reaction was adequately innocent.[23] Finally, Wu had won freedom to satisfy her eros—yet like many of her male predecessors, she would discover that desires may prove fatal.

The Zhang brothers were youthful men of musical talents; dressed in charming robes and wearing makeup, they came to Zetian in a fashion similar to their female counterparts. After a decade of stable rule, Zetian had gained her share of concubines proper, and when the brothers appeared on the scene, a new sexual rule was firmly entrenched. Thus an aged Zetian surrounded herself with the youths, ignoring growing complaints about their abominable conduct and threatening ambition, until a coup was organized by the chief minister, Zhang Jianzhi. The brothers were slain, and Zetian was requested to retire. In the manner worthy of a betrayed great mind, Zetian said to one among those who invaded her chamber during the coup: "You, too, are here?"[24] Thus ended Wu's two decades of power, first as mother-empress and then as emperor. The potential dangers of male and female imperial desires shared the same structure, then, and Zetian's fatal implication by her concubines was echoed later in Xuanzong's demise.

Wu had not risen above the bondage of desires, although hers this time was more senile patronage than passion, and the shifting from the masculine monk-lover to the effeminate brothers suggests implicitly the relation between power and desire. When a woman emperor took on effeminate consorts, the question was not her homo-eroticism, but rather that the object desired by a politically powerful individual was inherently defined as feminine. Here the internalized association between femininity and the object of desire is prominent. The dilemma of the woman emperor's passion is hence spelled out in this impasse: insulted by a masculine lover reluctant about his passive role, she succumbed to the charm of the less assuming figures of male entertainers. Under the reign of a woman monarch, the binary opposition between masculinity and femininity and their relation to desire remained intact.

Perhaps we should ask this question, one that has increasing weight in feminist studies: as one who reigned high in the empire, had Wu actually considered herself a man? This constitutes the central issue in the study of Wu Zhao and her significance as the only woman emperor in Chinese history. Except for the climatic exhibition of female energy that followed her reign, except for the self-respect and confidence Wu had infused in her contemporaries, especially among royal women and ministers' wives, had she succeeded in transforming the received conception on gender?

MONUMENT WITHOUT INSCRIPTION

Prior to the coup, for a long time the succession to the throne was heatedly debated, with both the Li and the Wu clans vying for the status of crown prince. The Zhou dynasty founded by Wu belonged theoretically to the Wu clan, and potential rebels of the Li were either exiled or executed; for a while it did seem that a Wu member would inherit the throne. Yet the patrilineal system had posed a dead knot: although the strongest contender, Wu Chengsi, had the right surname, he was only a nephew of Zetian; Li X'ian by contrast was her son, and as one minister reminded Zetian, in the ancestral temple, there was no place for an aunt. The fundamental condition of patriarchy, the patrilineal descent, stood as the last stumbling block. Li X'ian was brought back to the capital after years of exile and was ordained heir apparent, much to the relief of the courtiers. After his ascension, the Tang was restored.

In this manner, the Zhou dynasty came to its end. The only Chinese empire founded by a woman, the Zhou could not have sustained itself without the support of a matriarchal order. Percipient of the patriarchal mechanism, the innovative Anle had requested Zhongzong (Li X'ian) to name her heir apparent, thus breaking the chain of patrilineal heritage. When it was precisely the patriline that made the choice of heir so difficult and finally overthrew the Zhou, that a daring Wu Zhao did not perceive of establishing a matrilineal system and name her daughter Taiping her heir is regrettable in hindsight. For obviously, Taiping was much more capable than both of Zetian's emperor-sons and, with her characteristic competence, was instrumental in the ascension of her brothers. Together with Wu's daughter-in-law Empress Wei, Princess Anle, and the woman courtier Shangguan Waner (trained by Zetian into a first-rate official in charge of edict drafting and state affairs), Taiping embodied the exuberant female energies surrounding Zetian's exemplary presence. In this sense, Wu remained regrettably maneuvering within the existing order, allowing patriarchy to stand obstinate in its fundamental practice, while her granddaughter was ready to claim more.

Inspired by her mother-in-law's phenomenal career, Empress Wei plotted with her daughter Anle to install themselves as mother-empress and heir apparent. In an unprecedented move, they poisoned their father and husband, Zhongzong, seven years into his wayward rule, and Wei oversaw the empire briefly before she was defeated by Li Longji, who later succeeded Ruizong (Li Dan) as Emperor Xuanzong. After this coup/patricide, vigilance was set up against further female transgressions, and Tang women never regained the glorious height achieved by Wu Zhao.

With the abrupt end of this tumultuous yet prosperous dynasty, the process of Wu Zhao's erasure began. In the year 705, Wu Zhao died after decades of power.

Included in her will was the return to her title as empress, and a request for co-burial with Gaozong. The second request was met with resistance as ministers argued that Mound Qian was sealed with stone and iron, and to break through them would disturb the spirit of the dead. The memorial was overruled, and Wu Zhao secured her place next to Gaozong. Her edict to remove her title as emperor, if it was indeed her own will, points to a resourceful Wu Zhao apprehensive of the absolutism of patriarchy. By returning to the status of empress, Wu Zhao maintained her centrality; standing beside Gaozong, an emperor without the fear of posthumous deprivation, a self-made woman emperor retained her prominence. This is Wu's effort at not being driven further out of history, both physically and symbolically, by adopting the traditional, hence nonrefutable stance of the faithful wife. Ironically, it was again through usurpation, through breaking in the sealed mound, that Wu Zhao gained her place.

Time has made good Wu Zhao's insight: to this day Mound Qian stands, known principally as the tomb of Wu Zetian. With Wu's magnificent spirit hovering over it, the place exacted awe in the early days of Wu's death. When drought attacked the empire, Zhongzong sent members of the Wu clan to the mound and prayed for rain; when the rain did come, the son was overjoyed with gratitude.[25] On the magnificent Spirit Road stands the famous Monument without Inscription erected in honor of Wu. The blankness of the imposing monument has been interpreted variously, and it is the consensus among scholars that it was so willed for future historians to cast their verdict. Today the stone is inscribed with poems composed in later epochs, and Wu Zetian, as she is now known, emerges in these inscriptions triumphantly.

Although Emperor Wu of Han had erected a blank tablet on Mt. Tai after offering sacrifices to heaven, Wu's monument, by virtue of her unique career, acquires an altered meaning and is imbued with symbolic significance. Against the politics of patriarchal discourse with which Wu had engaged a lifelong battle stands this blankness, which defies language. Wu's monumental career must be judged from the distance of time, and her unprecedented role as a woman emperor could only be justified by a monumental blankness, which speaks for an apprehension well contested. Silently it stands against the sky, a symbol of women's exile from language. Wu's posterity will fill the blankness with visible and invisible inscriptions; this is essentially the monument's unspoken faith in history.

* * *

To assess Wu's achievement as a woman monarch, it is necessary to consider her policies on women. The single significant change in rites that Wu realized was the change of mortuary code for maternal mourning from one year to three years, equal to that for fathers, thereby raising maternal status in ritual terms. Although much maneuvering was done in increasing the empress's weight in imperial rites, in increasing the princesses' fief and stipend, and in bringing in ministers' wives in court ceremonies, Wu did not devote herself to a fundamental change of policies on women. Most of her efforts to upgrade women's status were made in her empresshood, while further policies were not enacted after she was enthroned. During her times, changes in the marriage institution or in women's rights to civil service examinations were inconceivable. Such changes required overall sociocultural transformations and were not to be accomplished by one woman's revolution. However, the audacious concept of a woman on the throne was perceived and realized by Wu Zhao. And before her, Empress Wenxian in the Sui Dynasty, exerting the radical virtue of female jealousy, vented much of her energy in curtailing concubinage. While Wu's literary talent was evident when she acted as Gaozong's deputy writer, while she had expanded greatly the civil service examinations and had made possible the participation of ministers' wives in court ceremonies, one wonders if Wu could have been equally daring in her conception of more radical transformations of women's rights.

Nevertheless, the symbolic meaning of a woman emperor and its psychological effect on women were significant. Wu's limited efforts at uplifting women's status should be juxtaposed to her violent battle with the patriarchal order, the triumph of which is emblematic, leaving a permanent imprint in history. After Wu, the surge of female power in the imperial circle continued relentlessly in her daughters and granddaughters. Both united and against each other, these women created a second wave of the women's revolution that twice threatened the Li clan. Modeled after Wu, they demonstrated unusual energies (although this time more to destructive aims) bringing the celebrated desires of Tang princesses to an explosion. A genuine women's revolution was in the making; more encompassing than Wu's personal revolution, this time it had the overturning of the patriline in mind. With their defeat, the residue of female energies subsided, and the Tang's grasp on women tightened. Soon, another female prototype presented itself in the image of the sensuous Yang Yuhuan, token of female victimization in direct opposition to Wu Zhao and her daring followers.

THE ERASURE OF HISTORY

As an isolated instance, the ascension of a woman emperor did not actually change the course of history, and with the defeat of her heirs, female force dissolved and women were barred from realizing an ambition once so vividly envisioned. The historical significance of Wu Zhao lies mainly in her very existence as a woman sovereign—this alone undermines the myth of female inferiority and questions the absolutism of centuries of female subordination. Once patriarchal order was reinstalled, however, this reign of a woman monarch was erased to reinstate masculine dominance.

The efforts to force Wu to abdicate gained momentum toward the end of her reign, and Wu received this advice with calmness and agile self-readjustment. Once, the sovereign presented her ministers with a twig of peach blossom in autumn, soliciting homage to her prosperous rule manifested by this auspicious omen. One official responded by stating that the ill-timed blossom was against the flow of cosmic energy, designating hence an inadequacy in the present reign. As he bowed and begged pardon, Wu complimented him as the true minister.[26] At another occasion, when a three-legged cow was presented as an auspicious omen, one courtier retorted that things countering normal order were evil, and the cow was but an ill omen of her troubled rule. Such a blunt critique changed the monarch's countenance, and she grew dejected.[27] Through denying these omens, the courtiers denied Wu's employment of portents, which she had utilized to a grandiose end more than a decade before. These possibly fabricated episodes could be seen as early efforts to question Wu's achievement, to make the woman emperor less than what she had accomplished. The disheartened response from Wu brought home the effect of such effort. Her task as the monarch remained daunting, and an aged Wu Zhao realized that her aim remained distant. As she was losing her edge, the remonstrations became bolder, and the process of effacement was gathering force.

The course of erasure started right after Wu's death when her edict for returning to Gaozong's mound was met with resistance. Furthermore, it was in naming, significant in imperial politics, that the erasure was most intriguing. While in retirement at Shangyang Palace, Wu was conferred with all due respect as the emperor Zetian the Divine by her son Zhongzong. In accordance with her decree from her death bed, she was given the posthumous title "the Great Divine Empress Zetian." From thereon, Wu suffered a progressive downfall in the shifting of her titles.[28] Such a long list of names (comparable to the list of titles Wu had given herself) exposes the process of historical self-adjustment and indecision on naming a female usurper, mother of two emperors, and the grand matriarch of all the Tang emperors from Xuanzong down to the last emperor. Ruizong's wavering attitude especially reveals the youngest son's hang-up with a less than kind mother. His bitter revenge by stripping Wu back to "Heavenly Empress" was reconciled by the much more generous "Divine Empress *and* Emperor," a title soon to be retrieved. From there on, Wu Zhao never regained her title of emperor.

The complex process of Wu's undoing was practiced in every field. At the restoration of the Tang, sacrificial rites, the colors of banners and ministers' robes, and names of official posts as well as the characters all returned to previous orders. *The Track for Ministers* was lifted from the civil exam curriculum, the cruel officials were stripped of their titles posthumously, and all the offspring of wronged ministers regained imperial favor. Wu's ancestral temple, along with the mounds of Wu Zhao's parents, were abolished, and her family members suffered near extinction after the defeat of Empress Wei's coup. The top level of the Bright Hall, symbol of Zetian's reign, was removed, making it (and Wu's self-glorification) considerably lower, and its old name Qianyuan Palace was restored.[29] This architectural transformation echoed the historical adjustments on Wu, as it was through deliberate modification that her place was redefined.

Thus things returned gradually to their previous order—with one exception. Under Xuanzong, an obstinate minister suggested that Wu's code of three years' mourning for mothers be abolished. In his opinion, this mourning code was a prelude to her usurpation, and arguments for its abolishment were squarely grounded in the precedence of the ethical status of father over that of mother, and in the assumption that observance of equal mortuary rites would threaten patriarchal authority and fail to contain female power. The painstaking debate was conducted at the court, and two years later, supported by the discovery of a Confucian record, it was determined that Wu Zhao's code should stay. A decade later, when the five rites were modified, it was further sanctioned.[30]

Nonetheless, this seems an insignificant triumph for Wu Zhao in the general process of erasure. In both official histories of the Tang, Wu Zhao enjoys annals among the monarchs, but as mere empress. The Song editors of the *New Tang History,* Song Qi and Ouyang Xiu, took pains to manifest their critique in her annals, which are marred consistently by an omen: "a hen transfigured into a rooster," a euphony commonly used to denounce female usurpation. Originally a portent presented to the mother-empress, this flattery is transformed back to its conventional derogatory meaning. In a more forceful manner, the *Old Tang History* presents a hostile eulogy to Wu's annals; the final poem that condemns her as a virtual demon has the effect of writing her out of history as a destructive force, leaving her legitimacy all but dismantled.

The structural organization of Wu's annals angered the writer-courtier Shen Jiji, who suggested they be replaced by Zhongzong's, making the then exiled crown prince the legitimate emperor.[31] This advice was followed by the Song scholar Fan Zuyu, in whose *Tang jian* (Tang mirror) events that happened in Wu's reign are presented in Zhongzong's annals, and the woman emperor simply dissolves. The patriarchal will to discard the undesirable is prominent in this mechanism of historical editing. Even in histories written in the twentieth century, Wu Zhao is often referred to as *Empress* Wu; her reign of fifteen years did not honor her otherwise.[32] In present-day speech, Wu is commonly referred to as Wu Zetian, a peculiar coinage. Different from official histories, it does not contain her as an empress; yet by replacing the dynastic name Zhou with her surname, her revolution and founding of a dynasty are forsaken, leaving her surname—the name of the father—as the principal identifier. Wu Zhao stands thus by herself, solitary in history, a monarch without a dynasty, a woman emperor without the law of the mother.

There are more subtle ways of questioning Wu's accomplishments. In *Chaoye qianzai* (Episodes from the court and the commoners), a curious entry records an episode in which Wu presented her ministers with the auspicious sign of the miraculous harmony between a cat and a parrot shut in the same cage. As the cage was passed along, the cat grew hungry and attacked the parrot and ate it. The entry ends with this remark: "The grand empress was quite ashamed."[33] Such an uncanny event presents a woman monarch frustrated by the embarrassing failure of her conceit. Her will to tame the cat (and the courtiers) failed disastrously, and the amateur historian shows in one single sentence the impossibility of having one's nature transformed. Both the cat and the ministers remained untamed; or, perhaps more to the author Zhang Zhuo's intent, as the cat, Wu remained a woman with all the capricious nature of one capable only of calamities. This dubious anecdote is adapted by Sima Guang in his comprehensive classic as historical truth, leaving Wu Zhao an ultimate loser.

As Wu's favored minister, Di Renjie suffered a similar underhanded critique. When Di visited his aunt Lu and offered to promote her son at the court, Lu repudiated his proposal sternly: "I have only one son, and I certainly do not intend to have him serve a woman."[34] The irony of the anecdote is that Lu, herself a woman, was contemptuous of Wu Zhao, and her contempt extended to the man who served Wu; the inferiority of woman was internalized well.

In the Marxist historiography of the People's Republic of China, efforts have been made to resurrect Wu's achievements, and increasingly she comes to be respected as one who had earned her throne well. Wu's inventions of the *dianshi* (court exam) and *wushi* (military exam), her contribution to stability at the border through stationing soldier-farmers at Anxi, and her willingness to heed the ministers' advice proved her insight and competence as a ruler. However, caught in her revolt against the patriarchal order, Wu Zhao presents us with a problematic situation not without its ambivalence, for her reckless assault on her enemies and the historians' crude portrayal of her vices had inevitably taken some toll. Because of this, a feminist rereading of her historical significance is essential. It is through women's collective reassessment of their predecessor that the blank monument's faith in history is truly answered.

The case of Wu Zhao remains an ambivalent one, and when patriarchy regained control and things returned to their normal course, one wonders if her victory had not been too costly. Wu's glory contrasted to the continuous injustice suffered by her contemporary women, which speaks to us of the inner split among women and enlightens us on the inequity between classes. The countermove of the relentless repression of women in later eras testifies to the fact that without a total reversal of consciousness, without thoroughly unlearning patriarchal teachings, and indeed, without fundamental transformations of men, one woman's revolution will remain a bitter fruit for one. Had Wu Zhao identified herself more with power/man in her later years? What was the truth of her cruelty? What weight does she carry with contemporary women, who are facing radically different agendas? These remain questions that will be answered differently by women of different ambitions, and the monument remains silent with all its ambiguities.

Chapter 4

Sacrificial Lamb:

The Case of Yang Yuhuan

The Silence of the Sacrificial Lamb

In the kingdom of the lambs, according to an age-old custom, the whitest and most beautiful among them was sacrificed for the sake of peace and order in the land. Once when war broke out at the frontier, the king, most reluctantly, was forced to offer up his beloved consort to save his kingdom. The lamb, perfectly white and slightly plump, rose up to the altar prepared for her by her king and received in silence her death. Until today, no one knows what passed through her mind when the king's knife pierced through her perfect body and shed hot blood on the ground, when silence enveloped her like the net that caught within it those tongueless fishes whose pain remained forever quiet.

The periods of statewide recruitment of youthful beauties to enter the imperial palace were marked by intense distress and grief for families of enlisted girls. Annually, from households of auspicious clans to those of simple folks, girls in their early teens were selected to join the already large collection of women in the royal harem. Only the luckiest handful would enjoy imperial patronage and join the body of *neiguan* (inner officials) composed of over one hundred royal consorts divided into hierarchical ranks, with the empress sitting at the top.[1] They would then be engulfed in violent political intrigues, competing with each other and with the continuous flow of young girls offered to the aging monarch. Vying for their sons' status on which their future hinged, they were in constant fear of the total reversal of the monarch's will. Of the thirty-six consorts recorded in Tang official histories, fifteen of them met tragic ends.

The unattended rest would stay under strict surveillance and spend their lives in idleness and uncertainty, surrounded by sexually defunct eunuchs. Imprisoned in the forbidden city, they were allowed to see their families once a year. At the death of the emperor, those without children would be pressed into a lifelong service of his soul beside the imperial mound, "preparing for his toilet and pillow, serving him in death as in life."[2] Others would grow old in the Shangyang Palace of the retired

73

Court ladies, detail of a mural in Princess Yongtai's tomb.

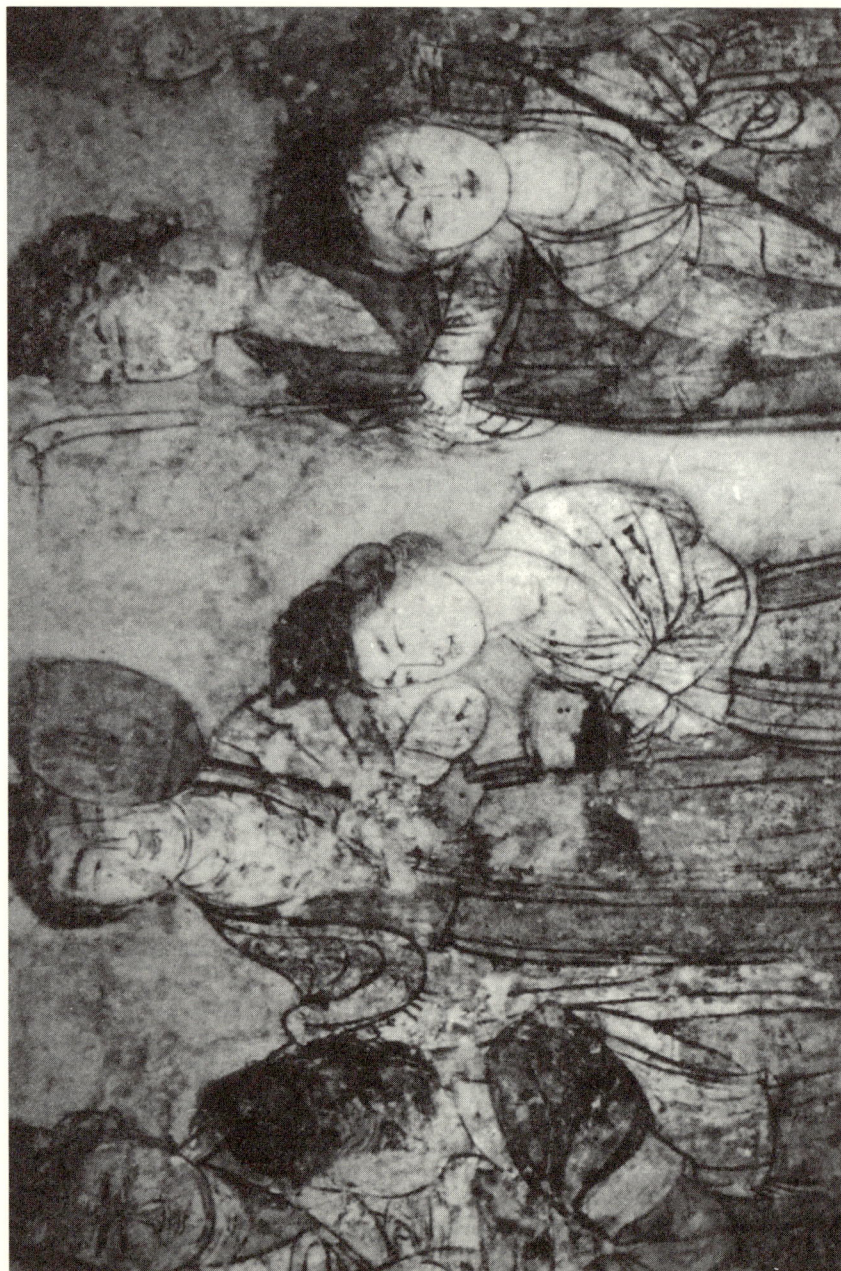

From *Tang Yongtai gongzhu mu bihua ji.*

emperor, displaying their antiquated costumes to sympathetic observers. When they died, they would be buried underneath the *gongren xie* (Slope of the Palace Women), the inconspicuous resting place for numerous women drafted from distant corners of the empire.

Among those of respectable background, the capable and talented would be assigned posts as *gongguan* (palace officials), who were divided into the Six Bureaus overseeing the Twenty-four Divisions in charge of duties in various spheres including food, clothes, medicine, books, music, bed chambers, adornments, treasures, gardening, accounting, banquet, chariot, lamp, and so on.[3] The more cultivated ones took up posts in the Inner Literature Bureau and were responsible for educating consorts and other palace women. Through various posts, these women found outlets for their intelligence and unspent energies.

The general impression of an inertia that characterizes the life of palace women should hence be checked by the knowledge of their professional activities that somehow gave their imprisoned existence a sense of focus. Considering the inner palace with its many female officials observing duties in domestic as well as ritual, legal, personnel, and financial affairs, the possibility of pursuing a career in the inner palace should be granted. The unanimous picture of palace women frozen in idle sorrow presented by the poets speaks for the ubiquitous propensity in the male imagination to see women only in terms of their frustrated sexuality.

At brighter moments, palace women rode on horseback in male costumes, accompanied royalty on hunts with bows tugged on their shoulders, engaged in athletic games to entertain the lords and ladies, sometimes playing against eunuchs and officials, and put on beguiling costumes for a grand performance of dance. In the unchecked climate of Zhongzong's reign, they were let out to enjoy the lantern festival and had the chance to escape.[4] Thus in the extravagant palaces, these women had their share of excitement and glamour. Together with their official responsibilities and the opportunity to learn from women tutors, life in the palace might not have been as totally despairing as it was painted.

However, these moments could not compensate for the more constant flow of uneventful life experienced in the women's humble quarters. The deprivation of the right to fulfill a normal life stood at the core of their doom, which became increasingly insufferable as they lost their youth. The collective frustration of these thousands of women (forty thousand at their highest under Xuanzong) registered a negative energy so palpable that the sovereigns were requested time and again to set them free to release the palace of an evil omen, the clustered *yin*. It is a challenge for the modern imagination to perceive the presence of these women, every one of them attractive in her own way, who were cut off from all ethical bonds, denied the urge for procreation, and who had lived a life of imposed celibacy since a tender age. A haunting image of these women is that of a white-haired palace woman, once the favorite of the monarch, who wore flowers all over her hair and sang in the blowing wind. Madness is explicit here, and this image exposes a more intense mode of feminine suffering.

Following our strategy in reading against the grain of patriarchal discourse, we should be cautioned against accepting uncritically the general sense of inertia in the portrayal of these women, who could have been unorthodox in their unusual mode of existence. At least in one incident, a palace woman attempted to assassinate Xuan-zong and was shot by a eunuch.[5] This transgression points to a capacity for action and a profound resentment that are all too often diluted into a docile feminine passivity in literary presentations of these women. Due to the circumscribed consciousness of the literati, records of the confined lives of palace women focus on their quiet distress in the lament mode, and their otherwise courageous or transgressing thoughts and acts are not documented. Applying the conceits of still ponds as reflecting mirrors and trees whose blossoms bear no fruits, poets present the barren beauty of these women, creating the general impression of them as trapped in perpetual sorrow and engaging in unproductive leisure, whose lives were a total waste.

Ironically, it was for their extraordinary beauty that these women were chosen to live out this inexplicable doom. Like those carefully chosen sacrificial animals, they were offered to satiate the singular lust of the monarch, and the slow passage of time in confinement spelled out the ritual of this collective sacrifice conducted on a hideous scale. Their sacrifice, because of its intensity and fearful irrationality, is metaphorical of the general sacrifice of dynastic women, when this continuous deprivation and confinement constituted a prolonged death on the sacrificial altar prepared for the fairest of the empire.

It was out of these women that one emerged triumphantly and posed for the history of this female sacrifice as a most memorable offering.

THE SACRIFICE

After the establishment of elaborate rituals in the Zhou dynasty, sacrificial animals largely replaced humans for state sacrifices. Although locally humans were offered to appease animal spirits or natural deities, the state no longer practiced human sacrifice. Mortuary human sacrifice returned in large scale in the Qin and Han dynasties, and mortuary female offerings lasted into late imperial epochs in various forms, when this practice acquired a delicate mask and was coerced through ethical pressures. Concubines especially were subject to such practices, and throughout the Tang, imperial consorts and the gentry's concubines alike were either consigned to the secluded life of Buddhist nuns or were pressured to take their own lives to honor their deceased lords. The case of Yang Yuhuan, however, was of a different nature.

At a particular moment in history, Xuanzong, while escaping from An Lushan's impending army, was requested to surrender Yang Yuhuan, his beloved consort, to appease the rioting soldiers.

His Highness replied: "We shall handle this ourselves." He entered the gate and leaned on his staff, and for a long time he stood with his head hung low. Wei E, Attendant

Overseer of the Capital, stood forward: "The rage of the mass is not to be opposed; danger lies close at hand, would that Your Highness decide." With this he prostrated himself until blood came out. His Highness said: "The Consort dwells in the inner palace, how could she have known Guozhong's plot?" Gao Lishi presented: "It is true that the Consort is guiltless, yet the officers and soldiers have already slain Guozhong: they would not feel secured leaving her by Your Highness's side. Please think carefully—when the army is secured, Your Highness too will be secured." Thus His Highness had Lishi lead the Consort to the Buddhist Hall and there strangled her. Her body, contained in a litter, was parked in the station courtyard. The general and others were called in to observe; they removed their helmets and armor, bowed, and implored pardon. His Highness reassured them and ordered this be known to the soldiers. All shouted, "Long live the emperor," and they bowed and took leave. Thereafter they began regrouping and made plans to set out for the road.[6]

Yang was placed on the altar to release tension and to induce action/wind, rather in the fashion of Greek tragedy. The killing of the chief minister Yang Guozhong (the consort's brother) prior to the scene was a collected act of violence that led to Yang's death, a death exacted by a consciousness that regarded women as the source of contamination. In the context of palace politics, it exposed resentment for the in-laws known to be conspiratorial, and for the women through whom they gained access to power. A cautious Empress Wende had pleaded Taizong not to give her brother a prominent position, and lacking such precaution, Yang courted danger.

At the immediate level, the sacrifice was offered to appease the violent energy unleashed by the soldiers, who had the blood of two ministers on their hands. Driven by their will, Yang was strangled, and her body exhibited as the testimony to the fulfillment of a ritual. At the symbolic level, the ultimate recipient of this offering was the ideology of female scapegoating, which found perfect manifestation in this incident, as the strangling of Yang Yuhuan becomes the most naked female sacrifice in Chinese imperial history.

By sacrificing his consort, Xuanzong, as his faithful servant suggested, was secured. By offering his beloved consort he offered part of himself, and like the deserted palace invaded by commoners and donkeys that he left behind, all boundaries were trespassed in this implacable national crisis.

THE WOMAN

Yang Yuhuan came to Xuanzong's service through a series of maneuvers. Originally a consort of the Lord Shou, Xuanzong's eighteenth son, Yang was sent to the palace belvedere, a preliminary move out of propriety for her transformation into the father/emperor's consort. We are told in her entrance to history of her lush skin and alluring appearance, and the few accounts in official histories present a picture of a talented musician and dancer with a slightly plump figure, who was of flippant wit and cravings (with seven hundred embroiderers enlisted for her wardrobe), was subject to flattery and easily swayed, and might have had a less than proper relationship with An Lushan. In all, she was presented as a woman with mental and moral weaknesses. By contrast, her many musical talents were not fully expounded upon; in miscellaneous records, her virtuosity in playing the *qing* (jade bells) is described as impressive, surpassing professional musicians at the entertainment bureaus, and her skill in playing *pipa* (the lute) was outlandish.[7] These and her talent in dancing seem her only redeeming virtues.

Yang's single recorded speech was made to entice Xuanzong's pardon: "All of my gold and valuables are bestowed by Your Highness, and are not worthy for an offering; only my hair is given by my parents, and I presume to present it to manifest my loyalty."[8] The offering of the lock of hair demonstrates a tendency to communicate with others physically: as metonym of the estranged consort's physical presence, the lock was made her deputy. This episode renders Yang a woman whose only possessions were her pleasing features, and she utilized them well. In a similar vein, the single poem left in Yang's name is about a palace dancer in whom her own image is mirrored, which points to a potential narcissism.

Yang's flamboyant siblings shared an excessive taste for sensual indulgence, and their pompous lavishness, much envied and criticized by their contemporaries, was a prominent extension of Yang Yuhuan, the center of this family patronized by an extravagant monarch. The illicit liaison between Yang Guozhong and Yang's sister, the Lady Guoguo, between the latter and Xuanzong, and between the consort and the overweight An Lushan have been alluded to with various degrees of verisimilitude. Episodes involving the last pair have a particularly interesting tinge: at An's birthday, Yang had the flippant wit of wrapping him in embroidery as a newborn. The general, who later would revolt and bring immediate demise to the Tang, stirred roaring laughter among women in the inner palace. In the above rendition, Yang was shown as moving suspiciously close to a future rebel. Again women were perceived as providing an opening that invites destructive forces, and it was out of this unconscious that An's intimacy with Yang was emphatically stated.

THE MYTHICAL BODY

In the process of Yang's secret reburial after Li Longji's return from his escape, a perfumed embroidery bag was found intact and was presented to him, now the retired emperor. From here on started an obsession with Yang in a pervasive mystification of her body. As legend has it, her stocking was found by an old woman near the Mawei station where Yang was killed, who made a fortune by charging interested viewers high fees, and Yang's physical metonym was regarded with fancy.[9] The one place loaded with metaphorical significance is the Huaqing Palace, the winter palace where Yang enjoyed the luxury of a lotus-shaped bath made especially for her in the early days of imperial patronage. To this day, the palace remains a popular tourist spot, renowned for the bath that had once contained her sumptuous body. The interest in this place moves shamelessly close to a collective lust of the mind, exposing not only an identification of women with locales, but a spillover of desire for a body long gone as a result of human sacrifice. Yang's body, then, is subjected to a double exposure: first examined by a male tribunal, then perpetually exposed to the curious gaze of millions who try to recapture its splendor through the now degenerate bath. Thus Yang's mystified body survives as perhaps the most celebrated—and lamented—symbol of female scapegoating.

The fate of Yang Yuhuan is the classic case of desire and punishment. As such, it became a thematic obsession for many Tang poets and writers, a phenomenon that betrays further truth about male desire and its sense of guilt. Her sacrifice is judged in these literary works as a cowardly act, and the Huaqing Palace, deserted, continued to be haunted by her presence/absence. In the well-known quatrains by Li Bo composed upon Xuanzong's summons, Yang is alluded to via misty clouds, dewy blossoms, and elusive goddesses. In an agonizing account, Du Fu describes the Yang sisters as goddesses shrouded by misty smoke.[10] Du Mu's "Huaqing Palace," commenting on the occasion of Li Longji's gracing of the palace years later, also employs the allusion of the goddess of Mt. Wu appearing as wandering clouds to embody the lost consort. Thus both before and after the cult of her mythical body was established, Yang's living flesh was made other than earthly.

In the lyrical genre of *yongshi* (laments on history), women appear as fragments of history, their physical being a synecdoche of the temporal and spatial dimension of events in which they had played a role. The ruins and their bodies are identified, and in a desolate mansion, shadows and sounds of their previous existence haunt the place with unexorcised memories. In this tradition Yang's literary persona is firmly entrenched. Her image haunts the palace with a sense of remorse, her mythical body remains at the center of its ruins.

In a more sentimental vein, the brutally terminated romance of Li Longji and his consort became a theme for public lamentations. Witness the narrative poem by Bo Juyi, "Chang hen ge" (Song of Lasting Regret), which opens with the Huaqing bath and a provocative depiction of Yang's lush skin and beguiling manner as she rose gently from the water and finishes with an account of Li Longji's search for her in mythical realms, which ended with the dreamy appearance of an ever-resplendent Yang Yuhuan. The wild popularity of this piece of a rather corny sentimentality attests to the populace's fascination with a frustrated royal romance. The reversal of fate notwithstanding, there is a reversal of positions involved in the people's sympathy for a monarch; the supremacy of imperial sexuality was toppled and transfigured into impotence in a state crisis, and for once, the commoners satisfied themselves with the image of a desperate monarch.

Yang's mythical body was transported across the sea to Japan, where a temple was built for her alleged remains, continuing the legend of a safely escaped Yang. Her sudden death had provoked a dissatisfaction in folk imagination, which set out

to amend it. The woman who had brought the kingdom's downfall deserved condemnation, yet paradoxically, by being executed, Yang was saved from historical
condemnation and aroused pity rather than fear. One and a half years after her
death, she was ordained empress by Li Longji: this was the highest gesture of compensation—and regret—from the defunct monarch.[11]

The death of Yang Yuhuan, whose last utterance was never known, marked the
decline of female power in the Tang. Compared to her predecessor Wu Zhao, the
role Yang had contented herself with seems degenerate. She remained the consort
who attained power through physical attractions, was good at intrigues, and had
exorbitant appetites—a quintessential "woman" in its derogatory definitions in
male discourse. Capacities other than those assigned to the pleasing feminine, which
Wu Zhao had in abundance along with the deadly will to realize them, were not
recorded in the consort. And her end, so sudden and powerless, is also a far remove
from that of the stronger Wu.

To speak of Yang Yuhuan, a name half buried in the many platitudes surrounding her, we must understand her as the creation of a society where beauty
with pleasing traits was regarded with fetishism—it was, besides the female virtues
stressed by the self-deceiving ethics, the most visible factor for women in procuring patriarchal patronage. Yang had excelled, yet the weight of the empire also bore
down on her; in her case, a woman's influence on the state was blown absurdly disproportionate. Because she was a sacrificial lamb, Yang's death symbolizes essentially the offering of women who were fashioned into creatures whose existence,
defined by pleasing, became a signifier without signified. Through the long tunnel
of imperial epochs, numerous women shared a similar destiny of sexual exploita-
tion and spiritual deprivation. Their lives were distorted for the pleasures of a few,
and by the demands of their patriarchs, they died quietly on an unnamed altar, like
those beautiful sacrificial animals, in a collective silence and passivity the injustice
of which was horrific.

Part Two

Internal Split of the Imperial Subjects

Chapter 5

The Making and Unmaking of Confucian Wives

Laughter of the Palace Women

Sun Wu, a famed military strategist, was invited to the king's court. Out of a frivolous curiosity, the king tossed the question at him: "You are good with soldiers. Can you train women to fight like one?" Sun replied without blinking his eyes: "Follow military principles and anyone can be trained." The king in a lighthearted manner decided: "Let me see what you could do with my ruthless women here." As the two spoke, dozens of palace women stood by, tending their wine and fruits, fanning them with long-stemmed feathers, and, peeping at Sun's unusually ugly face, now and then they held up their long sleeves and laughed quietly among themselves.

Upon Sun's demand, two sets of drums were set up in front of the court. The women all lined up, two of the king's favorite consorts were made troop leaders, and they were ready to receive orders. It was a strange sight to behold, for these women in watery sleeves and trailing skirts held those heavy, deadly weapons in their hands in various awkward ways. They stood wondering at the strange man by the drum with an almost violent look on his face; again they turned their heads and laughed, their slender bodies twisted into various lines of willows.

To suggest that the military genius was embarrassed by these charming creatures would be an insult. His eyes gazed out sternly, not at all bothered by their insolence. At long last he lifted his arms, and with a cutting precision beat the first drum roll. Upon this signal, the women were supposed to stand erect, uphold their heads heavy with adornments, and press their slender arms, so used to dancing, by their thighs. The pose was against everything they were born and raised for, and at this impossible request they all burst into roaring laughter. The square broke down.

The king himself too was amused, and his laughter joined the women's into an orchestrated music. Only Sun was furious. He stood by the drum and looked at these women whose bodies spoke of sensual indulgence, so alienated from his own breeding, and his will grew stern. Again he lifted his arms, waited until voices subsided, and hit the drum hard. It was like thunder pregnant with rage, and it grew faster with a terrible rhythm. The women were frightened; their bodies stiffened, their arms drooped down, and it looked like finally they were going to learn their lesson. One woman however was defiant; she was the king's favorite and the leader of the troop, her lithe body stood out and her face was large with character. She began to laugh, first alone, and then was joined by others, until their laughter defeated the drumming, and it stopped abruptly.

Expressionless, Sun turned to the king: "With your majesty's permission, I must have total authority to do what is necessary." The king restrained himself and put forward a likewise serious face—for he was quick to understand that this man had taken the joke seriously, yet it was too late to correct it. "Do whatever is required." With this, Sun ordered the troop leader taken to him. The outrageously beautiful woman stood face to face with him, and she was much amused. Sun proclaimed: "Whoever disobeyed must be punished so that it won't be repeated." And with this he ordered the leader be executed in front of the court. Before the king realized it, his daring consort had lost her head, and a deadly silence descended. When the drum beat started again, this time slow and deliberate, each beat sending low echoes through the court, the women began to move their bodies expressionlessly, their faces numb with invisible sweat. They turned their muted bodies around like stringed marionettes, and the drumming grew deep, filled with an ecstasy as it touched each curvy line of their bodies with precision and untold tenderness.

No woman would dare to make any more sound—unless, her body about to burst, someone began to laugh hysterically, driving the maddening drum to a panicked speed.

Due both to the aristocratic character of the Tang and, equally important, to the narcissistic tendency of the literati (with the exception of a few great poets), records of the common folks are extremely scarce in Tang discourse, with even the miscellaneous notes focusing on lives and gossip at the court and among the gentry class. It is therefore the rich collection of social documents from the Dunhuang caves that presents us with vivid phases of the folks' lives. Documents on the selling of children, the pawning of impoverished lands, the hiring of farming cattle, and the formation of support communities to share the burden of funeral, wedding, and religious festival expenses (along with pleas to resign from such communities due to further financial slips) inform us of the dire condition of the general populace. Without an adequate understanding of their existence, our impression of the Tang would be blurred by the images of free-spending aristocrats, ambitious literati, and extravagant entertainers who moved about in prosperous cities, while it was these much-deprived folks scattered in the remotest corners that constituted the foundation of the empire.

Among Dunhuang documents such as contracts, ceremonious manuals, and household instructions, those concerning marriage inform us of the folk conception of women's condition. Again, the understanding of women as outsiders permeates. While quoting the *Book of Rites,* which regulates that "families marrying off daughters should hold candle vigil for three nights as a token of mourning over separation; families taking a bride should refrain from having music for three days as a token of observing ancestral memorial,"[1] *Handbook of Dunhuang Marriage Ceremonies* attaches this remark: "In rites, there is remorse."[2] Such remorse is embodied in the return of thanks to wedding congratulations: for the bridegroom's par-

The bride kneeling in front of the parents–in–law in *Marriage Ceremony*, Yulin cave painting, cave no. 25 (middle Tang), north wall, east side.

From *Dunhuang shiku yishu*, pl. 65.

ents, it involved the thoughts of the ethical weight of transmitting the descending line and reverence for deceased ancestors; for the bride's parents, the daughter's leaving. Clearly, marriage meant different things for the two parties: for one, it signified continuation; for the other, sudden severance.

The alienation of women is further revealed in a twist of irony, when throughout wedding rituals in Dunhuang, the bride's beauty is compared to the Moon Goddess Chang Er, who stole the elixir from Yi (the legendary archer and her husband) and flew to the moon.[3] The various wedding songs that praise the bride thus signal an uncanny return of the rebel. This naive comparison conceals a not so innocent unconscious, exposing the would-be wife's alienation from the "home" of her husband.

The various divorce documents from Dunhuang bear an interesting title, *fangqishu* (letter for setting wife free). Echoing the Buddhist practice of setting animals free to procure blessings, this title deviates from the legal term *xiuqi* (terminating a wife). Either released or terminated by a home that is never hers—between a daughter who must leave where she is but a guest and a wife who faces the threat of sudden termination lies the fate of the ultimately homeless woman.[4]

This condition of alienation stands in direct contrast to the domestication of woman that traps her at the core of a household. Those who withstand the trials and tribulations of marriage, who sublimate their sexuality to become docile wives and dutiful mothers—in short, those who learn the patriarchal lessons well—would emerge as the anchors of their households and receive the name *neiren* (the one inside), a byname for one's wife. It is thus through the endurance of ethical burdens and exacting emotional turmoil that a woman emerges in a basically irrational marriage institution.

Alienation versus domesticity; an outcast versus someone "inside": these contrasting poles constitute the obscure dualism of a woman's position in dynastic China, and the Tang presents a complex reflection of such strange irony.

WOMEN ACCORDING TO LEGAL CODES

Besides contractual laws, the premodern Chinese legal system was essentially defined by a penal law that aimed to implement existing decorum. Since the Han dynasty, the fusion of Confucianism with Legalism led to the collaboration of rites and laws, rendering rites the basis of laws, and laws the weapon for implementing ethical ideologies.[5] Based on codes of previous dynasties and existing ethical norms in the *Classic of Poetry, Book of Rites, Book of Changes, Spring and Autumn Annals, Classic of Filial Piety,* and various Confucian canons, the *Tang Legal Codes* is the earliest extant Chinese legal document on which penal laws of later dynasties are based with various degrees of modification.

In the legal codification that designated each individual a prescribed position, obligations rather than rights were the guiding principles. This reflects the gradual shift from an earlier Confucian definition of complementary ethics to a one demonstration of the inferior's submission. Whereas filial piety was deemed mandatory, benignity was not stressed as parental obligation; likewise the mutual exchange of benevolence and loyalty in the ruler-subject relationship was ignored. This rendered Confucius's decree that each behave as appropriate to one's role—a lord/father is benevolent as the minister/son is submissive—overturned.[6] A categorical suppression of the socially subordinate moved in, and situated at the bottom of social configurations, women suffered absolute ethical demands.

The prejudice of Tang laws is obvious: in the sphere of the state, the aim was to guard the rights of the monarch; in the domestic arena, the rights of the patriarchs were under jealous protection. Likewise the husband was protected against the wife, the father against the children, and the master against the slaves.[7] A rigid hierarchy sustained by social stratification was hence manifested by the scrupulously laid-out degrees of sentences delivered to offenders of descending social status. The imperial clans and ministers above the ninth rank were shielded from certain forms of punishment (such as beatings and capital punishment), often replaced by exile for offenses not connected with political revolt. Prohibition of intermarriage between gentlefolks and slaves was regulated to safeguard social segregation; the slaves as property had no claims over their own lives and were prohibited from suing their masters in cases of the latter's criminal activities. In the context of ethical relationships, parent-child, husband-wife, and wife-concubine constituted sets of unequal pairs, with the superior's offenses against the inferior punishable by reduced sentences.

In the household, a patriarch had absolute precedence over his wife, concubines, and handmaids. Quoting the ethical metaphysics, "a husband is the heaven of the wife," the codes regulate a wife to serve her husband with reverence even in death.[8] Under this condition, a man killing his women by accident was not subject to punishment, and physical abuse was deemed his rightful measure to maintain order. In the domestic kingdom, women were to address the master as *fujun* (my lord), with the same reverence observed by a courtier. At his death, his women were to observe three years' mourning period, a length equal to that of paternal mourning. In the codes' wording, a wife was to "transfer the clothes she wears for her father to observe the mourning for her husband." Whereas the master and concubines should mourn for the wife for one year, no mourning was to be observed for concubines.

In the harem, the matriarch also enjoyed authoritative rights, and by legal decree, a mother-in-law killing a daughter-in-law by default would not receive a capital sentence, for to punish a mother on account of a wife would undermine the decorum of filial piety.[9] The wife had similar superiority over all other women. Among the wife, the *teng* (accompanied-concubine, woman from the same clan as the bride), concubines, and maids, the rigid observance of hierarchy ordained that each's offense to the other, to the husband, and to his parents was punishable by escalating degrees of sentences. Furthermore, a concubine was prohibited from being exalted to the status of a wife, nor was a maid allowed that of a concubine

It was not until a woman rose to motherhood that matriarchal authority became at her service. Motherhood was the essential recourse for women to acquire power, and this condition manifested their dependence on the procreative function. Ethical codes, when translated into legal ones, had the function of consolidating moral obligations forcefully and transforming individuals into docile beings. A slave might through a grand pardon or by a compassionate master be freed from slavery; men could through a relatively new channel enter into officialdom and attain higher status. For women, the legal channel of escaping oppression was mainly through motherhood, although it did not lift them entirely from the tyranny of the patriarchs, especially in the cases of concubines and maids.

The prescriptive power of decorum over legal codes has rendered imperial China dominated by an ethical order. Renowned for its disposition to bypass orthodoxy, the Tang remained an empire whose controlling basis was moral prescriptions modeled on the Confucian classics, and it managed to maneuver within this framework. In this chapter, through layers of presentations in different discourses, we try to piece together the realities of female existence in the era and examine how Tang women reacted to the codes that coerced them into the role of Confucian wives. Our task is not only to figure out the interaction between institutionalized ethical order and unleashed female energies, but also the effect of this ethical order on the Tang populace.

FRAGMENTATION, ABSTRACTION, AND DESEXUALIZATION: WOMEN ACCORDING TO HISTORIANS

We now arrive at women situated near the end of Tang official histories in "Biographies of Exemplary Women," followed by chapters on neighboring countries and traitors. Episodes of lives of these women, collected and edited by the historians, present images of the ideal feminine in patriarchal ideology, and they are the only female representatives, besides their advantaged imperial sisters, who appear in the official documentation of their times. What emerges in these truncated biographies is a naturalization of ethical codes in the handbooks of female conduct and the Confucian canon. Having internalized patriarchal teachings, these women often state their intention of serving vehemently their husbands and in-laws without questioning the rationale of such piety.

In these biographies, in the context of various virtues such as loyalty, filial piety, and bravery, chastity appears to be simply one among many manifestations of female virtues. One persistent virtue documented here, the resistance to rape, was perceived as a claim to female subjectivity, for the last words from women often stressed their fine lineage as inviolable. Although one woman addressed herself as "a gentleman's wife," the awareness of being "a minister's daughter" or simply "I," "an upright person," prevails, showing that at critical moments, Tang women resisted physical violation to safeguard their integrity. In biographies of later epochs, though, the obsession with female chastity became predominant, and it was emphasized mainly to ensure the husband's sexual authority.

If the resistance to rape was to protect one's autonomy rather than the husband's honor, the rejection of remarriage had been reinforced through ethical persuasions that stressed the husband's absolute superiority. The opening case of Pei Shuying cites the ancient formula: "My husband is my Heaven, I would betray him not." Although this is the only occurrence of this metaphysics for women in the biographies, other rejections to remarry or simply to outlive the husbands are delivered to proclaim an adherence to ethical dictation. Such is the power of discourse: these biographies would serve as models for women of generations to come, sinking deep into their unconscious and becoming fully internalized, until following these decrees became a natural inclination.

A comparison between the two histories of the Tang shows the tightening of demands on female chastity as mainly a trend in the Song dynasty. The only woman recorded for her literary talent in the old history disappears in the new; instead, we witness a nameless woman who urged her husband to sell her to sustain himself in a famine; the man, at her insistence, sold her for several thousand coins, and she was promptly killed and distributed in the market. This episode is echoed in a much-debated case of the governor Zhang Xun, who served up women as food to sustain the prolonged struggle against the An Lushan faction.[11]

Such extreme cases of cannibalism are juxtaposed with two incidents at the fall of Empress Wei, when a certain secretary and a censor killed their wives, who were Wei's sister Lady Chongguo and wet nurse, and presented their heads to the throne to clear themselves.[12] This act, in drastic contrast to the many women who refused to outlive their husbands in stolen existence, points to the dishearteningly unequal demands on the sexes on the issue of faithfulness.

The biographies of virtuous men in Tang histories are divided into two sections: "Loyalty and Righteousness" and "Filial Piety and Friendship," in which a different emphasis on male virtues is evident. The overwhelming records of men who died an honorable death on the battlefields contrast well with the large number of women who died in fierce protection of their physical integrity. Thus loyalty and chastity constituted a complementary pair of essential virtues, exacting separately the strictest observances from men and women, and in the replica state of home, chastity was demanded of the wives by the husband-lord. If the self-sacrifices of many women were their answers to an ethical calling, the brutal deaths men suffered were no less ferocious an adherence to the idea of loyalty.

In comparing the immoral measures taken to make people moral, we need to consider the normative demands on women imposed through different degrees of sanctions. In contrast to biographies of virtuous men and officials known for their distinguished careers, virtuous women appear to be truncated in their zealous self-sacrifices. In fragmented anecdotes, they are cited as icons of female models; subtracted to the point of abstraction, they become narrowly identified by one moral attribute. In sum, they become abstractions of patriarchal ideals.

In line with this fragmentation is the erasure of the female body. In the practice of pious daughters and chaste widows, cutting off the hair manifested a determination to sever from worldly desires, and women took to Buddhist nunneries as a gesture of avowed celibacy.[13] As a final retreat for women, Buddhist temples provided a shelter and extended demands for renunciation. In light of the destruction of facial features practiced by women to unmake themselves as objects of desire, desexualization was in many ways the precondition for female fortitude. While women gained social status through their sexual functions, it was ironically through a denial of the same functions that they procured their autonomy.

In these biographies, virgins adhered to their virginity through drastic means. As pious daughters, they stripped off adornments, damaged their faces, and at least in two cases broke off marriages to stay by their parents' tombs for permanent mourning. Although sons also dwelled by their parents' tombs during the mourning period, they did not abuse themselves physically to bar sexual temptations. With no obligations to secure the patriline through procreation, daughters were praised for watching over their deceased parents as perpetual virgins; through depriving themselves of all fleshly pleasures and future happiness, they became the faithful guardians of the dead. By an absurd social contract, women were cast at the two extremes of sexual desire, both as its emblem and as its annihilation. Echoing the imperial practice of sending palace maids to the deceased emperors' mound, the practice of these daughters is another manifestation of patriarchal will that weighed down on women. This uncanny association between virgins and death has a psychological depth, as the barren purity of one mirrored the tyrannical blankness of the other.

Prolonged fasts, cutting of the ears, plucking out of the eye, turning a deaf ear to music, and self-confinement had been ways for women to manifest their determination to live a chaste life. In a telling case, when a woman suspected it was her beauty that prompted a man to propose to her in her dreams, she cut off her hair and put dirt on her face to disperse her psychologically poignant dreams. Thus women repressed their sexual drive and removed themselves from the marriage market. Such practices had the effect of associating female virtue with deformity, whereas sensual indulgence and overt charms were saturated with implications of feminine vice in popular consciousness.

*   *   *

In these biographies and in other miscellaneous records of motherhood, sternness stands out prominently, exemplified by a mother unwavering in ensuring her son's uprightness. Such sternness contradicts the traditional binary opposition of a compassionate mother and a severe father. In many cases, behind a loyal official stood a mother who remained instructive: in his official robe she would lash him as if he was still a wayward child.[14] This image of perpetual mother entails two things. First, it shows the son–child as ever under his mother's moral admonishment and remaining psychologically immature. Second, when the motherly instructions were often directed toward adherence to loyalty, this maternal virtue in effect became the instrument for the exercise of state ideologies.

The boundary between family and state was vividly transcended in such maternal remonstration. This instrumentalization of female virtue brings to the fore other ethical parallelisms: between filial piety and loyalty, when the one served the purpose of the other; between the piety of a wife and that of a minister, when both surrendered their will to the lords. Both parallelisms testify to the state as the all-encompassing power with which all ethics must comply. When conflict arose between the interest of the family and that of the state, the latter always superseded.[15] In various incidents, the loyalty of a mother overruled maternal instinct, as the state loomed large over all other concerns.

The failure to mature psychologically has been a criticism of Chinese men by contemporary intellectuals, and mothers whose instructions and physical abuse were revered by their official-sons present the Tang version of male immaturity. With their sexuality twisted by a marriage system that resulted in a split between desire and decorum, and with the demand for unconditional filial piety, the women these men unwittingly submitted to were their mothers, who were responsible for the shaping of their characters.

Thus these women rejected the canonical definition of motherhood as characterized by gentle affection and, assuming the role of a tough father, they proceeded to build their sons. This is one example of female modifications on traditional ethics. When a son's achievement had decisive influence on the mother's status, especially when she was a concubine or a widow, the emotional investment she had in him must have been enormous. In this regard, she could not afford to abide by the role of a compassionate mother but must act aggressively. Such a role, together with Wu Zhao's usurpation of her sons' rightful positions, contributes to our understanding of the reality of motherhood as Tang women lived and defined it.[16]

SURVIVAL HANDBOOKS: A METAPHYSICS FOR WOMEN

While the character *nü* (a woman or a daughter) points to the woman's identity in juxtaposition to her parents, at her marriage a woman acquires the name *fu* (wife) that designates her many-layered relations to her husband, her parents-in-law, and her new siblings. Etymologically, the character is composed of two parts: *nü* for its radical, which holds a broom at its right. The attachment of this household tool changes the nature of *nü* into someone instrumental in home maintenance, and it defines the fundamental difference between the statures of a woman before and after marriage, weighing her down in domestic configurations.

Through the canonization of models of female chastity, the state maintained an impression of general order within the harems. To perpetuate this operation, collaboration from women by internalizing the harshest decree constituted the ideal form of female obedience. In a tradition carved out by the Han court lady Ban

Zhao, learned women of the Tang produced handbooks for female conduct, based on normative codes upheld in the classics. It is believed that starting with Ban Zhao, women's handbooks, by professing the principle of submission, further perpetuated female subordination. From another perspective, however, the genre, first conceived by Ban with an immediate concern for her daughters, served the purpose of preparing women for the trying role of Confucian wives. In this aspect, it embodied first and foremost a survival guide with a compassionate understanding of women's destiny.

From the opening section, "Lowly and Weak," Ban Zhao's handbook *Nüjie* (Precepts for Women) sets an urgent tone, informing women of their inferiority to orient them to an arduous life in marriage. Applying the dualism of *yin* and *yang,* Ban stresses the polarity between the feminine (low/weak/soft) and the masculine (high/strong/hard). Herself a widow, a court scholar, and a historian who completed the *History of the Han* left unfinished by her brother Ban Gu, Ban Zhao was sensitive to the changing ethics of the times, as the consolidation of Confucian ethics was at a decisive stage in the latter Han. Following the *Book of Rites,* Ban's injunction to women to regard one's husband as heaven presents a unique metaphysics for women, thereby drawing their world into a pathetically confined space. This metaphysics cast great shadows on female consciousness and was well internalized, as the women's biographies discussed above have shown.

In the section "Single-minded," Ban states the urgency of winning the husband's heart on whom one's future is entrusted. This is achieved through not physical attraction but proper conduct. In these instructions, a feminine self is sculpted in correspondence with ethical demands, which includes the bending of the self, when *qücong* (unprincipled obedience) to the parents-in-law is mandatory. With this, the image of a damaged woman emerges, whose own principle must be surrendered in absolute passivity.

Quoting the *Book of Rites,* Ban instructs that it is respect from the man and submission from the wife, not love, that create successful marriages. To maintain the hierarchy in the harem, intimacy is too threatening to warrant cultivation. This emphasis is essential for our understanding of the marital relationship in traditional China, and it entails a conjugal sentiment not easily defined. Upon this principle, the contradiction between rigid, respectful distance and intimate sexual encounter between the couple arouses modern curiosity, and one wonders at the actual dialogue exchanged between man and wife in the intimate space of their chamber.[17]

In two of the Tang instruction books for wives, *Nü lunyu* (Women's analects), by Song Ruoshen (with her sister Ruozhao as commentator), and *Nü xiaojing* (Classic of filial piety for women), by a minister's wife surnamed Zeng, the urgency in Ban Zhao's manual is toned down considerably. In exchange, detailed rules are laid down for total control of women's physical and psychological makeup. The theme of both books stays largely within the bounds of the designated sphere of the home, warning against transgressions.

The Song sisters, who shunned heavy makeup and remained unmarried, state the importance of the conjugal couple's "mutual respect as guests" and end the section "Serving the Husband" with the comforting prospect of co-burial. This may be the closest we can come to regarding conjugal intimacy in marital codes. In Zheng's terminology following traditional ethics, a couple's relation is compatible to solemnity between emperor and minister, respect between father and son, uprightness between brothers, and faithfulness between friends.[18] Echoing Ban's descriptions of the ideal conjugal relationship in which respect is the key sentiment, such terminology is sustained by the fear of intimacy within the chamber, which may threaten male authority, thereby dissolving the ethical basis of marriage.

Inscribed by a desire to negate the female body, to transform woman into her negativity, the manuals embody the painstaking effort of regulating the soul through containment of the body.[19] The control of the female body runs from its geographical confinement to sealing it up against sensuous stimulations. According to these body codes, when outside, a woman should "hide her shape and conceal her shadow" and become virtually invisible. Inside the household, she should "walk lightly and slowly, with hands dropped down and speak softly." In other words, woman is instructed to transform her body into a docile entity, containing all unspent energies. The result is a concealed female body, an invisible woman, who guards her lips from liquor and knees from opening wide, her ears and eyes against sensuous sounds and sights, sources of contamination.[20] Sealed off from the outside world and its temptations, the female body becomes an enclosed space. This total curfew is extended to pregnancy, when the mother-to-be is instructed to purify herself of sensuous stimulations, thereby providing a perfectly chaste womb for the formation of a male infant. According to the handbook, she must "refrain from holding evil instruments and should chant Buddhist sutra at night; always sleep straight and sit upright"—in short, the maternal body is disciplined into a purified vessel.

Preaching the importance of nonjealousy, Zheng falls short of offering psychological grounding for the complex situation, essential for the well-being of women ignorant of the cruelty of a polygamy in which concubines came in stock to supercede them. Instead, she cautions against contact with contaminating sights and sounds, proposing the containment of female desires and a puritanical disposition as measures against the grip of jealousy. This reminds us of the desexualization of chaste women in the biographies, and it appears that not only for women vowed to be chaste, but for properly married wives too, desire must be contained, while its manifestation is epitomized by biting jealousy, a most "unwomanly" vice. The total curfew of the female body culminates with this curtailing of female desires in jealousy, which erases the desires of one whose existence is shaped to serve the desires of the other.

The various overlaps between the *Women's Analect* and a popular household manual in the Tang, *Wugong jiajiao* (Lord Wu's instruction for householders), suggests the extent to which these female texts embodied patriarchal norms. Written in the liberal Tang, however, the handbooks exhibit various seams that expose an inner split within the texts, if not within the authors.

The very lack of a sense of urgency and the counterexamples of ruthless women cited persistently by the Song sisters arouse the suspicion that the manuals were written to counter the unwomanly conduct of the times, and that their aim, different from that of Ban Zhao (which was to warn women into total submission), was to coerce them into discipline. Ironically, the persistent appearance of women of bold, hilarious transgressions triggers liberating laughter from the readers, thus unleashing latent female energies. Women who ventured out on the streets, who scolded the in-laws, laughed loud laughs, and got drunk in banquets present a vivid contrast to the docile women who are paled by their uninhibited sisters. This undercurrent constitutes the unconscious of the text and threatens to annihilate the flow of the stiff-faced preaching. In contrast to the tamed woman, there is always another woman, a negative image to servility that poses a challenge to the orthodox. In a similar vein, Zheng's handbook, rejecting the notion that blind submission befits an intelligent woman, includes remonstration with a faulty husband as a female virtue, thus questioning the idea of absolute female inferiority, a tendency of Ban Zhao's earlier work.

The inner split of the texts points to the Tang's particular climate, with female energies threatening to burst out. In the folk tradition, a similar motion can be discerned in a text from the Dunhuang collection of Buddhist narratives (*bianwen,* a genre in the folk tradition associated with the popular form of Buddhist teachings). In the story, "The Shrewish New Wife," the free-spirited woman trampled on her husband, knocked off utensils in the kitchen, fought with neighbors like a water buffalo, and laughed like a well-bucket roller. Scolded by her mother-in-law, she indignantly asked for a divorce paper and started her liberated life. The text concludes that this untamed creature is so self-assured that it requires a "shedding of thousands layers of skin" to transform her.[21] With the various records on shrewish wives, the Tang's reputation for its unshackled female energy is palpable.

How exactly Tang women challenged the doctrines served up by their scholarly sisters is discussed in the following section.

THE BATTLEFIELD OF HOME

Readers of the Tang tombstone inscriptions might arrive at the conclusion that Tang women had submitted well to ethical and reproductive responsibilities, as the many inscriptions portray gentry women as faithful daughters, loyal wives, and dutiful mothers carrying graciously the burden of ancestral worship and educating the young. Reading these flattering biographies without knowledge of their social background, one is in danger of missing a hidden injustice. While the men's impressive titles are listed and the lineage and virtues of their wives given without fail, there is one obstinate omission: the nameless concubines.[22]

The injustice is dealt both to numerous concubines, household entertainers and maids as de facto concubines, and to the properly married couples. By deleting these women of lesser status, the lives of these gentry men and women lose their complexities: the pleasure and anguish surrounding concubinage, the intrigue among women, the inferiority complex that children of concubines suffered, all are lost in this deliberate neglect. The one truly difficult female virtue, nonjealousy, also loses its intense meaning.

From this omission derives an incongruity concerning the image of Tang women. In other modes of writing, wives of a very different character emerge: wives who would rather die than part with a fierce jealousy; who killed, injured, and abused their rivals in bitter competitions; who burned a concubine's hair, printed marks on her face, beat up the husband, destroyed his licentious banquet, and kept the man shaking with fear.[23] A husband's intense fear of a shrewish wife was a social phenomenon that men from emperor to minister readily admitted to in the Tang. Frightened men at the mercy of their willful wives—this is presented unabashedly in discourses other than the discreet language for the dead. If the wife had been cruel and the man cowardly, the gravestone remains silent on these issues; instead they were co-buried in a gratifying eternal companionship. Without the intense drama of intrigues and injuries, without the unequal war among women and their children, these biographies present but truncated family still shots that disguise a less happy truth.

As they appear in formulaic inscriptions, there seems to be only one woman: diligent, pious, capable of raising successful sons. With the exception of ones who died young, there are only mothers and grandmothers who, having fulfilled the duty of procreation, came to accept their condition of desexuality.[24] As for numerous women who suffered the severe neurosis of jealousy that lasted throughout their lives, who retreated to citing Buddhist sutras to curtail their desires and the intense agony they were made to endure, all these were obscured by the stones. With this, the power of discourse is manifested, for the image of Confucian wife erased the flesh and blood of women of various dispositions, and the ideal woman of ethical creation obliterated the real women, with their darkened psyches left unplowed.

The division of labor among dynastic women was borne out by their separate presentations in different modes of discourse. In the inscriptions, the concubines are excluded with discretion, while the many sensuous concubines and courtesans appear in private writings such as poetry and fragmented memoirs. Through their absence in funeral memorials, women of primarily sexual function are dismissed to maintain the ethical profile of marriage. And the wives, having fulfilled their procreative obligation, are granted a place in family history.

It would be culturally naive to interpret this practice as simply hypocritical. Legal sanctions on a concubine's obligations were carefully laid down to ensure the hierarchy of a properly married wife and a concubine purchased with a contract. The lack of legal protection had determined the concubine's nonexistence in formal documents, while her shifting status determined her absence from family biographies. As household properties, concubines were often dispersed or given away by their masters. Poor folks of the empire often pawned their daughters as leased concubines, and at the termination of the contract, if childless, the women were free to leave. Such drifting identity both offered the women freedom and stripped them of security in the household.[25] In this regard, the practice of concubinage presents one important dimension of class domination in which women of the lower class were literally sexual commodities. The disappearance of the concubines, then, is not so much the pretension of pseudomonogamy, but an honest reflection of their denigrated status.

The birth of a child consolidated a concubine's status in the household and was not without its complications. The honorary titles an official-son won for his mother went straight to the *di* mother, the wife, because the *shu* mother, the concubine, was a socially improper recipient of this prestige. This deprivation detached concubines from family history in the same way they were separated from their children in the lineage lists. In such operations, a concubine's children became family properties of which their mother had no share; it further distanced her from the wife as the designated procreator, and herself as the surrogate mother. In cases where plenty of descendants had already been secured before the purchase of a concubine, the production of children could be considered a by-product of her original sexual function.

On the theme of the making of Confucian wives, the position of concubines is a rather awkward one. Clearly the survival handbooks were designed for proper wives, not for concubines bought and sold. In the making of ethical wives, concubines constituted perhaps the most bitter obstacles without even appearing in the ethical guidance for women. If we must explicate, they belonged more logically to the process of the unmaking of Confucian wives, not only in the sense that they triggered fiery jealousy and threatened the wives' self-control, but in that their very existence posed an irrational demand on these women and upset the harmony in the household.

Due to a basic inequity, the battlefield of home was principally one between women, while men were infinitely implicated. Between women, physical abuse and vicious conceits were common; caught in between, the husband's was not a pleasant role, as situations could become vulgar when maids were involved.[26] On the other hand, this sexualized battle pitted women against each other, divesting the strength of their affinity as well as wasting their energy on violent emotions. In this sense, it betrayed the concept of conjugal relations as the basis of all ethical relations and posed difficulties to male cultivation that began with oneself and harmony within the family. It was precisely this threat within the harem that triggered the fear of female desires in male consciousness. Home as battlefield: this presents another self-defeating aspect of life in imperial China, as it destabilized men's moral control from the ground up.

The exile of concubines from tombstone inscriptions is consistent with the exile of women from history. When only certain types of women are recorded in official histories, when state ideology is bent on teaching and coercing, and when formal discourses are frustratingly biased, it is through private writings that one approximates the truth of women's lives in the Tang.

THE RADICAL VIRTUE OF JEALOUSY

Under the prescriptive ethic, the fundamental character of female sexuality in the general social and ideological context of imperial China was marked by suppression. Barrenness, jealousy, adultery, and vile diseases were four of the seven grounds for expelling a wife that bore degrees of association with her sexuality, with the last having a less direct, but nevertheless gravely negative sexual implication. Theoretically, a jealous wife deprived the husband of his legal right to fornicate both within and outside of the family that he established as the patriarch, while the other three offenses either threatened the continuation of or contaminated the patrilineage. These four offenses, together with gossip, theft, and physical offense on the parents-in-law, were established as early as the pre-Han era in the *Yili* (Rites of ritual) and consolidated in the *Book of Rites,* which set the tone for the sexual oppression of women for generations to come.[27]

One common strategy in arguing for the existence of female power has been the proposal that in the sphere of the household, woman had authority as the matriarch. This assumption both accepts the geographical limit on women and perpetuates the ideology that regards women devoid of sexuality as more legitimate. Tang women certainly did not buy into this compensation, and they refused to stay the course of desexualized mothers and quietly retreat to the background. Instead, they insisted on the legitimacy of female desire and fought vehemently for its gratification.

Immediately preceding the Tang, Empress Wenxian of the Sui Dynasty set the tone for female jealousy in an exemplary case of its triumph and defeat. Offering counsel to Emperor Gaozu as his equal, Wenxian was renowned for her wisdom; what gave her away, however, was a sternest jealousy. Once she took the liberty of removing a threatening consort, and Gauzu's reaction was strong enough: he galloped up the hill and refused to come down, and Wenxian realized, finally, that his will was stronger than hers. For the first time she realized that whatever her status and ability might be, she was deemed "a mere woman," as one minister had it. Her spirit was darkened, and although she continued to fight ostentatiously against concubines, Gauzu's and his courtiers' alike, she had known the taste of an indefatigable sexual inequality. Wenxian received her historical comment as one "whose virtue was deviant from that of the faithful wife": a fatal flaw that discredited all her other merits.[28] Because she was a "mere woman," wifely virtue was one ultimate criteria upon which she was judged, and failing it, Wenxian fell a heroic fall in orthodox history. Her enterprising endeavor against concubinage was not seen again, and even Wu Zhao left the issue untouched in her limited effort to enhance women's status.

Continuing from the exemplary Wenxian, Tang women's capacity for jealousy became a self-professed vocation. The legend of the Jealous Wife's Ferry presents a woman whose jealousy extended to the River Lo Goddess when her husband praised the latter's mythical beauty. Out of spite she drowned herself to haunt the river, demanding the lives of women prettier than herself.[29] Such folk fantasy associated with a locale surfaces a collective anxiety in which natural disaster was deemed the doing of a violently jealous woman, and the sentiment of jealousy was seen as feeding on itself with a destructive energy.

Such undaunted jealousy forces us to consider this phenomenon with care. Essentially, it was the struggles against unequal worth of genders that constituted the basis of this sentiment, when the wife revolted against the husband's right to polygamous sexuality. As men's value and sexual rights increased with the advancement of their careers, those of women decreased as they advanced in years. This was a lesson Tang women strived to unlearn through a tenacious vigil over proliferating male desires. When a general inequity determined the ways of existence of the sexes, the most fundamental inequity (concubinage) that destroyed the equilibrium of the sphere allotted to women (the home) became the source of anger and retaliation.

Female jealousy hence was an important phenomenon in Tang social history. In miscellaneous writings, episodes of jealous wives bringing anguish to husbands and concubines abound, and the reactions of these men were stereotypically hilarious. Restrained by a bad conscience, they looked pathetic in their failed attempts at sexual excursions. Thus women ridiculed men's desire in its orientation toward hedonism and its interest in entertainers or maids decades their junior. Sometimes female jealousy was publicly humored, as in the case of a servant's imitation of his mistress's jealousy, which triggered hearty laughs from the master.[30] In presenting these jealous wives, the joke was on the women as much as it was on the men; the wives' fearful will, sometimes scandalous, was often regarded with awe by the narrators, whose intent was neither to teach nor to coerce. The generous acceptance and ability to see irony as well as comedy in this bitter emotion illustrate for us the general mood of the times concerning female jealousy, a vice listed in the classics and the legal codes as one of the seven fatal offenses.[31]

The symptom of female jealousy, however, had a much more somber aspect than was generally admitted. One anecdote on female jealousy is particularly alarming:

> Yan, wife of the Guiyang magistrate Ruan Song, was extremely jealous. While Song was entertaining guests with several female singers, Yan, her hair all tossed up, baring her arms and feet, rushed into the banquet with a knife in her hand and scattered the frightened guests. Song hid himself under the bed, and shaken up, the entertainers escaped. [Song received hence the lowest ranking in his annual review.][32]

This outburst of jealousy boarders on hysteria and should be regarded as a psychological symptom that requires healing. Such a symptom signals the heavy burden the social condition of male promiscuity posed on women, and like the Victorian women, only the very healthy could *stand* marriage, while those unable to sublimate their sexuality succumbed to "severe, lifelong neurosis affecting the whole course of their lives."[33] The intensity of such a symptom invites us to rethink the farcical anecdotes of female jealousy scattered in miscellaneous notes, for clearly, in its usual strategy of disguising the unwanted, of concealing intense struggles between genders and classes, patriarchal discourse has again failed to present the much darker truth of jealousy that marked female existence. Instead of being a laughable, unworthy emotion, jealousy as it was experienced by Tang women should be recognized as a disease with all its tragic implications.

* * *

In the overall perspective of historical development, the outburst of female revolt was contemporaneous with the rise of the literati clique, which, once firmly entrenched, would further solidify institutionalized assessments of the personal worth of men and further deprive women of their social status. In the sociocultural transfiguration of the Tang, women had their historical chance of voicing their discontent with sexual oppression; it is nonetheless a voice that would eventually be stifled. In conjunction with female jealousy, we'd do well to consider the change of individual values on the political and social scales, for this sentiment was not an isolated symptom but interacted with the general climate of the times. Placed in the historical context, female jealousy was by no means merely a sexual issue but presented a much deeper symptom as well as the premonition of the advent of the general devaluation of women.

The voluminous unleashing of jealousy, then, together with the audacious indulgence of aristocratic women, draw a daring picture of female desires. That Tang women did not heed the warning of their scholarly sisters, that they differed drastically from their images on the tombstones, and equally significant, that Tang men did not abide by the legal codes, either concerning jealousy or the concubine's fixed status, are obvious enough. Less obvious is the psychological depth of female jealousy and women's apprehension of the threat of the rising literati. Since almost all documents are penned by men of letters from prescribed perspectives, an examination of male consciousness is essential to unravel the shadows it casts on the presentations of women. Furthermore, when men were seriously implicated in the battlefield of home and stood perpetually under the shadow of the ultimate patriarch, their subjectivity was inherently damaged, and their desires suffered an implicit split.

Chapter 6

Problematics of Male Desires

The impression some Westerners have of Chinese sexuality may have derived from an emphasis on the influence of Taoist sexual yoga that practices complementary gains for both parties, which leads to the misconception of wives as sexual partners with equal rights to pleasure.[1] While the upper class had indulged in the esoteric practice of Taoist handbooks, it was basically a deviance from orthodox codes, in which respect superceded love in marital relations, and the aspect of pleasure in conjugal sex was immaterial. Moreover, the theory of complementary gains was often overruled by masculine absorption of the feminine energies, rendering the female body an instrument for male longevity.

In both the Confucian definition of marriage and the Taoist practice of sexuality, love retreats to the distant background. One stresses the ethical purpose of transmitting the patriline, while the other emphasizes the masculine benefit from the feminine. The Confucian view on sexual mystery stresses immortality in one's progeny; the Taoist, transformation of one's own body chemistry.[2] The hierarchy between genders created hurtful distance within the couple, and on top of this, the practice of sexual yoga deprived men of normal perceptions of emotional ties. When women were regarded as an instrument for men's physical well-being, even as enemies against whom men must guard their *yang* energy, it was inconceivable that genuine affection could arise. As the practice of sexual yoga reached its peak in the Sui and Tang, together with growing numbers of concubines in the gentlemen's harems, symmetrical to the emotional jeopardy in the battlefield of home, Taoist sexual yoga posed physical, if not mortal, danger to male practitioners.

Perceiving the human body as a replica of the cosmic, Taoist sexual texts instruct man to study the nature of heaven and earth and put it into practice with his own body. In this metaphysics of sexuality, the embracing of *yin* and *yang,* imitating the cosmic copulation of heaven and earth, is believed to produce the state of immortality. This theory is further developed in the sexual alchemy after the Tang, in which a more complex theory suggests that male absorption of female *yang* essence to unite with the *yin* essence within himself will produce a form of spiritual pregnancy.[3] Applying the complementary hexagrams *li* and *kan,* which have *yang* on

101

the outside and *yin* on the inside, and *yin* on the outside and *yang* on the inside separately, sexual alchemy focuses on subtracting the *yang* within the female body for a higher fusion, and the male body becomes the laboratory of his spirit. Copulation with the opposite sex, then, is an expedient means of achieving immortality, accomplished by stealing masculine *yang* essence from the heart of *yin* to return to the adamantine state of pure *yang*. "Following the normal course of the *Tao* of man and woman, or *yin* and *yang*, produces offspring, but reversing it produces the elixir."[4] The mystical marriage of masculine and feminine principles within the body of the mediator would ultimately bring the practitioner into transcendental ecstasy, entering a paradise free of sexual desires. In the final analysis, it is the union both with *and* within oneself, rather than with the feminine, that this sexual alchemy is about.

This peculiar mysticism/pragmatism of sexuality has its psychological background. In the polygamous household, the patriarch, outnumbered by his many women, must uphold his *yang* dominance over the *yin* majority, and multiple contacts without ejaculation reinforced his right to dominance. The master was instructed to keep emotional distance from women, and not to corrupt sexual acts, conceived of as the battle of essences, with romance. The woman, the Other, the crucible, or stove as she is identified in later texts, is but an instrument, and although early sexual texts stress the recognition of a woman's right to pleasure in the bedroom, the Six Dynasties sexual text, *Yufang mique* (Secrets of the jade chamber), proposes that "those who would cultivate their *yang* must not allow woman to steal glimpses of this art."

As an ironic contrast to this statement, in earlier sexual texts such as the *Sunu jing* (Classics of Su Nü), sexual secrets lie with woman, as the Goddess Su Nü instructs the Yellow Emperor on secrets of sexual productivity. Echoing this, mystical ecstasy during sexual acts is recorded only in the woman's text, *Queen Mother of the West's Ten Precepts on Women's Practice*.[5] While early Mawang Dui texts of the Han are almost entirely free of theories prejudicial to women, women's status suffers a decline in later sexual alchemy, wherein for woman practitioners, immortality can only be achieved after her metamorphosis into a man by stopping the flow of menstrual blood, a process termed "killing the red dragon."

Such asymmetrical design produces damaging psychological effects on the male practitioner, who must guard himself against emotional investment in women, and for whom the pleasure principle is replaced with a transcendental pleasure, a function of the meditating process. The sexual act now brings man the union with his other self buried deep within the female body, and such inversion defeats the original design of human copulation as emulating the cosmic mating of heaven and earth. The inversion does not bring the union of the pure *yin* and pure *yang* as those texts suggest, but rather, that of the outer *yang* and the inner *yang*, when the whole act is conceived by a masculine will to a life that is purely illusive. Due to the emotional absence in the man's sexual act, the copulation originally meant as a channel toward salvation becomes a narcissistic, solitary act of the male self against itself. A despairing act of a futile attempt at immortality, it sheds off the intense passions that have made sex so much an obsession for mankind.

Utilized and bypassed by the masculine drive toward transcendental ecstasy, the flesh and blood of women are emptied out into abstract entities. With this, the most instinctive drive of the libido is transformed into unnatural, invested endeavor. The intimate touch of the flesh between individuals is deprived of its urgent meaning, and together with it, the chance of saving man from himself is lost. For a culture that believes *yin* and *yang* require each other to engage in a harmonious movement, to invest in this tilted-over relationship between the sexes, this total erasure and distortion of the feminine, is self-destructive and hypocritical, to say the least.

In a society where sensual enjoyment was phenomenal and ethical codes were openly transgressed, both women and men were allowed space for sexual expressions. However, a categorical difference between the degrees of freedom they were allowed to enjoy was obvious, and as ethical demands on women tightened in the late Tang, the distance between the genders' allotted status in terms of their sexual subjectivity widened. As the masters of households populated by women of varied standing, the ways men exercised or refrained from exercising their rights, together with the effect of pseudomonogamy on the construct of their sexuality, are essential for a feminist study of the era. When, within the harem, women were made to suffer injuries and self-denial, it seemed impossible for a man to maintain composure and stay above the intrigue staged in his own household. And as subjects of the vast empire that positioned each in a prescribed space, an inexplicable split within the masculine self appeared like a thunderstruck cleft.

DILEMMA OF THE DESIRABLE LITERATI

The Tang inherited from the Six Dynasties a high regard for the great aristocratic clans, whose heritage was ostentatiously coveted by the gentry, while the clans held on to their names by forming marital ties with each other, excluding even the imperial members. Under these circumstances, daughters of these houses became much sought-after tokens of prestige. Alongside this emphasis on pedigree was the rise of the literati, whose liberal lifestyles clashed with the clans, who prided themselves on their adherence to decorum, and the interaction of these two social forces, one steered toward stability, the other toward self-mobility, constituted the chance and finally the crisis for Tang women.[6]

The two periods dominated by pedigree experienced the syndrome of female jealousy vividly. Yet it would be facile to explain the rise of female consciousness as simply the result of political marriage when daughters of the great clans had a heightened sense of self-esteem. To apprehend fully this female self-advocacy, we need to place it in the larger context of changing social structures; more specifically, the coming into the political scene of the literati.

Historically, the worship of male beauty culminated in the Six Dynasties, when an individual was appreciated from a purely aesthetic, if not metaphysical, approach. At the Tang, the zeal invested in (sometimes effeminized) male beauty was replaced by appreciation of individual temperaments and overall bearing. Compared with the aesthetic appreciation of men of unusual grace, the appreciation of feminine beauty was seldom without a sense of anxiety. *Bo-Kong liutie* (Six scrolls by Bo and Kong), assorted fragments covering comprehensive fields compiled by Bo Juyi in the Tang and continued by Kong Chuan in the Song, has a section on feminine beauty; in contrast to its counterpart on masculine beauty, it quickly shifts to an anxious tone, warning against excessive female charms. While handsome men enjoyed generous compliments from strangers on the street, beautiful women, confined to their chambers, were subject to be tagged with a cautionary that rendered their natural gift suspicious. This discrimination made the appreciation of male elegance a tasteful practice, whereas that of female elegance was considered morally contaminating.

The gentry's invested interest in choosing sons-in-law was carried to a height in the Tang; by emperors and gentry alike, promising young men were jealously coveted. This phenomenon was entrenched in the culture surrounding the state examinations, when at its annual celebration, young men freshly adorned by the halo of success were observed with keen interest by potential fathers-in-law. Thus the value of aspiring talents rose both politically and in the marriage market, while an alliance was formed between two generations of men as they furthered each other's prospects through the trafficking of women.[7]

A potential crisis was inherent in this opportunity for mobility, when a wrong decision might prove disastrous, to which the unfortunate case of Li Shangyin attests. By marrying into the family of his powerful patron's enemy, Li made himself an outcast for both factions of the Niu and the Li, the two most powerful cliques in the Tang. In other cases, whether to ally with the powerful by dispensing with one's lawful wife was a taxing issue for the feeble-minded, and with the rise of their value, the literati faced new trials when tempting marriage propositions exposed their moral weakness.

Herein lies the inherent conflict in the psychological makeup of Tang literati. Torn between ambitions and ethical callings, between personal advancement and emotional responsibilities, they produced various literary works that expose their inner split.[8] The split of male subjectivity lies not only between desires and decorum but also between their political ambitions and moral burdens. The aristocratic society, the harem, and Confucian ethics made various demands on men, and while they benefited from a changing climate, it was inevitable that they should pay dearly for their expanding privileges.

The counterbalance of men's and women's worth in the Tang was precisely an imbalance: if men enjoyed social mobility through strenuous efforts, women were trapped by their fathers' names. This constituted a countermove in the sexes' rise and fall in this critical turn of history. The great clans' practice of selling daughters to unequal partners by taking "compensation money" to make up for the latter's inadequacy was so common that from Emperors Taizong to Gaozong edicts were issued to prohibit such an unseemly custom.[9] For daughters with a high value in the marriage market, a psychological imbalance was in effect. Sold by their fathers to unworthy partners, daughters of the great clans were caught between pride and shame, and their often unorthodox behavior should be understood as a symptom derived from this psychological tension.[10]

The countermove between the literati and prestigious clans and, together with it, the delicate (im)balance between the literati and the clans' daughters, was upset by the decline of the clans at the late Tang and further destroyed by the expansion of the elite in the Song. While in the Tang, betrothal gifts normally far exceeded the dowry, the expansion of the local elite in the Song triggered the need for stronger interconnections among the group through transactions of daughters accompanied by a handsome dowry.[11] The elite's increasing value had great impact on women, now facing a prohibitory rhetoric from the neo-Confucians, while commercialization and the widening market in women also affected their status.[12] The historical significance of the rise of men's value, then, proved to have a negative impact on women, and the seemingly tasteful appreciation of a young man became threatening from a woman's viewpoint.[13]

On this note, the phenomenon of the impious daughters-in-law that culminated in collective female jealousy should be interpreted as women's struggle for self-worth, and in the context of the literati's growing value, female jealousy intensified. It stood at the threshold of the entrenchment of the elite, sensing that juxtaposed to men's growing value was their own inevitable degradation. The ultimate meaning of the jealous wives, then, should be understood not only as a revolt against men's categorically higher sexual freedom but also as vigilance against the rise of men's value over women, and it entailed much wider social as well as psychological significance.

* * *

In the self-promotion of the literati, an important facet was involved besides their liaison with prestigious clans. If the courtesan's career depended on patronage from the literati circle, that of a literatus depended on the patronage of men of consequence. The circulation of their literary compositions into the hands of the influential had a similar effect as the circulation of a courtesan's lyrics (and that of her patrons') among those interested.[14] In this manner, recommendations based on linguistic merits brought young scholars recognition in the capitals, which usually preceded the actual verdict of the state examinations. While the fame of a courtesan was translated into her livelihood, that of the literati was translated into civil careers and subsequent political power. For both parties, a similar mechanism of building one's reputation upon linguistic creations was mandatory, when the dire necessity of finding a patron could be fatal for an unresourceful literatus.[15]

Outrageous as it may seem to compare the self-promotion of the literati to that of the courtesans, by drawing an analogy between their ways of self-establishment, the absolute value of words in seventh- to ninth-century China is evident. We should also notice the different (and similar) ways men and women related to language. The pride and plight of the literati, so much a part of the paradox of the era, were firmly rooted in the creations of belles lettres, and they were driven, much like the courtesans, to adorn themselves with words.

INNER SPLIT OF MALE DESIRES

While a woman's ethical status was defined essentially by her domesticity, that of a man involved a much wider sphere that included his position in relation to the state, the monarch (his symbolic father), his father, brothers, and friends. The challenges to a man's moral integrity hence involved extensive aspects in which the demand from the closest vicinity, the harem, posed the most immediate challenge.

Implicated by the downfall of Prime Minister Wang Shuwen, the iconoclastic Liu Zongyuan was downgraded as governor of the depleted district, Liu Zhou. Liu's wife died young by a traumatic delivery, and he wrote in a letter with heart-rending anxiety about his failure to secure a descendant line.

> Solitary and childless as I am, in this wilderness without gentry's daughters, I could not find a suitable marriage; the world too is unwilling to associate with a criminal.
>
> Although I do not presume to hope to return and sweep my parents' tomb, or retreat to my ancestor's house and spend the rest of my days, if I could only move up north a little and be somewhat rid of the swamp air, find a marriage mate to procure my offspring, and have someone to leave them to—even if I die, it is like a sweet sleep, and I will no more regret.[16]

These words are a perfect reminder of the procreative function of marriage and discrimination against marriages between parties of unequal standing. The solitary figure of Liu, in conjunction with Wang Wei who, widowed, found solace in Buddhist doctrines, and Li Shangyin who refused an entertainer offered to him as solace in his widowhood, shows a puritanical facet of the literati at odds with the general impression of Tang gentry creating around themselves a populated harem.[17]

Countering the epoch's indulgence in the sensuous, Buddhist asceticism did not prevail in the Tang, and the case of Wang Wei certainly does not represent the norm. Other famous men of letters were less inhibited in exerting their rightful desires: In mourning for his deceased concubine, Wei Zhuang describes her emotional disturbance whenever the topic of acquiring another concubine was brought up. Both Han Yu and Bo Juyi surrounded themselves with versatile entertainers/concubines, and while one of Han's concubines escaped to seek better fulfillment, the aged Bo sold one of his against her earnest plea.[18]

Although concubinage was a luxury out of reach for the financially underpriv-
ileged, ethically defined monogamy undermined by the actual practice of male
polygamy constituted the basis of marriages in premodern China. This particular
practice had fundamental contributions to the shaping of the character of the marital relationship and with it, that of romantic love. The unique version of Chinese
monogamy, operating within and dictated by strict ethical considerations, had a
decisive effect on female sexuality, as we have seen. Ironically, it simultaneously
shaped and misshaped male sexuality and emotions in ways that had important cultural consequences—the lack of more strictly defined love poems in the otherwise
strong lyrical tradition being but one symptom derived from such social practice.

While respect outweighed affection in the Confucian blueprint for marriage,
under ethical dictates, filial piety overruled conjugal affection, and parental discontent could be a decisive cause for expelling a wife. An outright injunction is found
in the *Book of Rites*' section "Neize" (Inner regulations): "A son loves his wife.
Should the parents be displeased, expel her. The son resents his wife; his parents
say: 'She serves us well.' The son then should fulfill conjugal decorum with the wife
without fail after the parents' death."[19] In some cases, brotherhood also overruled
the marital tie, when a wife was divorced for having caused a split among brothers.
As an outsider, a wife who caused disputes in the family and disrupted its harmony
was considered antagonistic and could be promptly removed.

Under the pressure of this normative code, men resorted to moderate, stereotyp-
ical ways of confessing feelings for their wives, and conjugal love with all its intensity was not adequately recorded either in private letters or lyrics. In a self-serving
poem to his bride, Bo Juyi cites virtuous ancient women who showed admirable
courage in sharing hardship with their husbands and proposes that they "harbor
poverty and simplicity/and age together with delight."[20] Yuan Zhen's well-known
"Daowang" (Mourning for my wife) also stresses with gratitude his late wife's moral
support during lean times. Besides these expressions of bonds between materially
starved couples, to wives in absentia men expressed distress over prolonged separation, and usually familial affection outweighed romantic feelings in these letters.

While a man's affection for his wife was under constant surveillance, his emotional ties with concubines were likewise under ethical pressure. Preference for
concubines who were often younger and more attractive is perceivable, yet the
inequity within the harem rendered love for the lesser woman unethical, pointing
to the man's moral weakness. The preference of beauty over virtue had long been
criticized as a vice by Confucius, and a gentleman was urged to exhibit moral superiority by respecting a virtuous but otherwise unattractive wife and keeping away
from the capricious concubines.[21] When moral demands confronted desires, the
more decidedly Confucian elite would forgo natural inclinations to fulfill higher
callings; in rare cases, they might even become willing martyrs of this moral habit.[22]

In the houses of men of large appetite, private entertainers saturated the space
with music and dance, transforming an ethical home into a sensuous site. The separation of love from an enslaved sexuality underlay this condition in which the traf-

ficking of emotion was suppressed, and the relationship between the master and concubines was defined by an owner-property bondage. When women were exchangeable commodities, however self-infatuated, a man's feelings for them necessarily failed to have the quality of love between equals; consequently, poems composed for entertainer-concubines often are tinged by fetishism, transforming these women into sensuous objects.

Private entertainers whose status fell between that of a concubine and a maid, who were not tied by ethical bonds to their masters, had a history of taking to the road, or eloping, which exasperated the more possessive masters. Ironically, by acquiring concubines decades their junior, male sexuality became vulnerable precisely because of its expansion. In a similar vein, the legal sanction on the concubine's status created tension between emotion and decorum. Du You, editor of the comprehensive *Tong dian* (Compendium of rites), who exalted his concubine to the status of a wife, had to weather sarcastic criticism from his contemporaries, an embarrassing situation that he shared with other high ministers. In this manner, the politics of sexual inequity created vulnerable spots in men both as moral and emotional subjects. When women were divided into strict categories, it was difficult for men to simply follow their feelings without paying a high price demanded by an absurd social contract.

Underneath this tension was a psychological split between a man's feelings (*qing*) and sexuality (*se*) caused by the irrational pseudomonogamy. Caught between the double bind of ethics and natural drives, conscientious men were urged to conceal their desires from the orthodox-minded to avoid scorn. They were required also to maintain composure in terms of their emotional makeup. It appears that a man respected his wife and adored his sensual concubines, while at both ends he was not encouraged to extend to them love such as we know it today.[23]

To do justice to marital affection, which must have had its intense moments, we must turn to the jealous wives, whose zealous protests and disheartening frustrations solicit recognition of the emotional bond between the conjugal pair. Such intense female jealousy also enlightens us on the ethical necessity of defining the marital relationship as one of mutual respect, which is in essence an effort at containing excessive emotions that would result in an overspill of female desires. It is through this great show of emotional upheaval that we gain insight into the realities of Tang marriage, with conjugal intimacy as its undefined core, much as the literati, for one reason or the other, chose not to reveal it.

LONELINESS OF THE LITERATI

In an era that enjoyed sensuality with uninhibited appetite, the constant temptation of women who enticed with songs and wine was difficult to resist. For the ill-fated scholars who struggled to maintain a living, the sights and sounds of private entertainers crowding the many social banquets must have been painfully stimulating. As possessions of the state or of powerful men, these women aroused desires that must more often be frustrated than satisfied; in this manner, they wove a sensual surface without providing actual fulfillment, thus severing sensual pleasure from its consummation for the less fortunate. Inherent in this situation is another problem: fascinated by luring entertainers, the elite confronted their wives in a very different environment. Through social segregation, women were placed in contrasting categories that came to identify them, and as a result, men's perspectives were colored by this radical compartmentalization, which was further sanctioned by both legal and ethical codes that dictated strict divisions.

The phenomenal success of the courtesans, together with the fact that in courtesanship intellectual appeals outweighed physical attractions, brought to the foreground the elite's yearning for intellectual companionship in women. Encouraged to develop their intelligence, Tang courtesans had a high reputation for their sharp minds, while women trained to be docile wives were cautioned to refrain from cultivating their potential, when feminine virtue did not encompass talent. Yet one must not unreservedly grant the courtesans' existence as an answer to the literati's need for compatible lovers, for accepting this would suggest that the majority of gentry women were inadequate, and that women of divided spheres complemented each other to create the image of complete women. To accept such a proposition, which unfortunately had its qualified truth, is to suggest that wives, whom we have seen as capable of passionate emotions, were sexually undesirable and intellectually incompetent. It has the danger of falling into the trap of the male utopia of complementary lovers: one chaste, the other wild; one spiritual, the other earthly.[24] If Tang wives were not as "chaste" as formal discourses would have it, neither were they entirely incompatible with their husbands.

This caution is not without its ambivalence: while helping us see the exaltation of courtesans as partially a cover-up for proliferating male desires, it also presents such social practice as weighed with deliberation. This practice of categorizing women was another function of patriarchal mechanism: the division of women into ethical and sexual beings ensured the stability of a proper home and the pleasurable atmosphere of social gatherings, at the same time satiating male desires with their wildest fancies.

Tang literati and courtesans shared their historical moment marked by the centrality of embellished words; when talent sought out talent and fed on each other's creations, when poetic creations became an obsession and a survival game, it was inevitable that men and women sought solace from each other as they wrote to impress as well as to conform, and for both parties, this act of conformity entailed a complexity difficult to unravel. Because of these special circumstances, romance between members of the two groups had long been a reservoir for obsessive anecdotes, and it is through reading these tales that we learn of the literati's capacity for loving, in ways different from their feelings for wives and contracted concubines. Perhaps the literati, pursued by the need to promote themselves, understood the delicate position of courtesans; perhaps in these women who, driven by the need to please, busied themselves with poetic compositions, they found a *zhiji,* one who knows the self.

In miscellaneous records, intense affairs between the two parties are profuse. The following is a telling case: a local official at Guangling who was not particularly brave or successful loved a wine entertainer in vain. When after twenty years he returned to his previous post and found her again at the banquet, still serving the wine, his sorrow was such that he could not hold back the tears. A poem was composed and the woman was made to sing it, and the man left the banquet dead drunk.[25] In another episode, when an official was shifted to another post, he cried so heartily when parting with a certain entertainer that the host official, embarrassed, gave the woman away.[26] Similarly, when the singer a certain governor loved was enlisted by another province, the man composed a lyric for her to sing to her new master, and the singer was sent back promptly by the obliging official.[27] As state property, official courtesans were at the mercy of local authorities, and with an institutionalized courtesanship, to feel genuinely for a woman was often to inflict pain upon oneself. The sorrow of parting with a courtesan hence was a common poetic subject, presented sometimes by an observer in a tone of gentle ridicule. That courtesans were deprived of free will is accepted; that the officials, grown men with high self-regard and reasonable establishment, should expose themselves to such emotional turmoil, is less expected.

Herein lies the dilemma: the realities that made courtesanship rationalized rendered it both a source of pleasure and of pain, simultaneously fulfilling and frustrating male desires, scorning their impotency in the face of this peculiar game. For the less resourceful and the cowardly, love for these women may never be fulfilled. It is in this context that one reads the amorous poems by Li Shangyin, who by some strange destiny may have been the one poet who embodied the underrepresented tragic character of male desires in the Tang.

It would be misleading, however, to presume the literati as being always frustrated by enticing courtesans who remained unattainable. In their celebrated relationships, the predominant mode presented in writings by the elite was that of betrayal, exposing thus the harsh truth of their liaisons. In the narrative especially, angst and a profound sense of guilt are often concealed behind the seemingly self-righteous tone of the story.

As courtesans' patrons, the elite were often regarded as their potential rescuers, who could either purchase them out of the profession (in the case of commercial courtesans) or request for their deliverance from the official roll. Sun Qi, author of *Beili zhi* (Records of the northern quarters) who had wandered the many houses of the courtesans' quarters in the capital, was looked upon as such by a courtesan who was on intimate terms with him. To her plaintive request, Sun answered by stating that to take a courtesan was improper for a scholar who has passed the civil examination. After Sun's refusal, the courtesan became doleful in her public appearances, affecting those surrounding her, and she remained melancholic after marrying a merchant.[28]

From the obsessive theme of betrayal in the narrative and the peculiar poetic image of the boudoir woman cast in a state of perpetual waiting, we may conclude that after the original excitement had worn off, most literati sobered up and left the courtesans, who had become simply inconvenient. The illusion of compatriot spirits was too fragile to sustain the weight of practical considerations, and the elite must move on. Just as a marriage proposal from a powerful clan might pose a moral challenge for the rising literati, betrayal to courtesans carved out another moral wound when these ethically alienated women posed hindrances to their ambitions.

The many facets in the literati's relationships with courtesans expose the complex layers in their psychological construct, and the difficult problem of male desires is seen with all its complexities in this convoluted liaison. Members of the new class presented themselves as both pathetically repressed and yet at the same time capable of inflicting violent pain on the other party for self-preservation. The many chances and temptations thrown at their feet posed moral challenges that proved perplexing for the fainthearted. In the last analysis, caught in an obscure design of the instrumentalization of women, the problematic of male desires is too excruciating to suffer closer scrutiny.

This problematic reveals essentially the vulnerability of Tang literati, when the feminine as the Other cast hovering shadows on these gentlemen's consciousness and impaired seriously their composure. In a unique operation that persisted at weakening, repressing, and damaging the objects, it was unexpected that the subjects themselves should also be imperceptibly wounded. The patriarchal machine of overcoding desires was more pervasive than normally believed, when all was implicated in its mechanism of psychic suppression, which served the general purpose of social repression for the achievement of a faked sense of order.[29] Caught between the despot's looming phallus and the collectively weakened Other, masculine subjects experienced a neurosis that heretofore had not been adequately extrapolated.

With this vibrating effect that rendered both genders handicapped in their desiring, the dialectic of the subject and the object was evidenced, and the subject found itself emotionally and morally dependent on the object, and in the end, their carefully kept distance proved illusory. "The subject swallows the object, forgetting how much it is an object itself."[30] As the difficult condition of Tang literati entails, the binary opposition of the subject and its Other requires thorough revisions, and the primacy of the object ought to be proposed to counter that of the subject. Strictly speaking, the object as the subject's abstract opposite is delivered out of an illusive conception of a tyrannical hierarchy that is now proved destructive. And in order to offer healing for this deep-seated symptom of the inner split of male desires, whatever made the illusion necessary "ought to be removed,"[31] until the subject stops creating faked images of the object, until the subject and the object stop positing insufferable pain/burden for one another.

Chapter 7

Icons of Flesh

Let us picture the sight of many women who were part of the tapestry of the fermenting empire. In the vast rural areas, among the millet, in the mulberry fields, and in the woods were peasant women who labored hard to make ends meet. With huge, heavy loads of crops or firewood on their bony shoulders, they presented the harsh side of life as lived by numerous imperial subjects. Although in the southern provinces, women picking ferns and washing silk by the river, who roved the boats and picked lotus singing, were portrayed by poets with a romantic tinge, the truth of their lives could not have been all that pleasant. With the absence of men during wars, more heavy labor and the tax fell on these women with a crushing weight. Due to the aristocratic character of the Tang, records (either in visual language or in words) of peasant women are extremely scarce, with a few poets turning their sympathy (*or* idiosyncrasy) to their impoverished lives and depleted appearances. Instead, we are left with more detailed documents of upper-class women.

With the return of every spring, gentry women came out from their secluded chambers and sat in the peony bushes with their scarlet skirts hanging on the twigs to make shelters while they enjoyed the lush blossoms. Major Buddhist ceremonies where sutra were chanted and Buddhist stories were performed were also attended widely by women. Visits among households were not uncommon among official wives who socialized among themselves. However, although Tang women did come out on the streets, unlike their Northern Dynasties predecessors who ran from house to house for family matters, they were more commonly sheltered behind the walls in their boudoirs.

It was women of less-usual standing who were more visible in public spaces in the urban areas. Commoners in the two capitals were often treated to the sight of exuberant palace women who accompanied the monarch's entourage in gallant outfits, the extravagantly dressed princesses and ladies who dropped their jeweled adornments on the pavement and galloped away. Equally stunning were those female performers who were widely seen on the streets of major cities showing their impressive talents, from juggling and tightrope walking to sword dancing, providing inspiration for the elite and creating a vibrant cultural atmosphere. In the wine shops, foreign women with their exotic costumes served wine to self-intoxicated guests, and in various hotels, restaurants, and small shops, women were seen running businesses in small scale.[1]

Among these professional women, the more unconventional were the self-styled witches who organized rituals for exorcism or pleading for rain, and provided uncanny services of divination. Buddhist nuns too were frequent guests at houses of fervent believers to offer consultations for matters concerning procuring blessings. Patrons for these two groups of women sometimes included emperors who somehow needed supernatural guidance. Taoist priestesses, with an ambiguous identity that stood between a religious adept and an independent courtesan, were perhaps the most intriguing among Tang professional women because of their sexual freedom, lyrical talents, and their liaison with famous men of letters, with whom they sojourned in scenic spots.

In more sensuous sites, singing girls, dancers, and courtesans (both private and official) provided alluring entertainment for the elite and merchants, constituting the largest number of professional women exposed to the public gaze. Weaving a sensuous aura in the era, these women became the obsession of Tang lyrics. Precisely because of their exposure to the traffic of desires, they occupied a central place in male eros, in direct opposition to the Confucian wife who was addressed by her husband as "the one inside." Because of their special function, courtesans also stood dangerously at the very fringe of ethical configuration.

A HIGH DRAMA AT THE HIGH TANG

In the fifth year of Kaiyuan, in the reign of Xuanzong and at the peak of the high Tang, something unprecedented happened at the state examinations' annual celebration. Thousands of onlookers observed with the keenest interest as promising examination graduates roamed the Qu River on a boat in the company of versatile courtesans. When the painted yard went down, all thirty men and all the courtesans—whose number was uncounted—drowned.[2] That on one spring day at the height of the era, with their careers about to take off and their beauty at the ripest, these men and women should drown in the middle of an extravagant celebration was too much of a high drama for history. This episode belonging to the culture surrounding the examinations has one significance: by perishing thus dramatically, the courtesans for once shared the literatis' end. The separate roads the two parties normally were to take—the men ascending to the road of bureaucrats, the women continuing their profession, becoming concubines or entering the Buddhist or Taoist convents at old age—were severed, and the courtesans were never closer to the literati than in this shared death.

In discussing the liberty allegedly enjoyed by women of the Tang, the climate of an open society demonstrated by the mingling of literati and courtesans has often been presented by endorsing scholars. Compared with officials in later dynasties whose sojourns into the courtesans' quarters were limited, Tang officials socialized extensively with courtesans. The institutionalization of official courtesans who were necessary ingredients at official gatherings was inaugurated at the Tang and continued well into the Song, contributing to a sensual surface of officialdom.[3]

In the case of young upstarts who staked much on state examinations, association with courtesans acquired something of a legendary dimension. Part and parcel of the glamour of the *jingshi* examination for graduates was the flattering attention from courtesans and romantic liaisons with them. The ascent of the literati to the social scene was historically contemporaneous with the arrival of official courtesans; in this historical juncture, the two parties developed a relation predicated on mutual appreciation as much as on mutual interests, with the women clearly in the subordinate position.

Records in the tombstone inscriptions indicate that gentry women were widely educated and often well-read in the classics; surmising from cases in which a woman either drafted essays for her husband or pleaded on his behalf, wives who were intellectually compatible to their elite husbands were common. Without disclaiming the legendary intellectual appeal of courtesans and their alleged friendship with the literati as compatible companions, we must caution against dividing women into groups that have no meeting grounds. The fact that some courtesans were originally daughters of respected families who, implicated by a kinsman's crime or through either poverty or bigotry, wound up in the courtesans' pleasure dome, warns us against facile discrimination. The line that separated them from Confucian wives is thin indeed, when their social and biological functions were altered by a sudden turn of fate, forcing them to adopt a radically different self-definition.

Official courtesans provided a boisterous atmosphere and tasty conversations and fulfilled a particular social function, and together with private entertainers and the unearthly priestesses of ambiguous identities, they embodied the temptation of hallucinatory romance and took center stage as the objects of male desires. With the half-cultural, half-erotic affiliation between the elite and courtesans as eloquent evidence, the proposition of a liberal Tang is persuasive enough. On a closer look, however, it is a half truth that requires plenty of modifications and putting into context.

UNEQUAL TRANSACTION OF WORDS

Much has been said about the countermoves between the literati's political endeavor and their affiliation with courtesans, when the latter provided a vibrant stage for their liason with the powerful. It has been suggested that the courtesan culture influenced not only the literary scene, but indeed Tang literature itself.[4] The ways of courtesanship provided fascinating anecdotes, and the creative energy generated by the singing girls and the many dancers at sumptuous banquets was an important stimulus for Tang literature, which turned to an indulgence in sensuality in its later stage. One aspect specifically deserves our attention here: the supreme efficacy of belles lettres and its politics in the liaison between courtesans and their patrons. In the previous chapter I show that in different discourses, Tang women receive rather varied representations, and it is in literary works, together with some tale-telling anecdotes in miscellaneous writings, that we gain visions of the realities of their existence. Poetry and the psychologically poignant narrative especially contain the harsh truth of a courtesan's luck.

Courtesans were not only the creators and receivers, but also the subjects of the lyrics exchanged in their quarters. This intimate relation between women and poetry, partially expressed by the vigorous practice of poetry exchange in the courtesans' quarters, may have fatal consequences. In *Records of the Northern Quarters,* Sun Qi presents us with an array of courtesans of distinct characters and fortunes. In his eyewitness's account, the quarters were as much trafficked by patrons as by lyrical compositions both serious or buffoonish. In the epochal admiration for poetry, courtesans learned the necessity of acquiring written words as their trophies. They would aggressively seek patrons' lyrics and have them inscribed over the chamber walls, and by several accounts, a courtesan's reputation was easily swayed by a literatus's verdict, which traveled rather like the omnipotent communication media of today.[5] Such stories reveal a sobering reality of the literati-courtesan liaison: when the enamoring aura had worn off, the harsh truth of courtesanship as business was exposed. Anecdotes of the persuasive power of the literati's words also reveal the peculiar tension between fame and desire; in the exchange of poetry, language was at the service of insinuating yearnings. Such dangerously intimate relations with language correspond well with the courtesans' exposed identity as object of desire, when both desires and language are defined by absence.

Physical charms were not the essential criteria through which Tang courtesans earned poetic advertisements. At the banquets, it was rather the quick-tongued courtesans with intellectual appeal that were admired by the word-crazed elite. The most famous of all the Tang courtesans, Xue Tao, whose fame was based mainly on her poetic talents, bears this out. The weight attached to courtesans' linguistic competence can be measured fully only in the context of the inflation of belles lettres in conjunction with the literati's escalating value, which provided an immediate background for the appreciation of female entertainers whose poetic or conversational skills were considerable. This phenomenon contributed to the overall impression of the Tang red light district as an unusually graceful and enticing place. With the rapid economic growth in the Song, the profession's connection with the markets became entrenched, and the flamboyant courtesan quarters of the Tang gradually shifted to the commercialized environment of later dynasties.[6]

However the display of lyrical exchange might embellish the courtesans' profession, under the surface of high cultural activities, it was nevertheless a profession through which women's bodies as commodities were transacted. In this context, the function of words as exchange tokens went further in the shaping of a courtesan's fortune. One favorite anecdote concerning the flamboyant poet Du Mu records an outlandish request from Du, who confessed of spending a decade in the dreamy milieu of the courtesans' quarters. In this incident, Du had invited himself to a banquet held by a retired officer renowned in Luoyang for his over one hundred charming entertainers, and upon seeing Purple Cloud, he decided that she deserved her name and "should be given" to him. Another poet, Liu Yuxi, having recited a poem expressing the amorous effect a singing girl had on him, was promptly offered the singer by her master.[7]

When the reward for a gifted poet was a beauty, one is invited to draw the superfluous conclusion that the worth of a man's talent was categorically higher than that of a courtesan who, however well equipped with lyrical virtuosity and a name established upon it, was but one commodity for exchange. But entertainers were deemed private property in equal standing with horses, and such an unequal transaction is expected when a basic inequality defined female existence. The lesson of inequity came harshly, however, when an entertainer realized that alas, she herself was but one exchange item in this seemingly harmless practice of lyrical exchange.

INSCRIPTIONS ON THE BODY

Until the Six Dynasties, the characters for entertainers and musicians, *ji* and *chang,* retained the radical *ren* (human being). The explosion of the population of women entertainers in the era must have prompted the need to append the *nü* (woman) radical to the characters.[8] This etymological transformation, in line with our discussion above on the attachment of a broom to a woman in the character *fu,* entails an inscription of the feminine on the entertainment profession. Thus *ji* and *chang* in historical development became increasingly restrictive and derogatory in their references: originally designating performers of either sex, the characters came to denote first versatile courtesans with embedded sexual functions, and then prostitutes as we know them today. This gradual descent points to the specification of gendered roles, and once the woman radical was inscribed on these characters, woman's role as sexual object became firmly entrenched.

Besides this ideologically poignant linguistic coinage, on the immediate level of the flesh, inscription on women was also evidenced in the following case. On a famous courtesan's thigh, a youthful literatus left his imprint of a poem.[9] In writings concerning courtesans, actual consummation of relationships with patrons was seldom explicitly mentioned, and with this episode of a fetishistic act, we finally have a taste of what it was like at a courtesan's private chamber. This act of writing on the body brings home our suspicion that at the bottom, courtesans were in truth both metaphorically and metonymically related to the words transacted in their business. Ultimately, it was her very flesh that partook of the transaction.

In this episode, a courtesan's body was written over with words and was seen by another: a double exposure. Perhaps in a devious way, the calligraphy that had graced the female body was deemed a compliment so immediate that it actually enhanced its value, and the body revealed it with pride, not shame. The response

Dancers and acrobats in *Entourage of Lady Songguo*. Dunhuang cave painting, cave no. 156 (late Tang), north wall, lower portion.

of the other patron is also intriguing: bemused, he wrote another poem to ridicule the young man's urge to write on a lithe thigh. On the public property that was a courtesan's body, the imprint of another did not trigger jealousy but rendered the body the site of sharing/lyrical exhibition; the aesthetic detachment on the part of the literati was indeed remarkable.

The reader need not be reminded of the numerous inscriptions on the lofty cliffs of Mt. Tai left by illustrious emperors and poets, which are no less than the testimonies of a collective desire to leave inscriptions on nature, to simultaneously attest to and transcend an ephemeral existence. Absurd as it may seem to refer to this impulse to illuminate the devious act of writing on a mistress's body, the second poem by the patron compares precisely the inscribed thigh to Ci'en Tower, on whose walls examination graduates were accustomed to inscribe their names as a gesture of triumph. This blunt analogy presents another facet of the culture associated with the civil service examinations. For some, success in the realm of the flesh served as a form of compensation for political failure; for the ambitious, success in romancing the courtesans complemented well their political victory, with the female body as a replica of that great tower, the conquering of which was mandatory.

The relationship between courtesans and poems as exchange icons, then, becomes intriguingly complex. A courtesan's flesh was covered by lyrical lines and was transacted together with the words, and in the process of transacting, both the body and the inscription were consumed, each heightening the other's value. The obsession with words reached a climax here, and not only could a beauty be won through poetry, not only was language incentive to desires, but the flesh itself was made a linguistic vehicle and was threatened to be usurped. A body inscribed with a poem is no longer itself: was the man not satisfied with mere flesh and felt the urge to transform it through pictographs? The imposition of the human upon nature exposes an anxiety over the latter's untamed strangeness, as well as a latent desire to possess. The act of transforming a courtesan's flesh has layers of meaning (and nonmeaning); it would not deserve our pondering here if not for the fact that it belongs unmistakably to a culture in which exchange of words and women had become so confused that finally, the words *came to be* the women in a fetishism that fetishized both the words and the feminine body.

Tang poets had boasted of and competed their popularity among the singers; the liaison between the literati and the courtesans was set against their intertwined creative activities, and the floating icons of words and musical notes provided a perfect breeding ground for the lust of the minds, when words were transformed, held back, and chewed in the singers' mouths, and wove the core of the sensual surface in great cities. When women were the producers, receivers, and now singers of lyrical texts, poetry clearly constituted the single discourse with which Tang women had intimate relations and in which they received the most private renditions.

While the narrative *chuanqi* unveils the collective unconscious of the elite, Tang poetry presents, alongside its daydreaming of a steadfast mistress, emotions that have a more private and immediate sense of reality. While its length promises swift traffic, its formulaic rhapsody is compatible to the fetishistic attractions of feminine charms. Its fragmentary format, a perfect vehicle for emotions associated with the (lightweight) feminine, contrasts well with the stiff-faced tombstone inscriptions from which courtesans are exiled.[10] In the poetic subgenre of boudoir lament, amorous women appear frozen in perpetual waiting, captured in the texts as tokens of love; the intimacy between women and poetic form is thus pushed to the extreme. In this manner, the playful practice of exchanging poetry with courtesans inadvertently came to embody a metaphorical character that confused and identified the verse with the women, the consequence of which we have already seen.

FREEDOM FROM THE PERIPHERY

The various nuanced terms denoting feminine roles, such as *fu* (wife), *qie* (concubine), *ji* (entertainer), and *ji'* (entertainer-concubine), are significant for our understanding of Tang courtesans' ethical status. A man who chose to maintain an upright profile would emphatically state that he had for domestic purposes taken a concubine, not an entertainer, for the latter in a master's house remained an exchangeable item, while a concubine had a relative, though fragile, ethical attachment to the house.[11] The courtesans' status for marriage was not regulated in the legal codes, but in common practice they were taken as entertainer-concubines, often kept aside from the household. The ethical status of a "married" courtesan, then, was understandably very shaky.

These difficult situations manifest the particular position of Tang courtesans, who were placed at the center of male desires and at the periphery of ethical configurations. They also explain the meek image of courtesans presented in lyrical pieces as creatures subject to abandonment and perpetual waiting. Yet a reading of miscellaneous records presents us with a different picture of these women, who often made good the myth of their liberal existence. The most eloquent example is presented by Zhang Zhuzhu, who through her determination and clever intrigues drove off a potential master and married a local boy with low social status. Other courtesans humiliated guests who could not pay up fees; one who was especially shrewd slapped her patron's face and the man, bearing the imprint, was looked upon with dismay by his peers. It turned out that not all courtesans were cultivated or submissive, and some would offend their sensitive guests with blunt words. These incidents present the courtesans in private quarters as beyond the confines of the literati's wishful imagination that subdued them into inert icons of flesh.

Nor were the desires of these daring courtesans turned obstinately to the literati, much as the men would have it. When purchased by the rich, they did not observe prudence, and they often had liaisons with musicians living in the same quarter. Even the gifted Yan Lingbin, who implored verse from the scholars to honor her impending death, associated herself with a neighbor musician, and her patrons regarded this as a humiliation that contaminated the elegant air of their patronage and refrained from discussing it.[12] Such silence alludes to the elite's propensity to disregard these women's different set of psychological needs. In their portraits of courtesans, the literati often failed to show the more mundane side of these women, who could be ruthlessly resourceful. Compared with the refined and amorous courtesans in literary discourse, these professional women appeared to be robust and not easily defeated in their desires.[13] Situated at the margin of orthodox society and at the core of male desires, they embodied a *jouissance* associated with the exuberant sensuous and the erotic; the *jouissance* belonged after all to themselves, although given the social construct, it was inevitably saturated in bitter resignations.

For a truly bold manifestation of female desires, we turn to palace entertainers under the Entertainment Bureaus, which provided entertainment for imperial members. Women in the two bureaus, the left one specialized in dance and the right one in singing, were kept under imperial command without being confined in the palace or sexually subordinate to the monarchs, and they enjoyed a sexual freedom unique among their contemporaries. One prominent practice was the bond of what they called "brotherhood," when these women performers formed communities of "blood brothers" and addressed each other's (true) husbands as "wife." Allegedly following the Turkish custom, these women shared the new "wife" among themselves, stating that out of brotherly love they "would like to have a taste of this new wife"; the "husband" granted this wish without jealousy.[14] This intrepid act presents a radical female desire, when performers of special talents—some were acrobats with the highest expertise—reversed sexual roles not only by changing gender denominators but also by making a husband a shared object: the use of the word *taste* certainly gives the act a connoisseur flavor, common in the appreciation of women among men.

One could and perhaps should ask if this did not actually make the shared man the beneficiary. Two things should be considered in this regard: first, he was referred to as a wife, and considering the heavily coded meaning of gender terms, this linguistic shift had the effect of putting him in a subordinate position, with the women taking the lead as aggressors. The r' of roles could not have been overlooked by these women, who had the imagination to make the linguistic reversal in the first place. Second, such a proposition is based on the presumption that men are the active agents in sexual relationships, blind to the fact that they could as well be enjoyable objects. Arguably the most versatile performers of the empire, when the single most visible profession for women was that of entertainer, these proud women, with the characteristic liberal temperament of performers, fashioned this practice, unusual by any standard.

Enacting the role of courtesans and associating with gentry of a Taoist inclination, Taoist priestesses embodied another outlet for female desires.[15] Without direct control from the brothels or state officials, they were simultaneously economically independent and socially vulnerable. The esoteric learning they acquired, their unique autonomy, and the vaguely defined relationship with their patrons contributed to a mode of living that set them apart from women coerced by various forms of institutions, chief among them the family, the principal site of female oppression. This particular condition might have contributed to the fact that of Tang women who took up poetry composition seriously, among the most established were two Taoist priestesses. They are discussed when we turn to women poets in the last two chapters.

In the popular consciousness was a distrust of the Buddhist nuns' celibacy, when less than doctrinal behaviors among them were not unique.[16] In the narrative, these nuns sometimes are portrayed as women warriors, avenging wrongs through miraculous acts. Tales like these show the extent to which, in the collective unconscious, these women were deemed deviant from what they appeared to be and were transformed, accordingly, into unworldly beings. Occasionally, these nuns allied with the political figures and achieved dominance.[17]

The profession of witches also provided opportunity for lower-class women who made a living by providing supernatural services. They appear in various chronicles, social records, and poems, and their esoteric practices in the superstitious Tang were extensive.[18] Occasionally, this profession provided opportunities for women who had political ambitions or a big appetite in matters of choosing sexual partners.[19]

From the few instances recorded in miscellaneous writings, we can infer that besides courtesans, both the Taoist priestesses and witches, and to a much lesser extent Buddhist nuns, created for themselves a lifestyle that presented a comparably liberated way of living in its deviation from that of common womenfolk. That they had to resort to religious or cult careers, allocated to the social fringes, suggests that to achieve freedom, Tang women took to the less traveled roads. From courtesans to priestesses, it was through a sexually exploitive profession that escape from an ethically repressive life was possible. From a marginal position, they proceeded to shape an existence that would grant them autonomy otherwise unthinkable. In direct contrast to this choice was the celibate existence in the temples for women determined to shun marriage and domestic constraint. At both ends, women resorted to finding freedom at the periphery; ironically, it was through either denial of or recourse to their sexuality that Tang women forged a way out.

Part Three

Self-Representation of the Tang

Chapter 8

Logic of the Unconscious

Fall of the Supernatural Feminine

Originally, the right to copulate with the supernatural feminine was the kings' alone. In their dreams, beguiling goddesses appeared to offer themselves for the royal pleasure, and the power of worldly kings was thus manifested. As time passed, men of letters presumed to avail themselves of this privilege, and women of strange origins were enlisted to satiate their various whims.

At first these unearthly women, announced by their uncanny scent, came and went as wished in the scholars' dreams, in their private gardens and lonely abodes in the mountains. Soon, finding these women faithless, the scholars resorted to capturing them in the prison house built by the language of dark pictographs, until a vast population of esoteric women was collected, and in each heavy book that lay on the scholar's desk, a fox-woman, a dragon's daughter, or a beguiling flower spirit was imprisoned. At midnight, she slipped out from her prison upon summons and was intimate with the scholar to his heart's content, saturating the room with her eerie scent, her jade pendant, her perfumed robe scattered on the floor. In this manner, the scholars succeeded in making these mysterious women yield to their desires without fail, like those docile, punctual wives trained by the Confucians. And the fall of the supernatural feminine was hence complete.

I. LOGIC OF THE TANG NARRATIVE

In the self-celebrating splendor of the Tang, men of letters diverted from the major literary activity of poetry composition and tried their hands at prose stories, a genre hitherto on the periphery. In the boisterous Chang'an and Luoyang where commerce prospered with urban centralization, where Buddhist scriptural narration vitalized storytelling performances as popular entertainment—where there seemed to be a keen interest in the fantastic associated with the rise of the metropolis, writers in the capital elite circle began to create tales that would become the mirrors of their times.

The narrative, scarce in the early Tang, reached its peak in the middle Tang and headed for an anticlimax in the late Tang.[1] This venture into the fictional may be explained by various sociocultural stimuli. The stylistic inspiration from the classical prose movement, a need for self-promotion by circulating writings that demonstrate an array of literary techniques into the hands of the prominent, the urge to absorb contemporary sensitivities such as the Buddhist vision of emptiness, the Taoist cult of the immortal, and the changing politics of the times—all are part of the general milieu behind the creation of these tales.

Chuanqi (Transmitting the strange), as the genre is named, has its predecessor in tales from the Six Dynasties in which dark, primal forces are predominant. It continued to develop along this line until the subterranean elements were shifted to the psychologically realistic mode in the middle Tang, then replaced by a resurgence of the fantastic toward the end of the era. What at first seems paradoxical in these narratives, which contradicts their supernatural bent, is their claim to refer to real events, a claim operated by a convention of literary *vraisemblance* that creates an illusion of fictional probability. In the mode of historical documentation, the tales adopt a biographical format with a commentary closure, taking precedent from a historiography bent on interpreting events rather than simply chronicling. This combination of the historical with the fictional should not be dismissed as a rupture between form and content, or as a conflation of ideologies. The presence of the narrator as a participant who vouches for the truth of the story is more than a mere access to points of view; it naturalizes the tale by leaving a prominent signature in the text. This practice inscribes simultaneously the story within the author's social milieu, and the author within the text. Thus the writing of these narratives should be conceived of as a sociocultural act that equates the fictional with the real.

Such a convention manifests the deliberate confusion, a collective effort from both the authors and the readers, that makes the supernatural natural. Another level of *vraisemblance* is at work: By relating to a body of works that follow similar norms, thereby forming a literary genre, the tales become intelligible.[2] By virtue of the large corpus of the genre, tales in which human beings communicate with spirits in unlikely ways become probable and indeed expected. The persistent naturalization of the unnatural points to a network of obsessions that creates the texts' own law, an implicit theory of realities to which they conform. The widely practiced witchcraft and Taoist magic, the obsession with unintelligible phenomena in miscellaneous writings, and the indiscriminate records of supernatural events in Tang official histories all reveal a nonrational perception of reality that serves as the basis of the logic of the narrative.[3]

One may thus claim that it is the demand of the discursive field that determines the raison d'être of events: in other words, these mythical events are the product of the demands of signification; they are not the cause, but the effect of the theme.[4] The formulaic quality of many less-accomplished tales certainly endorses this argument, and we may perceive the genre as being predicated on its own invention. This line of argument, however, will trap us at the level of generic probability, forcing us to leave aside the psychological basis of the discourse. Bearing in mind the social climate of the era, the discursive effort at naturalizing itself should be seen together with its psychological underpinnings that continue to work against the laws of realities.[5]

By a literary conceit, the presence of these authors, most of them administrative officials (some enlisted in the Department of History), was felt with immediacy by readers who were largely their colleagues or members of the in-circle elite. If this small circle of readership and its homogeneity give rise to a suspicion that these narratives are self-generating and self-reflexive, such a suspicion, albeit legitimate to a certain extent, should be checked by an awareness of the folklore influence on the genre. However saturated in an elite mentality, many of the tales are rooted in folk legends, Buddhist lore, or Taoist cults, some transformed from storytelling performances, thereby exhibiting a healthy absorption of the folk tradition.

Let us spell out the dialectical forces that inform the structure of Tang narratives: history versus fiction, moralization versus superstition, and elite versus folk tradition. These contradictory forces find a meeting ground in tales that ignore ideological conflicts in a syncretism that characterizes Chinese religions as well as philosophies. Our purpose here is not to tease out the various strains of contradiction but to expose the embedded ideologies that create an illusion of unity for the discourse. Interpreting the literati as sharing a collective unconscious whose genealogy can be traced along the lines of literary tradition, I study these texts as cultural self-representation, as the embodiment of male desires and subsumption of female desires, and as the tale-telling reservoir of repressed realities.

A Split of the Self

As Tang narrative can be considered a discourse written by and for people from a similar milieu, its heroes, much like their authors, are often portrayed as well-versed and imbued with Confucian virtues. These protagonists, different from the archetypal romance heroes in the Western counterpart, are armed with words, a symbol of their self-assertion and the channel through which they associate with the world.[6] The Confucian aversion to brute force might have shaped this heroism of *wen,* cultivated refinement, and when violence is required, a double sometimes in the disguise of a foreign servant or an unusual maid comes to help out the protagonist.[7] The peculiar unlikeliness of these doubles, who are socially inferior to the hero, together with the latter's weak character, have been observed by Western critics.[8] The exaltation of the scholar-hero's moral uprightness and eloquence over martial force seems a self-deceiving heroism that falls short of the model of the assassins who at the time of the Warring States had presented an admirable union of mental strength and martial skills.[9] In the six arts taught in the Zhou Dynasty, archery and charioteering came before the study of books. With increasing stress on canonical knowledge, a separation of physical strength from intelligence has been criticized in intellectuals since Confucius's time.

Since Qu Yuan's *Encountering Sorrow* in which the ultimate ideal was embodied by goddesses roaming in the mystical world whom the self tried against all hope to approach, women as the Other were transported to the realm of the supernatural, enacting the role of the frontier of the unknown. This topos of woman as the sym-

A Tang woman. Detail of a mural in Princess Yongtai's tomb.

From *Tang Yongtai gongzhu mu bihua ji*.

bolic Other gains momentum in the Han rhymed prose, where the feminine is persistently employed as a rhetoric trope for the strategic end of the text. There is a decisive turn in the representational modes of the feminine in the prose: the symbolic feminine here is in possession of two opposite physiognomies, one that continues to be ambiguous and unapproachable, tormenting the self with an existential tension, and the other (its mundane counterpart) that becomes the sensuous seductress threatening the self-composure of the narrator, the renunciation of whom testifies to his moral triumph.

This figure of a split feminine finds its antithesis in the much quoted "Gaotang fu" (Ode on Gaotang), attributed to Song Yu, in which the poet recounts the sexualized epiphany of the goddess of Mt. Wu who condescends to give herself to King Huai of Chu in his dream. This legendary union suggests that copulation with the supernatural feminine is a privilege reserved for kings, and the goddess's self-bestowal is the manifestation of the court poet's will to elevate a human ruler above natural forces, bringing about the appeasement between the natural and the human through a linguistic act. The triumphant hunt of King Xiang (heir of King Huai) in the territory of the shrine that commemorates the goddess is a further symbol of the metaphorical unification between the king and the goddess.[10] Through this act, the negative relation between power and sexuality is transformed into one of identification, as royal sexuality stands beyond the machine of repression.[11] As the motif developed in the Six Dynasties texts, however, although works by accomplished poets retain self-surveillance and distance themselves from the intensely desired union with the ultimate feminine, erotic encounter with divine women is no longer restricted to the kings in the hands of more daring poets.

Anthropomorphism of feminine spirits gives the pretext to the longing for a communion with the supernatural through sexual consummation; at the same time, it gives rise to the despair that comes with an apprehension of the unconquerable distance between the human and the divine maiden. This despair, taking its cue from Qu Yuan whose divine woman is arguably a symbol for his political idealism, comes to acquire an existential dimension when the removal of the ideal Other registers an internal split, a sense of the self's inevitable separation from itself.

The propensity for aligning the feminine with natural elements reveals a tendency to place the feminine at the frontier of the incomprehensible, a space that is neither inside nor outside. She is identified either with the incomprehensible, as in the case of the supernatural woman, or with disruptive forces of chaos, as in the case of the temptress.[12] Seen in this light, the internal split of the self is nothing short of the inherent rupture of the feminine from the masculine, or the exile of the feminine from the male psyche. This alone can explain the irrational demand of the self's yearning for and inevitable separation from the ideal feminine. In a complex psychological construct, the idealized feminine is placed within the masculine self, only to realize its inherent alienation. The ideal feminine sits within the masculine self like a white abyss, an unconquerable lack within.

If the anxiety over supernatural women is derived from an intrinsic sexual politics, its antidote, the temptress and her rejection, is equally convoluted in a psychological network. In a famous piece from the rhymed prose, "Dengtuzi haose fu" (Ode on Master Dengtu's erotic drive), attributed to Song Yu, the court poet boasts of his rejection of a rare beauty next door. The equally renowned "Meiren fu" (Ode on a beauty), attributed to Sima Xiangru, recounts the poet's erotic encounter with a seductive woman and his narrow escape from losing a battle of wills. These temptations threaten the court poets' self-control, who must demonstrate to the king their perseverance when their relation with the king is charged with erotic overtones. Such political romance has a long tradition. In the lyrical convention shaped by Qu Yuan, the poets either adopt a feminine voice to show humble subordination or conceive of the king as an elusive lover, an ultimate object of desire. The rationale for these metaphors is the Confucian political idealism of a sage-king, and the trope of a lover-king is derived from this conflation of (masculine) loyalty with (feminine) chastity. The application of sexualized tropes, which makes the king–courtier relation a (hetero)sexual one, bespeaks the burden of the family-state romance that had lost its idealistic flavor since the Han dynasty and testifies to the increasingly subservient state of mind of the courtiers.[13]

For a court poet to attest to his noninfatuation with the feminine, then, is to demonstrate his moral control. When we remember the king's privilege to fornicate with the supernatural, together with the existence of the many castrated in the palace, the necessary linkage between the exaltation of the royal phallus and the demand for sexual restraint of court poets is evident. On this note, the demonstration of male chastity at the court reveals an incipient sexual politics at the royal presence. Compared with ministers at the court of Tang emperors, these early poets were subjected to a politics that might have put them in a more perilous position.[14]

An understanding of the feminine as the estranged supernatural and of the intricate role-playing between the king and his courtiers are essential for a critique of Chinese literary tradition; more importantly, they direct us to an insight into the political unconscious that informed the literati. Although Tang narratives present a rather transfigured version of this unconscious, our awareness of it is essential for an initial study of the genre.

Copulation with the Supernatural Feminine

In Tang romances, the feminine presents itself often as a symbol of repressed fear. Inadvertently, woman takes on various unnatural forms or appears as a reincarnated man punished by retribution; in short, she is scarcely herself. By contrast, the narrators recount supernatural events that they have allegedly witnessed, confusing the fictional with the real, bridging Taoist heaven and the human world. As they strive to render the tales realistic, they appear always *as* themselves, the erudite literati who merely record what they have seen. What prompted these authors to make women alienated beings, thereby placing them in diametrical opposition to themselves as totally authentic, is culturally specific and demands our examination.

The presentation of supernatural women as the symbolic Other reached a new height in the Jin poet Tao Qian's "Xianqing fu" (Ode on stilling the passions), in which the unapproachable beauty becomes a metaphor for a desire that encompasses transcendental dimensions, tormenting the self with a frustration that recurs eternally, creating an intensified sense of the temporal force. This despair over a symbolic figure of desire is markedly different from the sentiment of Tang literati-heroes, who are plagued neither by a sense of impotence nor by self-censorship, and whose most presumptuous desires are gratified, thanks to the complying supernatural feminine and her gift of immortality. The role of the temptress underwent a sea change when the sanction on sexual drives was relatively relaxed, and when marginalized women, especially courtesans who were referred to by their byname, "goddess," were readily available *and* dispensable. This linguistic conflation of goddesses with courtesans further illustrates the changing character of the divine women and their domestication; with the dispersal of the supernatural feminine into the most mundane, a radical conception of sexual politics was envisioned.[15]

Should one conjecture, then, that contemporaneous to its sensual indulgence, a sexual liberation was in effect in the Tang? When Chang'an was the center of Asia, absorbing freely exotic merchandise and dynamic entertainment, when every luxurious banquet was populated by performers whose beauty was a good match for the talents of the presumptuous literati, a puritanical sentiment toward relationships between the sexes seemed self-frustrating. At odds with these social circumstances, Buddhism with its doctrines against sensuality was in constant confrontation with the extravagant Taoist cult, which sought earthly immortality through alchemy and sexual interchange.

The truth of the unrestrained consummation of appetites in these narratives, nevertheless, lies deeper in the compunction of conscience that accompanies it, however deep-seated and in disguise. As we probe deeper, the narrative's ideological transformation from its predecessors acquires further complexities. If erotic encounters with the supernatural may be interpreted as a phenomenon of Taoist influence, the existence of the fatal fox-woman complicates the picture and invites us to read the stories in a larger cultural context. The drastic change from a despair of perpetual distance from the supernatural feminine to an all too easy possession of both her physical charms and her gift of immortality is not simply a manifestation of a new religious climate or a liberated sexuality but testifies to a more intricate consciousness.

Confusion of Desires

The impressive number of tales describing a scholar's erotic encounter with an ethereal beauty, sometimes right in his study, may be stated hyperbolically as a partial crystallization of the cliché "In books stand the mansions of gold, in books hides a face like jade." This cliché reveals the belief in the power of books in bringing worldly fulfillment, and specifically the faith in the Confucian canon, which comprised the textbooks for the state examinations. An obsession with the examinations and things associated with them emerges, sure enough, as the major concern for our literati-heroes.

Readers of Chinese folk literature will notice the excessively popular Song folktale, "Legend of the White Snake," and the public's overwhelming sympathy (evolved around the eighteenth century) for the snake-woman's betrayal by her human husband. Ironically, all sympathies go to this creature created out of a collective anxiety over feminine charm, thereby defeating the moral injunction of the tale. The embedded ideology is turned against itself—the snake-woman born of aversion is presented as virtue itself, and all efforts to extinguish her are condemned. This inherent schizophrenia reveals an unreconciled antithesis of desire for and fear of feminine seduction, while the moral repression is expelled with a vengeance.

An irrational dichotomy of sympathy and fear, together with a belief in perfecting the canons, may serve, however incompatible, as two points of reference for our study on the nature of desire in Tang narrative. In analyzing its literati protagonists, it is impossible to separate their amorous desires from either a longing for political glory or a primal yearning for immortality. As they confused the infatuations with courtesans with political ambitions and were encouraged to equate political success with profitable marriage, or belles lettres with material gain, literati in these tales also have the propensity to confuse romantic conquest with financial and political success. Love in itself, in other words, is seldom the conclusion of the romance.

The belief that beauties and riches would come as the trophies of strenuous canonical studies constitutes the basis of these confusions, and it works hand in hand with the traditional fascination with mythical females, which undermines and complicates simultaneously the inherent logic of the discourse. It is mainly through the imagination of a Taoist earthly paradise, itself infused with paradoxes, that such self-deluding conflation of worldly gains with otherworldly creatures is conceived. This confusion of desires is symptomatic of Tang narrative and, coupled with the dialectic of sexual drive and its repression, constitutes its many problematics.

II. SUBMISSION OF THE FEMININE

Legends of Departed Souls

As the earliest artistically conscious creation in the genre of fictional writing, Tang narrative had not yet expelled the animism of a mythical mind in its perception of all things and beings as an integral part of human existence, exerting power over human lives. This may explain its propensity to apply anthropomorphism to common household objects, fierce animals, and terrestrial and celestial elements. A quick, indiscriminate reading of its large corpus leaves one with an impression of intercommunication among all beings, when familiar objects such as an ink stone or an old broom possess human attributes and engage in prolonged conversation when all is quiet at night. In the imagination of the era, the boundary between human and nonhuman is erased to stage a carnival dance of all.

This is nonetheless not an innocent dance; things all too often take on feminine attributes and become objects of obsessive desires. While spirits of masculine gender are less often rendered with a psychological interior and do not inspire the author's fancy, feminine spirits of animals and plants are charged with a symbolic significance that dominates the Tang imagination. The echoing creation of amorous spirits in the tradition of the supernatural woman exposes further a collective lust of the mind, in which the projection and reflection of desires are full of intrigue. The division of the feminine into body and soul, and further, the subtraction of its spirit from its physical being, create a precarious precondition for male desires, a phenomenon manifested in the portrayal of several feminine spirits.

A local official who left his mistress behind for a good eight years in the story entitled "Legend of Li Zhangwu" returned to where he held his former post and, finding the woman long dead, did not hesitate to reunite with her soul, which haunted the house as a testimony to her unappeased passions. In "Lihun ji" (Record of a departed soul), Qianniang left her body behind when she was promised to someone other than her dejected lover, and the consummation of their love was left to the doing of her strong will, which led her spirit to wander away from her flesh. The passions of both women are not isolated cases: in other tales, women are presented as capable of obstinate desires, a trait disproportionately scarce in the characterization of male protagonists.

It is tempting to attribute this asymmetry to the realities of the times, when women's worth was entangled with the politics of class and power, as we have seen. While ambitious men climbed the social ladders and conquered the empire with their belles lettres, women, confined to the boudoirs, were wont to become obsessive mourners over a wrecked love. Yet to interpret these fictional women as representative of social realities is to fall prey to these authors who were conversant with the taboo of excessive (male) emotions and the threat of female sexuality. As a literary discourse, these narratives have the function of exhibiting the collective unconscious of their times, and we would be seriously misled to take them simply as apt reflections of social realities. The truth of this emotional imbalance between genders is complicated by a psychological double bind and a mechanism of transference, which deserve our careful extrapolation.

The separation of Qianniang's body and soul in pursuit of her lover was the precondition for the fulfillment of the man's desire, for, like many heroes in the narratives, he lacked both the courage and the means to win his beauty. Thus Qianniang's body lay sick at her parents' home, and at her soul's return five years later, her body rose up and rejoined the soul in a perfect fusion. In this succinct story of the soul's quest for love, the purity of the plot hinges on the divine miracle of the

reunion between body and soul, and the soul's absolute need to free itself of physical boundaries under the demands of love. The naturalization of the tale as an
actual event circulated among contemporaries can be seen either as an observance
of literary convention or as a verification of the popular taste for a woman's
departed soul. Through the popularity of the tale, an unusual fetishism proclaims
itself, and in its later renditions, the departed soul of the feminine acquires altered
meanings.

The subtraction of a woman's spirit from her body satisfies male desire precisely
because such a split intensifies his passions for her. In "Legend of Li Zhangwu,"
the woman's devotion is attested to by both her death from amorous craving and
her steadfast soul's wait for Li's return. In this uncanny fancy, the reunion between
a man and a ghost in a deserted house, touched by the horror of the approaching
dead, is presented as a memorable event.

> At about the second watch, the lamp southeast of the bed suddenly turned dim three
> times. Zhangwu knew that some change had occurred and he had the candle placed
> against the wall at the east corner of the room. Soon he heard some noise from the
> north corner, as if a human shape was slowly approaching. At five or six steps away,
> he could discern its shape: judging from the clothes, it was the hotel host's daughter-
> in-law, Yang. She had not changed, only her movements were weightless and swift,
> and her voice soft and crisp. Zhangwu got off the bed and held her hands, caressing
> her with the same tenderness as before. Yang said to him: "In the underworld, I have
> forgotten all my relatives, my thoughts for you alone remain unchanged." Zhangwu
> made love to her just as before, with the only exception that she asked several times
> for someone to watch over the stars: once they came out, she must leave.[16]

Li's consent to meet the dead was prompted by both desire and regret; character-
istically, his feelings for Yang intensified in a crescendo as her passion manifested
itself first in her death, then in the persistence of her soul, and finally in this agonizing reunion. Juxtaposed to the Li who came to visit the old place by sheer
chance, the Li who continued to return to the haunted house should be understood
as a man who loved better a spirit whose passion had been fully contested. Here the
peculiar appetite for a woman's soul purified by her devotion is brought to an
unprecedented height, when an embedded sense of guilt played so underhanded a
role that the reader is invited to conclude that it was Li's conceited ego, rather than
his compunction, that continued to send him back to the feminine soul trapped in
her fearful faithfulness.

We notice hence a necessity to transform woman into something other than herself as a precondition for her to obtain acceptance. From transformation to acceptance, from creation (of the fox-snake-woman) to rejection to resurrection: these
are the shifting points of transference in the narrative. When their camouflage is
uncovered, these texts reveal themselves as being governed by the logic of wish
fulfillment and daydreaming.[17] Desiring women's unwavering devotion, the elite
transfer such desire to women, sometimes with ostentatious naiveté. In the patri-

archal imagination, the feminine's most cherished existence is as an object desiring man's desire; denied access to self-representation and the pleasure that might be specific to it, the feminine is caught in a mirror that mimics perpetually the reflections of male desires.[18]

Such a mode of discourse suggests that women in love were dangerously vulnerable: in their isolated boudoirs (however well-tempered in verse), without access to the high road to success or to society, they had limited ways of self-fulfillment and even fewer emotional outlets. For women of the Tang, romantic feelings, because of their unconventionality, provided the possibility of living creatively, as opposed to the existence of a Confucian wife procreating, alongside various concubines, children for the paternal lineage. Passion then became a particular form of fulfillment, and the inward turning of a thwarted love became fatal.

Again, to accept this suggestion without scrutiny is to fall prey to the conceit of the collective male desire that demands women sculpt themselves into icons of chastity. We must bear in mind that we are gazing at images of women reflected in the mirror of masculine eros, and whatever the social realities, it is through this mirror, with all its wistful contortions, that we have with us such legends of departed souls. Ultimately, this obsession with feminine souls is expressed through a dark psyche controlled by fear and the apprehension of a preeminent punishment that are coexistent with pleasure.

The movement of male desire is full of anxieties, and the overwhelming number of tales depicting gruesome female spirits reveals its deep structure. In one common plot that reverberates with variations, a man is invited into the house of a beguiling woman and frolics with her, only to discover later that she is the ghost of a woman long dead. The initial enjoyment of the woman's unearthly beauty is shifted to a ghastly disclosure, and the reader is pulled between opposite strains of lush, sensual language of sexual attraction and the repugnant closing images of the dead. Although in some instances, consistent with the genre's bent toward material pragmatism, the man is adopted as son-in-law by the aristocratic family of the dead woman, in the majority of the tales a sense of regret permeates the end, if not an acute sense of disillusionment and a chilling premonition of death.[19]

The obsession with the dead points to a sexual drive distraught by its opposite principle, when the obstinate will of the female ghosts exposes ironically not a will to life, but an inherent death drive. The banal circumstances of the stories are made barely intelligible by this stark convention, as the principles of pleasure and reality crash against each other, and the text is torn between opposite movements toward sexual gratification and its ultimate frustration. At the linguistic level, the creative drive is constantly frustrated by the grotesque, which brings it to an abrupt end. Although employment of the horrifying may achieve an artistic effect, the often crude and formulaic disclosure defeats this potential. Thus the creative drive is circumvented by a countermove that terminates its daydreaming, directing it back to a sobering truth.

This psychological underpinning is embedded in the generic obsession with the feminine souls who arouse and then stifle the erotic drive, bringing home the intricate pull of fear and anxiety. Plagued by the preconscious, eros crosses with the death drive, and the obsession with feminine souls, however programmatic sometimes, exhibits a drive that leans toward masochism.[20] The pleasure derived from reading these tales is foreshadowed by this masochism, as the reader acquires the expectation of each tale's harrowing antithesis. The tales that warn against indulgence in the flesh hence are saturated in a complex working of the unconscious that foresees agony in pleasure, enlightened by the premonition that the reality principle would always strike back.

The Original Fox-Woman

In the erotic imagination of the masculine in dynastic China, the fox-woman acquired centrality, and the effort to discard her, like the existential effort of approaching the goddess, is morally mandatory and emotionally excruciating. While the supernatural feminine in early writings constitutes a split within the self, the fox-woman, originated from a psychological rupture, is a curious externalization of the fear of female sexuality. One strives to cleanse the unwanted within oneself, and the function of scapegoating is underwritten by the reality that whatever needs to be exiled is often an integral part of oneself.[21] Precisely because of this, the expelling of the fox-woman inflicts pain on oneself. The acts of reaching toward the exiled and refuting what is firmly within oneself thus compose two opposite movements enacted by the unconscious, which poses the feminine as negativity.

In a desperate move, the feminine is transported by a principle of animism to appear as creatures of an appalling origin. In "Renshi zhuan" (Legend of the woman Ren), Shen Jiji presents a protagonist who is to become the archetypal fox-woman. Ren, who set an unblemished standard for future fox-women, was of exceeding charm and virtues and possessed invaluable esoteric knowledge. Out of gratitude she chose a downcast married man because of his unrequited feelings for her after his discovery of her identity—for a certain courage was required to continue the liaison with an allegedly harmful fox spirit. Herein lies the dilemma: a suppressed desire has rendered the creature borne out of fear irresistible and the test of will all the more demanding. Moreover, the succumbing to temptation is rewarded rather than punished here, defeating consequently the moralizing purpose of the fox-woman. In such manner the struggle between desire and repression continues, as the mind probes and understands itself through the act of writing.

The creation of this externalized repression conceals the movement of a deeper desire: the craving for wealth. Through her esoteric skills, Ren gained large profit for her lover, with which the man purchased an official post and from there on ascended to prosperity. Chastity, the essential female virtue, also found a perfect expression in Ren, who demonstrated unusual strength in defending her sexual integrity. Below is the episode that begins with the discovery of Ren by a relative of her lover, Wei.

> Wei led her out and observed her under the light: clearly, her beauty exceeded its reputation. He adored her rapturously, and embracing her, he tried to invade her but was met with resistance. He forced himself upon her and she became anxious: "I will succumb. Please slow down a bit." Once Wei let up his hold, Ren resumed struggling, and this went on four times. Wei then exerted all his might to contain her; spent, her sweat came down like rain. Ren thought it was unavoidable; she stretched out and stopped resisting, her look was miserably changed. . . . She sighed: "I pitied Zheng. . . . He is built with a man's body, yet he cannot protect a woman—wherein lies his manhood? You are rich and have enjoyed luxuries since youth, possessing beauties prettier than I. While Zheng, a poor man, has but me to please him. How could you bear to snatch away from someone who has less?" . . . Wei was a righteous man, and hearing this, he gave her up, stretching out his robe and apologizing: "I dare not."[22]

Having won Wei's respect, Ren later satisfied his lust at the expense of two unnamed women whom she submitted to him, thereby preserving her virtue. Thus before her sudden death by a group of hunting dogs, Ren managed to uphold a model of female chastity defined by physical resistance and upright eloquence.

A woman like Ren is by any standard beyond reproach; her convenient death when Zheng was on his way to his new post removed her from the picture after having fulfilled her functions, and the men continued with their normal course. In his closing remark, Shen Jiji states: "Even amongst women today, Ren puts some to shame." Projected from the axis of destruction to that of perfection, such is the paradoxical character of the fox-woman. Through her psychic power and conformity to human ethics, the most dangerous becomes perfectly desirable: the male unconscious has indeed molded an impossible formula of desire and fear.

In a similar vein, a complex structure of desire is perceptible in the presentations of the mythical feminine who, much more generous than their predecessors, provide the literati-heroes with immediate sexual gratification and passage to immortality. The story "Pei Hang" presents us with an archetypal romance in which the hero conquered a series of obstacles and finally won his beauty. The obtaining of beauty, however, seldom marks the end of a romance; ideally it leads to further political and financial gains, and ultimately to immortality, as is the case here.[23] We can thus infer that arranged marriage, the practice of concubinage, and the large supply of entertainers and maids diverted men from the basic instinct of pursuing a woman for romantic reasons. Where the sexes experienced a radical disparity in their social status, woman, however desirable, became a mere mediator between the hero and his higher ambitions in the literary imagination.

Couched in Confucian mores, the "Legend of Liu Yi" offers a perfect example of such imagination, in which a dragon-princess intensely desired a scholar, Liu Yi, who had saved her from her plight but in a moral indignation refused to take her as his reward. When the dragon-princess was finally wedded to him, she presumed to identify herself only after she had borne him a son. These are her own words: "A woman weights lightly, and cannot secure your heart to a lifelong companionship; through your love for your son hence I entrust my hope." This female desire, timid and wrought with agony as it is presented, is important for our understanding of the prescribed logic in the genre, in which a mimicking echo, a painfully distraught self-perception, characterizes the female persona.

Through his virtuous feat, Liu Yi, who had just failed the state examination, procured not only enormous wealth by selling the outlandish gifts from the dragon-king but eventually gained the dragon-woman herself, and consequently an immortal life in the mythical realm. A tale of wish fulfillment compensating for mundane failure, the story exemplifies the entire spectrum of male desires inherent in the discourse. Self-conscious and camouflaged by Confucian morality, this famous legend reverses the order and makes a mythical woman desire a man, rendering all profits, worldly and unworldly, part and parcel of his moral practice.

The departure of Tang narrative from Han rhymed prose in its rendition of supernatural women is now complete. As the story of Liu Yi suggests, Tang literati, either in an overblown confidence or out of a failed ambition, believed themselves to be utterly desirable to mythical women. The luxurious world of the Taoist paradise became available to appease the disillusioned, as supernatural women provided them with its easy entrance. The inevitable question begs itself: what did women mean to men, after all, when in story after story women were presented as simply a means to an end? The absence of romance with love as the male protagonist's sole destination, together with the absence of a body of love poems in strict definition, forces us to rethink carefully the cultural construct of the Tang, and the structure of its unconscious.

This self-conceit of the masculine was adequately checked as history progressed, when political upheavals after the year 755 brought prolonged chaos and gradually decentralized the state, prompting a sense of disillusionment. A propensity for cryptic sensibility, even decadence, revealed itself, which was counterbalanced by a fighting spirit for lost glories.[24] This shift of sensibility explains the unprecedented fruition of the tales of the strange in the middle Tang, and a sense of belatedness is revealed with poignancy in tales of dreams of history.

Dreamers of History

The dialectic between dreaming and waking, tied in with the Buddhist teaching of the world as illusion and the enlightenment on nonstriving of philosophical Taoism, has been an important literary theme since the Six Dynasties. The famous "Zhen zhong ji" (Record of the pillow), by Shen Jiji, and "Nanke taishou zhuan" (Legend of the south tree prefect), by Li Gongzuo, written in the early middle Tang, can be interpreted as metaphors of the totality of existence, in which human pursuits are compared to the anxious and futile activities repeated each night in our dreams. In the short span of the cooking of the millet, a man has won all the glories of the world, lost them, and died in a dream of initiation. Heavy with religious connotations, these dreams of epiphany might also be created out of historical frustrations.[25]

The dreams of later literati, however, are of a different character; anxiously conscious of historical memories, they are filled with alluring beauties identified by past events. The use of the past as a high model was a common practice in ministers' remonstrations with the sovereign, and the present was often regarded as a fall from grace compared with the idealized past. Already in Confucius there was a sense of belatedness when he lamented the lost solemnity epitomized by the Duke of Zhou. This yearning for the past found further justification in the middle Tang, when chaos brought adversities and all ambitions suffered bitterly. From a sense of impotence rose these dreams of history that transported the literati to a world in which glory was still possible, and from which moral lessons of history were delivered. The principle of substitution puts unwelcome reality on hold, and the *chuanqi* authors' concern for giving their stories a historical outlook turned to the concern for history itself, now that its harsh truth had been delivered.

In "Zhou-Qin youji" (Record of traveling through Zhou-Qin), Yang Yuhuan, with other femmes fatales of early dynasties, appears to the dreamer, who has the fortune of sleeping with Wang Qiang, the Han consort given to a Tartar khan as a covenant of peace. Wang bore the khan fine children and was forced to marry her stepson after the khan's death. Hundreds of years later, by a literary command, she gives herself again, full of shame and most reluctantly, to a presumptuous Tang official. As a token of the irony of history, Wang Qiang's value as a woman is manipulated to its extreme. In "Qin meng ji" (Record of a dream of Qin) by Shen Yazhi, the legendary Nongyu was wedded to the dreamer identified as the narrator himself, who enjoyed brilliant military and administrative careers at her father's court. In another tale by Shen, "Yimeng ji" (Record of strange dreams), literati exchange accounts of their dreams of ancient beauties in their gatherings, sharing extensive poetry readings. The echoing dreams of these scholars point to a collective yearning that finds its gratification in nocturnal communications with the past, embodied here by historical beauties.

These beauties, who have become tropes for historical events, who embody the signs of time in their ancient costumes, are ideal mediators through which these belated literati become one with the past. Communication with the past seems most complete when conducted through physical union with a woman who presents the tangible site of history. From a critical perspective, the wish to possess women of past sovereigns represents one particular version of the Oedipus complex in which the political son, the minister, presumes to have the wife of his supreme father. When family and state romances were conflated in state ideology, when ministers were under surveillance in terms of their sexual self-control, it was natural that their psychology would include such a sacrilegious deviation.[26] From sharing with the king the right of copulation with the supernatural feminine to usurpation of a past emperor's sexual territory, the literati had surely transgressed far. It appears, then, in Tang narrative, a genre through which the most conceited desires are channeled, that writers had their moments of toppling the existing order in ways quite different from those of the modest historians.

The tears shed by these past consorts as the dreamer took leave to wake up from his gratifying dream are again the result of a transferential act; in the present's profound yearning for the past, the past is in turn presented as full of longing for the present. It is in such descriptive detail that the basic function of these narratives as wish fulfillment manifests itself with all its nuances. The supernatural feminine, the animal spirits and past consorts, all come to share a yearning for our literati-heroes, and through their submission, the authors find expression for their suppressed desires.

Is this a heresy of self-love that exposes the literati's mental impasse and their inability to satisfy their emotional needs except by way of linguistic creations? Is such exhibition of wayward desires a sign of an inherent state of mental impotence, or a collective narcissism? More accurately, by a linguistic inversion, these writers undo ethical-political suppressions forced upon them as imperial subjects and expose a grandiose lust of the mind, which ironically points simultaneously to their fundamental vulnerability, both sexual and political, and their desire to overcome it, however clandestine their method may be. Precisely because of this inherent agon, these tales appear as regrettably deformed in their askew logic.

Dissolution of Desires

The sense of belatedness intensified in the late Tang, and as mentioned above, the narratives were increasingly written in the mode of the fantastic and had lost their grip on the realistic as the dynasty headed to its downfall. Their exuberant displays of obstacles and martial skills are hinged on a craving that has lost its original drive, and tales written toward the end of the epoch propose ever more obstacles to be conquered by desperate protagonists. The series of obstacles presented in "Pei Hang" is a phenomenon of the late Tang, for compared to the convenience of having mythical women imposed on the literati-heroes in earlier tales, Pei's strenuous effort at winning the woman is unique. "The Legend of Wu Shuang," the tale that makes the obtaining of a beauty from a family past its prime so impossibly difficult and costly that it seems like a tour de force, also belongs to the late Tang corpus. The overcoming of obstacles in "Hongxian" (Red line) and "Nie Yingniang" (The woman Nie) is made miraculously easy by female knight errants of supernatural powers, and as such it loses all sense of immediacy.

Typical then of late Tang narratives is the contradiction between ostentatious struggles and the lack of an urgent longing. When the hero relies on his double to accomplish his goal, one hesitates to give credit to his emotional intensity. Tales depicting spirits of animals or household vessels break all the boundaries, yet in the authors' obsession with wordplay, the focus is shifted from a sharing of destinies between myriad beings to a display of linguistic virtuosity.

Even in matters concerning female chastity, we see a significant transference in which human decorum is transported to the supernatural sphere. In "Mingying zhuan" (Legend of divine correspondence), thematically the most interesting of late Tang stories, a dragon-princess was under the threat of losing her avowed chastity by the proposal of a second marriage. She appeared in the dream of the local official where her temple was honored, stated her case, and asked for a list of dead soldiers to fight the battle over her chastity. A gallant general was summoned to lead the uncanny army—for that, of course, he had to die first. This comedy of a supernatural war with an unlikely ethical cause has a subplot: in compliance with the epochal sentiment of disillusionment, the general was dejected by his trivial post and welcomed the opportunity of a grand battle, wherever it might be staged. Later he accepted with pleasure the underworld position offered by the dragon-woman, which required his death to be irrevocable. One must notice how the struggles, together with the desires, are now so dissipated that what one fights for is an ethereal woman's chastity, while engaged in the battle are mythical dragons and dead souls. In other words, everything disintegrates into the incorporeal, while only the general's yearning to fulfill his ambition stands as a genuine desire locked in with the contemporary climate.

The transmission of a heavily coded ethical value to a dragon-princess is obviously an imposition of the human upon the supernatural. Although supernatural women have been endowed with human emotions, even trauma, it is unusual that this particular one should adhere to a virtue the strict observance of which is the creation of a patriarchal state. The battle over a dragon-woman's chastity, then, presents the ominous register of a tightening ethics in the late Tang. The appearance of this tale marked a change of consciousness, when the empire was slowly moving toward its end. The shadow of an old glory still stood, but it was already the residue of the original, just as the battle over a nonexistent woman's politically constructed chastity was fought by airy soldiers. In effect, everything was at a remove from the genuine, and the great battle was but a luxurious fabrication. One senses in these transfigurations an imagination that has lost its centrality, and, dressed in exuberant costumes and working its way through a supernatural labyrinth, it nevertheless expresses a desire that no longer knows itself.

A Tang woman in front of a mirror. Detail from Ladies with Fans, attributed to Zhou Fang.

From Gugong bowuyuan canghua, pl. 5.2. (detail of pl. 5).

Chapter 9

Desire against Decorum

Before its relapse into the ossified mode of the fantastic and its further departure from realities in the late Tang, the narrative presents us with a couple of tales charged with social and psychological dimensions, which have the effect of securing the genre's status in literary history. In this chapter, I focus on a reading of three of the renowned romances, which are both artistically and psychologically intricate, in which self-reflexivity both of the literatus-hero and of the text explores the movement of desire further. The social realities of sexual relations discussed in part 2 find support as well as counterevidence in these tales steeped in the mode of realism, whose protagonists, talented literati and versatile courtesans, have captured the popular fancy with their fabulous liaisons.

EXPLANATION OF A JEALOUSY

"The Legend of Huo Xiaoyu" has the poet Li Yi, whose biography can be found in official histories of the Tang, as the protagonist. Much like the historical Li, the man is well-known for his talent; while in search of a rare beauty worthy of himself, he was introduced to Huo Xiaoyu, daughter of a deceased lord and his expelled maid who had retreated to her former profession of courtesanship. In their introductory meeting, it was made clear that their mutual appreciation resided in the exception of Li's talent and that of Huo's beauty. The thought that a beauty was an appropriate reward for his precocious mind, an idea contagious in his times, did not escape Li, and he was excited over obtaining the unsurpassable Huo.

Yet political career and social status were essential for a man's self-esteem, and Li consented to marry the daughter of a prestigious clan. Huo, sensing an impending separation, pleaded for some more years of companionship, and Li answered with a faithful oath. The rest of the story is a classic example of male betrayal and female agony. Huo suffered publicly when all efforts to reach Li failed, and by an indignant stranger Li was brought to her at her deathbed. In her insecurity, in her relentless suffering until death closed in upon her, and finally in a prophetic inter-

143

pretation of her dream, the text presents a woman of extreme delicacy and single-mindedness, who gave herself to an agonizing love.[1]

Huo's desire was fraught with anxieties, yet this had not subjected it to repression, as anxiety did to male desire, embodied by the invention of fox-woman. A woman's relationship to her desire is presented to be neither as reflective nor as antagonistic as a man's, and her ability to suppress, rationalize, or transfer her desire to a compensatory object is presented as fatally limited. Enmeshed in mourning, female protagonists in the narrative acquire the symptom of melancholia, when depression and pain cluster in their silenced bodies and become internalized. In Freudian psychoanalytic terms, the symptom is derived as a result of an incomplete process of mourning, which builds a vault for the lost object in the body, and the mourning becomes perpetual.[2]

The tale closes with Huo's soul haunting Li's conjugal bed, subjecting him to severe jealousy: a trait that ties the man back to the historical Li Yi, whose jealousy was infamous. The danger of female sexuality—namely, its intense dissatisfaction—is prominent in Huo's spirit, which embodies the crystallization of guilt at the dark corners of male consciousness. Taking Huo's obstinate spirit as a ruse to explain Li's jealousy, an emotion pervasive among women of the era, is a telling transmission. It points to an imbedded logic that male jealousy is a curse received from female jealousy, that for a man to be so improbably jealous as Li Yi, a supernatural explanation is enlisted. A monumental jealous soul of the feminine is used to explain a monumental jealousy of the masculine; it is indeed a peculiar cross-dressing of desires.

The well-circulated tale goes beyond the curiosity about the origin of a man's sickly jealousy and points to an apprehension of collective female trauma. Huo's revenge is the revenge of the weak, of a woman who from a deteriorated body raises a willful spirit as her weapon to avenge herself. The necessity of Li's betrayal, given the social construct of the time, and Huo's irrational self-destruction, might have been the partial truth of romantic relationships in the era—especially one between a literatus and a courtesan. It is out of guilt and fear of retribution that "The Legend of Huo Xiaoyu" invents itself, and hands down it is the quintessential image of a woman in love (*and* pain). The mechanism of wish fulfillment becomes obsolete here, when the other axis of desire, that of punishment, looms large in the nightmare that is Huo's fierce soul.

This haunting soul has influenced the creation of female spirits in all their horror and perversion in Mirasaki Shikibu's *The Tales of Genji,* in which Lady Rokujo's possessive soul compulsively harmed Genji's other women. It is in the context of the pervasive number of women in later eras (and other countries) who, believing in the power of spirits as their final weapon, took to suicide as a way of reprisal, that the universal significance of "Legend of Huo Xiaoyu" can be fully grasped. The revenge of the weak is full of its pathos, and the appetite for a woman's faithful soul is made to stand on its head in this total reversal of the meaning of a woman's departed soul.

A COURTESAN'S DESIRE

The origin of "Li Wa zhuan" (Legend of Li Wa), has been traced to a story called "Yizhi hua" (A twig of flowers). The text presents us with a young scholar who appears to be the only man in Tang narratives willing to stake everything on eros. It also presents us with Li Wa, an antidote to Huo in her emotional independence. In this popular tale, the promising student who arrived at the capital to attend the imperial examination forsook his ambitions and familial obligations when he chanced to meet one of the most sought-after courtesans in the capital and headed straight to his ruin.

Having squandered everything and been deserted by Li, the young man, gravely deteriorated, was taken to the undertaker's shop where he was hired for funeral services.

> Whenever he heard the mourners' doleful songs, he would regret that he could not change places with the corpse, burst into violent fits of sobbing and shed streams of tears over which he lost all control; then he used to go home and imitate the mourners' performance. Being a man of intelligence he very soon mastered the art and became the most expert mourner in Chang'an.[3]

This vocal skill won him considerable fame as the whole metropolis gathered one day to watch the competition between two major undertakers; it also exposed him to his father who, lashing the prodigal son relentlessly, intended his death to save the family from humiliation. The man suffered further physical deterioration and became a beggar, until one day in heavy snow he bumped into Li. Li retired from her courtesanship, nurtured him back to health, helped him prepare for the examination, and in other words, brought him back to the track to imperial officialdom.

To have a member of the elite sing in the undertaker's parlor, to have him so degenerated in body and will that he sinks to the bottom of the social pit, reveals a salient interest in the doings of fate, one of the obsessions of Tang miscellaneous records. In a society in which the division of classes was keenly observed, the crossing of boundaries constitutes a challenging act. In "Legend of Xie Xiaoe," Li Gongzuo stages an encounter between himself and Xie, a figure from folk legend, thus bringing a scholar-official of the gentry class into close contact with a legendary woman of the merchants. Here in "Legend of Li Wa," the young man receives an identification so degrading that his father wishes to annihilate him. If Li Gongzuo's is a literatus's act of uniting with the folk through fiction, the "Legend of Li Wa," with its origin in popular entertainment, presents the commoners' wish to bring the elite down to them.

The young man scored first in the examination and was subsequently assigned an important post—this is where Li Yi left Huo and where Huo should have resigned herself. With her characteristic independence, Li Wa accomplished the task without sentimentality, reminding the man not to "injure his prospects by an unequal union." The tale ends with the reunion of the father and son and the father's decision that they propose to Li Wa. The couple was duly married, and both their marriage and Li's performance as a wife and a mother were perfection itself.

Although the young man suffered all possible injuries, it is Li Wa who, in her strength for action, is the hero of the story. The thrust of the text is not toward the eventual glorification of the man, much less his reunion with his father, but the marriage of a courtesan with a newly posted scholar, a miraculous conclusion. In hindsight, the downfall of the young man creates the precondition for the rise of a resourceful courtesan.

The text exhibits an unconditional surrender to the power of a femme fatale, ignoring all warnings against passions, and a belief in the good that would eventually derive from such a surrender. The social phenomenon of courtesans providing literati with a milieu in which they found a cutting edge to the political world constitutes the backdrop of the story. The text exposes the complex mechanism of desire in the relationships between literati and courtesans and speaks, for once, for the fulfillment of female desires at the expense of man. As one major variation on the folk tradition by a literatus, the tale contains a folk wisdom; without claiming it to be an injunction from below, it seems reasonable to propose that in a happy incident, the elite and the folk joined hands to answer a long-neglected call for a gratification of female desires.

A FURTHER SPLIT OF THE TEXT

Among Tang narratives, the single most influential text may be "Huizhen ji" (Record of an encounter with a goddess), or as it is otherwise known, "Legend of Yingying," penned by the famous poet Yuan Zhen. It has been critically argued that the tale springs from Yuan's youthful adventures, a theory that seeks support from his biographical data as well as from his erotic and autobiographical poems. Critics have since drawn on the debate between the intricate relation among Yuan the author, the narrator, and Zhang the protagonist and have analyzed the text's psychological underpinnings in light of Yuan's motive of self-justification.[4] Yuan's personality as seen from historical records is also manipulated for the argument that Yuan, as Zhang, was a man of a compromising character.[5]

Finding correspondence between a literary work and its contextual events has long been common practice in traditional Chinese literary criticism. With its unusually vivid descriptions, a text as psychologically dubious as Yuan's invites conjecture about its empirical origin. Although an uncritical acceptance of this autobiographical reading could do damage to our approach to the text, we may yet otherwise benefit from the textual problematic in all its complexities. When the genre's intelligibility relies on a literary *vraisemblance* and its claim to reality is considered a mere ploy, the persistent question of the probability of the text as having its basis in real experiences testifies to its significant deviation from and unique position in Tang narrative.

Another romance of betrayal, the text is marked by its subtle portrayal of the protagonist Cui Yingying, who represents a unique and rather mysterious version of the boudoir feminine. Nothing Yingying said or did in the narrative falls easily into the conventionalized ways women carry themselves, and her coyness and sensibility are more genuinely felt than in most heroines. Characteristic of the literati narrative, the tale records various literary exchanges, especially those from Cui. Zhang's infatuation with her writings and her musical talent is explicit:

> Cui was well versed in calligraphy and prose; Zhang asked for her works many times and was always refused. Often Zhang would show his own works to provoke her, yet she paid them little attention. Generally what Cui revealed was artistically perfected, and yet she appeared not to know its merit; her words were quick and eloquent, yet she refrained from ordinary social exchanges. Her feeling for Zhang was deep, yet she never did correspond with him in verse. Often she looked resplendent in her sorrow and remained quiet and impenetrable, as if unaware of it; her joy and anger too were scarcely revealed. One lone night she played the zither and her sorrow plucked the impassioned strings; Zhang stole in to listen, but when he pleaded with her to continue, she stopped. Thus Zhang was ever more infatuated.[6]

Cui's writings, her music, and even her intriguing silence become metonymical extensions of her physical being; together they constitute her as an object of desire. The desire for a woman's talent is most blatant in "Ode on Han Peng," a Tang *bianwen* story based on a tale from the Six Dynasties collection, *Soushen ji* (In search of the spirits). In the story, a king so coveted a woman's brilliant verse that he schemed to make her his queen. In Heian Japan, a court woman's verbal wit, her calligraphy, her poems, and her musical skills were all part of the charms that contributed to her value. The Tang emphasis on a courtesan's conversational skills, the importance of poetry exchange in the courtesans' quarters, together with the infatuation with entertainers' virtuosity, also attest to this scenario.

Writing for Cui was a private act that she hid from other's eyes the same way she internalized her emotions. The fact that her writings remained unread, her seeming indifference concerning her talents, and more importantly, her enigmatic language as Zhang experienced it, all reveal a second degree of female alienation: the alienation in language. That her first message should be misunderstood by Zhang and, ironically, that the not at all ambiguous wish for a union in her anguished letter should be ignored, together with Zhang's infatuation with her compositions, suggest the extent to which female writings were exiled to the realm of enigma by male consciousness, to be manipulated to its own aims.[7]

As metonym of the object of desire, female language was not regarded as an instrument for communication; rather, its splendor was an end in itself, a thing to be consumed. Hence Zhang was urged to exhibit Cui's letter, a letter full of desperate pleas for Zhang's kindness, as if it were a trophy. The responses from the

literati circle were typical: they congratulated Zhang for his aversion to a dangerously contaminating beauty, and the narrator came up with sixty lines of verse
describing an erotic encounter with Cui as a goddess.[8]

Documentation of public reactions is a common practice in the narratives. In
"Legend of Feiyan," after the concubine was tortured to death for her infidelity, several poems were produced to comment on this event, upon which Feiyan appeared
in the dreams of these poets to rebuke or to thank them for their opinions. Beneath
this display of public opinions is the fact that a woman's self-expression in whatever
form—a letter, a death sworn to love—was subject to public tribunal. What was most
private became public, and Cui's letter that exposed all her previously restrained emotions, once circulated thus, lost its value of communication and became simply an
oddity, a female desire exposed under voyeuristic gaze.

The psychology of our literatus-hero is complex. What Cui concealed intrigued
Zhang, yet what she revealed most clearly, namely a wish for a proper union, was
ignored. The story is one of misunderstanding: Zhang misunderstood Cui first out
of his expectation of a conventional love affair, and then out of his assumption that
she would remain silent about her own desire. Such misunderstandings are self-
delusions nurtured by conventional romance, and they play a central role here, as
the lovers engaged in writing and reading love poetry, while approaching the acts
of writing and reading from different angles.[9]

The abandonment of Cui presents another archetype of patriarchal intrigues.

> Upon inquiry, Zhang stated the ground of his decision to abandon Cui: It is a general
> rule that what Heaven has destined for an extraordinary beauty is that she should either
> bring harm to herself or to others. Should Cui be united with someone with wealth
> and position, she would use the favor her charms gain her to be cloud and rain or
> dragon or monster—I can't imagine what she might turn into. . . . I have no inner
> strength to withstand this evil influence, and that is why I have resolutely suppressed
> my feelings.[10]

If such a statement is not supported by the previous logic of the text and seems like
an ironic jest, frustrating the reader with the discrepancy between expectations and
denouement, it is yet perfectly in line with an unconscious that regards feminine
charm with suspicion.[11] Zhang's self-serving moralizing was accepted by his circle—indeed he was congratulated on his self-rectification, and the narrator
recounted the affair as a moral lesson. The literati seemed to agree among themselves, yet the split within the text demands further examination.

We may go back to the historical background of the production and reception
of the genre. As pieces circulated among the literati, whose rise was a result of
changing social structures, a class consciousness among the new spiritual aristocrats
might have had some influence on the narrative. As a collective creation among
friends (witness the circle of Han Yu and Bo Juyi) who generated ideas among
themselves, the narrative had an immediate readership, including the powerful

patrons, and in the texts social decorum and ideologies preceded private concerns.[12] In this sense, the genre as a public discourse more conscious of social conventions than of creative needs deserves our consideration.

In the case of the "Legend of Yingying," it is the happy correspondence between ethical demands and his private interest that legitimizes the protagonist's logic. Nevertheless, a discrepancy between his conscience and social practices steals in to create an inner split. After Cui's letter was made public, the text evolves from a private mode of discourse into a public one, and the narrator's voice takes center stage. Directed by a self-deceiving logic, the text takes pains to present a woman of refined sensibility, only to have her rebuked for her destructive potential. If Cui's enigmatic temperament caused Zhang's anxiety, this is the only psychological basis that the text actually provides for his statement of rejection. In other words, from infatuation to sudden moralization, the text moves too fast to be credible.

The overt enthusiasm of the narrator arouses suspicion and invites the conflation between him and the protagonist.[13] The rupture of the text, then, should be traced to the author's psyche and interpreted as a projection of a need to reconcile with himself through (re)writing and remembering—hence the attempt to exonerate Zhang by endowing him with virtues that are never contested, and the scholars' eager consent. This mechanism of the psyche alone can explain the enigmatic image of Cui—perhaps in his memories (and fear of memories) not untainted with remorse, the woman becomes slippery in her loving and suffering. In the presentation of her silenced existence, we see lurking underneath it the commotion of a mind that struggles to find peace with itself.

Pertinent to this is the problem of the representation of women. With no access to self-representation, women are left to the erotics of editing; the consequence of their being assigned a marginal space in patriarchal discourse is grave indeed: it leaves them at men's mercy, and the truth of their consciousness can never be restored.[14]

With this we seem to have come full circle to the conclusion arrived at by other critics about the autobiographical nature of the text. However, I am only offering an explanation that would shed light on the inexplicable split in the text. The unconscious works as the driving logic behind these tales, as the movements of "Li Wa" and "Huo Xiaoyu" exemplify; the supernatural turn of events of the latter and the anticonventional ending of the former after all are departures from the main gist of the tales. Yet while these texts are governed by an ideology of which they are not self-conscious, the moralizing of "Yingying" discloses the text's awareness of the dialectic between desire and repression, or rather, of its riding on the wings of an ideology that is on its side. The resort to an ideology that saves the hero's integrity (and very possibly the author's conscience), destroys that of the text.

In the last analysis, whether or not we take Yuan Zhen as the disguised protagonist, the gap between an unprofitable romance and social norms has induced the split in the text, and it is precisely this gap that becomes the organizing principle of the narrative and, more essentially, of the literati eros. A split in the text originates from a split in the self, as the literatus stood as the guardian of his desires, betraying himself to his irreconcilable remorse.

The psychologically telling tales reveal for us in less naive ways a literatus's unconscious, as anxiety and guilt are no longer transported to an imagined creature but come back to haunt him with a vengeance, transforming realities into something disturbingly unstable. A jealous soul of the feminine, memories of a betrayed lover—these come too close to home for the authors to retain composure, and we begin to sense that they are suffering from a contrition, caught in a desire confused with its conflicting aims. With these tales, we come closer to an understanding of the different degrees of sacrifice offered on the altar of this empire, exacted through the machinery of the ethico-political complex and wielded by a technology of power that sets out to carve out the domains, the structure, and the direction of desires over which neither men nor women have claim.

Chapter 10

In Feminine Voice

BOUDOIR LAMENT OF THE LITERATI

In a conspicuous convention in the Chinese lyrical tradition, boudoir lament, or *guiyuan,* poets follow through schematic expressions of a woman's amorous yearning from behind a female persona. Composed in a tradition in which the feminine voice is essentially a male construct, the lament presents a stylized feminine token exchanged between poets and predominantly male readers.[1] As such, the romanticized mourning of the feminine becomes an exotic item under a penetrating voyeuristic gaze. This particular mode of writing, both universally practiced and specific to Chinese literature, with its thorny political connotations, is an essential theme for a feminist study of the problematics of sexual difference.

This lyrical convention portrays women in a claustrophobic interior, frozen in an inward-turning gaze at an absent lover. A typical boudoir lament presents with stock idioms an abandoned woman in her scented chamber, suffering from a neglect syndrome defined by masochistic tendencies and self-absorption, exhibiting the debilitating effects of love. It often ends with the woman's vow of eternal faithfulness, spelling out the discordant relationship between genders.[2] This fascination with woman's mourning over a disenchanted love is universal: in world literature throughout the ages, the abandoned woman has preoccupied writers' imaginations and embodied the very condition of abandonment.[3] However, its Chinese version presents a unique tradition in which an obsession with and conventionalization of the theme intertwine under specific cultural demands.

The impact of this poetic practice is keenly felt in that, in the hands of women poets, it has inadvertently come to shape their self-expression. The usurpation of the feminine voice thus comes full circle. At the same time, this mode has taken its toll on male expressions of amorous sorrow. Since literati have expressed the agony of love in feminine voice for centuries, in their own amorous mourning this voice intrudes and takes over. Couched in the tradition of allegorical exegeses since the Han, where romantic lament is read as rending plaint by a disenfranchised courtier, the lament and its reverberating effects strike home with a vengeance.

151

This lyrical subgenre found its origin in the Nineteen Old Poems of the Han dynasty and was implemented in the literati's *yuefu* (imitation folk songs) through the Six Dynasties. Later it was incorporated into the *gongti* (palace poetry) of the Southern Dynasties, which takes ravishing palace women as its subject, shaping thus an eroticized lament. Merging palace poetry with poems on objects, *yongwu,* the Southern Dynasties court poets present women as exotic items confined in luxurious chambers, and the probing into the chambers amalgamates with the probing into their minds. In the late Tang, the lament on history, *huaigu,* intersected with erotic poetry, *yanti,* in the hands of Li He and his followers, and a new breed took shape with a sense of the pressing vicissitudes of life. Temporal progression gains existential intensity here and achieves ontological dimension.[4] Focusing on palace harems, *gongyuan* (palace lament), an imperial parallel to the boudoir lament, bewails the fate of palace women incarcerated in the chambers of a disconsolate palace.

In its *yuefu* format in the Han and early Six Dynasties, boudoir lament enjoyed a prominent status; almost every major poet engaged in its sustained practice. This creative interest concentrated itself on the palace lament in the middle Tang and returned in joint force with the erotic in the late Tang, taking sensuous pleasure as its aesthetic principle. In this chapter, I focus on the problematics of the lament in its various forms and ramifications in related poetic modes, with three major poets, Li Bo, Du Fu, and Li He, as our focus, followed by a coda on Wen Tingyun.

There are various possibilities in interpreting the obsessive lament. As political allegory, the minister-concubine complex is read into the feminine mourning of a lost lover/lord; in this reading, the female persona is projected back to the poet, himself a forsaken protégé. As a manifestation of an androgynous psyche, the poet's feminine self, the lament may also simply be understood as an expression of empathy for women's collective plight. More critically, we may decode it as a strategy to usurp feminine voice and thereby dictate its proper tone; in this reading, androgyny becomes a way to claim power. Ultimately, the lament presents a perception of the feminine as the embodiment of lack, cast in perpetual mourning of absence itself. All these interpretations should be accounted for in a comprehensive discussion of this poetic mode that has engaged generations of poets' imaginations.

This feminine mode of lament, widely practiced and essential for its revelation of the literati psyche, occupies a peripheral position in the poetic tradition. The aversion from expressive romantic sentiments and the tendency to slight writings associated with the feminine certainly are behind the logic of such positioning. In the hands of Li Shangyin, poems of erotic and secretive sentiments (*yanqing* and *youqing*) achieve artistic maturity; they are often read as political allegories by commentators, probably as an apology for their overtly delicate sentiments.

That classical Chinese poetry does not preoccupy itself with the theme of romantic love should be recognized as the result of ethical mores that emphasize conjugal respect, rather than affection between man and wife. Thoughts for departed friends overwhelmingly outweigh those for absent wives, in which familial rather than romantic sentiments are characteristic. The narratives have shown us how an unequal social structure made women dispensable; under the circumstance, profound yearning for a woman was exceptional. When women were bought and sold as household attachments, it was difficult to desire them with a hurtful intensity. The theme of courtly love and its quest for an ideal lady, to an extent echoed in the yearning for divine women in early Chu shamanistic poetry, in certain love songs in the *feng* (wind, folk songs) of the *Classic of Poetry,* and in the rhymed prose discussed above, in general finds no equivalent in Chinese poetry at the more mundane level.[5] With a few exceptions, in the Chinese lyrical tradition the controlling principle of love poems is absence and remembrance, and yearning is savored for one lost, rather than for one to be won.

In poems addressed to courtesans, one notices a confusion of the women with memories of the past—they are not treasured for what they are, but for what they represent. However, it is careless to make any categorical statement in reading Tang poetry that exposes subtle sentiments of the elite, who were bound up in a sociocultural complex that required them to resort to roundabout expressions of love. As we shall see, the entangled love poems and boudoir lament, expressions of imagined obsessive feminine, are both the symptom of and cure for male sexuality in a radically unbalanced gender relationship.

AN ALLEGORICAL BEAUTY

Besides its obsessive practices and formulaic styles, what sets the Chinese version of the theme of abandoned women apart from other traditions is its political exegesis. Couched in the background of the minister-concubine complex, the poetry of abandoned women is sometimes interpreted as the voice of a disgruntled courtier. Such a reading, insipid as it may be, points to a culturally significant political unconscious. Indeed, one intriguing debate in Chinese poetic criticism centers on whether it is the commentary on the *Classic of Poetry* (with its propensity to read love poems as political satire) that inspired Qu Yuan's feminine voice in his "Encountering Sorrow," or if Qu's adaptation of a feminine pose encouraged the allegorical readings of the folk songs.[6]

In the boisterous court, courtiers, rendered effeminate in contrast to the emperor, were made to entertain with verse. Li Bo, the unconditionally admired genius with a propensity to take flight in Taoist wanderings, was recruited to the court of Emperor Xuanzong and had composed upon demand a handful of poems praising the seductive charm of the consort Yang Yuhuan. Li's brief career as a court poet provides an intriguing picture of the conflicts of a true poet at court, and his poems, set to accompany banquet music, reveal that both poetry and gifted poets were at the disposal of imperial pleasures.[7]

With many Tang poets, Li shared the ambition of ascending to political glory and a sense of untimeliness, *buyu.* The daring poet with a contempt for the ruling class was not above feminizing his voice in a political context to adopt the humble gesture of one seeking patronage. In "Number Fifty-Two" of his fifty-nine poems in the ancient style, Li expresses an anxiety over time and his unanchored life.

> Can't bear to gaze at those autumn weeds—
> Soaring and drifting, nothing to cling to.
> Light and wind consume orchids and herbs of fragrance
> White dew dots on mallows and greens.
> My fairest awaits me not:
> Grass and leaves perish day by day.[8]

The last couplet echoes the following lines from the much quoted original by Qu Yuan:

> Days and months rushed on, never lingering
> Springs and autumns sped by in endless successions.
> How trees and flowers were fading and falling
> I feared that my Fairest's beauty too would fade.[9]

Traditional commentary has interpreted "Fairest" as the king, with the self mourning over its abandonment. Li Bo's poem, using identical diction, expresses a similar sentiment with a heightened sense of helpless drifting.

Confucius has said as much: "Not to take offense when others do not appreciate you, is this not being a gentleman?"[10] For the scholars, *zhiji* (one who knows the self) is a rare gift that one receives once in a lifetime. In a letter to Ren An, Sima Qian quotes from *Zhanguo ce* (Record of warring states): "A gentleman dies for one who recognizes him, a woman adorns herself for one who adores her." This is not mere rhetoric: in historical records of the assassins, accounts of fatal devotion toward one who regards oneself with esteem are profuse. The analogy between a grateful man and a pleasing woman is culturally telling, and this need for recognition, intensified by submission toward the monarch, supports the rationale of the political allegory of a pleading courtier as an abandoned woman.

In a poem entitled "Zeng Pei sima" (For Magistrate Pei), Li Bo ends with these lines:

> Surely I deserve to be cherished
> With beauty hard to come by in this world.
> To you I sing through shining teeth—
> Turn to me, without fail.[11]

Possibly written in jest for an entertainer fallen out of favor, a common poetic game, the poem empathizes with an abandoned woman and, furthermore, identifies with the feminine psyche. Granting the tongue-in-cheek aspect of the poem, we should also consider the text as a conventionalized plea for a much-desired patronage, when different styles were required while addressing people of hierarchical ranks.[12] The presence of this poem in Li Bo's anthology testifies to his programmatic acceptance of the tradition of feminine persona. The candid expression of self-worth and the plea, understood as lyrical convention, release the poem from embarrassing self-abasement. Such excessive mannerism (or mannered excess) is a telltale sign of a socially sanctioned mentality that found disguise in the humble feminine.

This feminine persona stands opposite to "Number Fifty-Two" quoted above, in which the masculine self searches for the lord-beauty. These two contrasting poses draw the essential contour of political allegory that can be traced back to Qu Yuan. The "beauty and fragrant plant" metaphor in "Encountering Sorrow" takes the lord as the ideal lover, and the lyrical self shifts from assuming the role of a court lady competing for his favor to that of a man pursuing the "Fairest." Such shifting genders put the sexual identity of both the lord and the courtier in jeopardy, fashioning a treacherous composite difficult to disentangle.

The allegorical "beauty" clothes political desires in decorum, just as the pursuit of woman is legitimized by the marriage institution. The *Classic of Poetry* begins with a stately song on courtship, testifying to its centrality in Confucian ethics. For a more poignant rationale for this allegory, however, the pursuit of woman should be understood as the quintessential quest, with the feminine as the essential object of desire.[13] The exaltation of the king to an ideal beauty adds to it a transcendental dimension in line with the theocratic nature of kingship, as a sanctified Son of Heaven stands as the political ideal for conscientious ministers. Through this ideological complex, the lord is legitimized as the ultimate object of desire, from a moral-political standpoint.

On the other hand, the deployment of a concubine's stance embodies the essence of humility, and the absolutism of female dependency gives such conceit symbolic weight. The symbiotic opposition between the genders makes the subservient gesture of woman both the regulated and regulating code of social stratification. This normative dichotomy mirrors the stratification between the lord and his subjects, and the two ethical pairs arrive at a fusion in this conceit. By adopting the pose of a deserted woman, by wielding the humility of the weak and hiding behind an approved mask, the minister-concubine complex finds its convenient ramification in this literary convention.

One needs to speak either of the lord or of oneself in feminine terms—the woman-as-the-trope syndrome reverberates far with unlikely ramifications. These literary conventions go far beyond the symptom of proliferate feminine tropes and suggest intricate cultural meanings.

THE SUPREME OBJECT OF DESIRE

The fate of thousands of women encapsulated in the palaces with the remote hope of imperial exaltation preoccupied Tang poets' imaginations. Numerous *gongti* poems lament their tragic fate, which is reminiscent of that of the ministers, when both were subject to imperial capriciousness. The more observant poets among officials bear witness to this forbidding condition, in which they too played a perilous role.

It was Li He's unconventional imagination that broke new ground for this subgenre, exemplified in the following piece, "Gongwa ge" (Song of a palace woman):

> Candle flames hang high over an empty gauze
> Night in the green house, pounding red lizards . . .
> Mole-crickets mourn the moon under the balustrades
> Gate nails of bronze beasts locked up a lady Zhen . . .
> May my lord be bright as the shining sun
> And set me free—riding on fishes, parting sea waves. (*LH*, 129)

In canonical expectations, the poem depicts insomnia, chill, the beatings of time, and a nature echoing human sadness. The red lizards are pounded into powders and dotted on a palace woman's skin, leaving a mark that diminishes when she loses her virginity.[14] The allusion to Lady Zhen (empress of the Emperor Wen of Wei), locked up after falling out of favor, delimits a palace most austere. The request to be released separates itself from the boudoir inertia and the subservient political allegories, and riding on fishes, a lively mind breaks loose in a speed and method provided only by the sea animals.

The force of this image is fully felt when placed against expressions of intense thirst for imperial favor. A poem by Li Bo sets the picture in a nutshell. It bears an intriguing title: "Handan cairen jiawei siyangzu fu" (A Handan low-ranking consort marries a kitchen servant):

> Once I bid farewell to the jade terrace and descended
> All was gone as dispersed morning clouds.
> Often I remember the city of Handan:
> In the deep palace, I dreamed of an autumn moon.
> The lord is not to be seen:
> Vexed, I waited till dawn. (*LTB*, 154)

Variation on a piece by Xie Tiao, the poem's ironic title is not sustained by its formulaic tone. The concubine passé sinks to the bottom of the imperial ladder, indulging herself in memories of a painful yet glorious past. The arresting strength of the end couplet moves beyond memories of the past and attests to a state the concubine still submits to; having been given to a servant, the concubine views the lord as ever more awe-inspiring and painfully desirable.

The hovering image of the lord put all desires under his shadow—in the imperial city, in juxtaposition to the monarch, metaphorically, all men's sexuality was dwarfed. The eunuchs presented the surface of this sexual tyranny, while thousands of palace women forbidden sexual trespasses and obliging courtier-concubines constituted its deeper layers. The comically low status of the husband here is essential to expose the shame of this fall, and a past consort is presented as fixated on a yearning for the ultimate lover/lord. Supporting this fixation, a commentator states that this is in effect the poet lamenting his fate of royal abandonment.[15] With this, the absolutism of the machine of imperial desire is fully contested.

In a more subtle reading, the ironic title suggests this poem as Li Bo's comment on the convention of palace lament. By producing the situation of the marriage of a consort with a kitchen servant, Li creates a curiously melodramatic effect, mixing the comic with the starkly pathetic. In this reading, the woman's voice complies with the condition of sexual subjugation to which Li Bo is sensitive, and the gaze fixed on the palace embodies the abstraction of an existence under the imperial shadow. A subtle critique is inherent in such a reading, when the woman's mourning, caught between the comic and the tragic, receives an ironic twist.

In the ministers' relation to the despot, the urgent situation forbids such poetic distance. Consider Li's greatest admirer, Du Fu. After a brief career at the court during the An Lushan rebellion, Du Fu began his years of traumatic wandering. Below are two poems composed during the early years of his drifting.

I.
Last year this morning, we held up the imperial bed
At the fifth watch, three roll calls and into the court we went.
Driven to this heart-rending place
My thoughts are of the enshrouding mists and scented visions . . .
Who longs for the day when sorrow will end?
Day by day, sorrow grows with the shadow of the sun.

II.
Remember yesterday, on duty in the bureaus with ease.
Last year today, I served the dragon's countenance.
Unicorns poised above incense-burners' smoke
Peacock fans opened slowly, shadows returned.
The jade stool alas points at the north pole in Heaven
Your red robes pose at the center of court ceremony.
Solitary minister—my heart is about to break
Sorrow pit against wintry clouds, snow over mountains.[16]

In typical Du Fu style—unabashed sorrow infused with profound pathos—the twin poems are exactly what the commentator claims Li Bo's poem of the consort to be. Addressed to his old colleagues at the cabinet, the poem states the lyrical self's yearning for the distant imperial presence, and its envy for those present at the solstice ceremony. In familiar diction, it describes fondly the palace's scented air, a misty quality tied in with the metaphor of the dragon-emperor hovering as its elusive center.

The couplets on holding up the imperial bed and serving the dragon's countenance present Du's single-minded loyalty, revealing him as the sage-poet whose love for the empire extended from the sovereign to its suffering people. Both the characters *peng* (to hold with both hands) and *shi* (to serve, even sexually, as in master-servant and lord-concubine relationships) are expressions of humility. With the term *imperial bed,* a standard metonym for the emperor, the convention of putting the monarch-subject relationship in gendered terms is imminent. Through the heavy-handed expressions of stress and this heavily connotative mannerism, an acute dejection and thirst for the royal presence are explicit, with the sovereign at the center of pressing desires.

These twin poems demonstrate the strange parallel between released consort and alienated minister, when both gaze stubbornly at the palace with a yearning not easily resolved. Without the disguise of the fantastic, the linguistic transgression we experienced in the narrative is toned down considerably in poetic discourse. A regular exchange and offering at the court, poetry carries the burden of a decorum excessive for modern tastes. It is this excessive awe supported by a self-serving humility that shaped the feminine voice in political laments and, ultimately, the consciousness of impaired male sexuality.

In the end, we are enlightened to the realities at the core of the empire's deployment of power and ideologies, and to how those ideologies reinforce one another. The hovering imperial desire has strictured the confines of masculinity, which in turn further constricts the confines of femininity.[17] It is in this sense that a careful analysis of the feminine persona sculpted by the literati is mandatory for a feminist critique. As we read these poets who dictate the domain of femininity, the inherent structure of their own subjectivity informs the basis of our extrapolations.

WRITING FOR THE SILENCED

Famous for his uninhibited temperament, Li Bo did not hesitate to don the mask of the abandoned woman in *yuefu* style. In his hands, poignant portraits of the female psyche are created, and his somewhat belated practice of this convention provides it with regenerated freshness. The following quatrain, "Yuanqing" (Resentment), is a succinct case in point:

> A beauty curls up jeweled curtains
> And sits quietly, knitting her slender brows.
> Clear are traces of her tears
> Yet whom does her heart resent? (*LTB,* 579)

The piece contains all the basic ingredients of boudoir lament: a woman, a sense of confinement, inside/outside (the curtain), inertia, and a metonym of the woman (eyebrows). With admirable economy, the movement of penetration delves deep into the woman's mind. Caught in the boudoir, a woman and her amorous sorrow are pre-conditioned, as the rhetorical question coins an internalized union between woman and pain. Yet through the forceful word "resent," the woman, unlike other boudoir women who merely reflect male desires, removes herself from a state of passivity.

The rhetorical question is essential: if regular laments claim to know the woman inside out and take the liberty to usurp her voice, here the professed ignorance of the woman's secret is genuine. No longer a compulsive sufferer, she turns her gaze back to whoever is looking on and startles that gaze with a vehement emotion, retaining her secrets.

In traditional practice, poems composed for wives are usually titled "Zengnei" (For one inside), in contrast to the more vague "Jiyuan" (Sent to one far away), addressed to courtesans or concubines, and occasionally to a remote wife. Both "inside" (a byname for wife) and "far away" characterize a woman's position: she is simultaneously inside the harem and far away from her man on official duties. In general, poems were composed for wives during a painfully long separation or after their untimely death.[18] We must note the uncanny coincidence with which these three conditions—inside, far away, and dead—constitute the symbolic positions of woman. Placed within the ethical home, she stands as the anchor for a drifting husband; being far away, she is identified with an unapproachable ideal and the nostalgic concept of home; and being dead, she embodies past memories, anxiety over time, and, ultimately, the pressing comprehension of an ephemeral life. Being distant and dead, woman registers the sense of an inexplicable lack.

In the twin poems entitled "Qiupu jinei" (Sent to my wife from Qiupu) and "Zi dainei zeng" (Sent to myself for my wife), Li Bo writes both to and on behalf of his wife after years of separation. These two poems differ considerably in tone, with the first focusing on the sorrow of separation and aging, and the second, in the style of boudoir lament, stressing a humble longing: "Circling as the moon in heaven/You shed not your light on me" (*LTB*, 579). This asymmetry is amplified and somewhat confusing in Li's series of twelve poems entitled "Sent to One Far Away." The vagueness of the title conceals the actual identity of the addressee, and usually poems titled thus are more romantically inclined; the emotion in this series is hence uncharacteristically intense.

The diverse styles of this series raise questions about their grouping, yet as a series, they provide fruitful examples for an analysis of the nature of love poems couched in the lament mode.

In fresh makeup, she sits against the setting sun
And gazes forlornly at the empty gold screen.
This thought presses me to write this letter
Hoping it be airborne by the flying geese. [Number 2]

In spring wind, a jade face fears fading
Flowers fall by the screened window, scattered.

Green chamber—hollowed by a bright moon . . .
Embroidered words pledge a pure heart:
Until now it seals up sorrow, unbearable to behold. [Number 8]

Embroidered bedding curled up, this dreadful insomnia.
For three years she is gone, her scents yet unspent . . .
In my sorrow, yellow leaves fall
White dew wets the moss, so blue. [Number 11] (*LTB*, 567–70)

Alternating between male and female voices, the series presents degrees of gender
ambiguity that confuse the reading. A hybrid of love poem and boudoir lament, it
thereby challenges the dividing line between them and brings to the fore problematics of gender expression.

In classical Chinese poetry, love poems are often either camouflaged as lament
or supported by the lament mode (as is this one), and expressions of feminine sorrow transport the self's own eros. Boudoir lament as substitution/sublimation can
be understood best in this sense. In this regard, sympathy for and imagined passion
of the other are the two axes around which a lament/love poem evolves itself, on
which hangs the masculine eros in disguise. In the hands of average poets, aversion
from identifying the self plus a frivolous sentiment create the function of
voyeurism, which is symptomatic of most laments. To call such poetry love poems
seems lacking in discretion, without discriminating between a fancied feminine sentiment and genuine yearning.

The problematic of gender expression is complicated by the fusion of male and
female voices, when neutral references such as "jun" (you) and "meiren" (a beauty
or a lord), and this "I imagine that you are" pose, are profusely used. In number 8,
the quiet chamber alludes to (by canonical expectation) a woman perceiving with frail
mind things around her, and a man perceiving her in his mind's eye. Such intertwined
perspectives create confusion and make the identification of the voice's gender futile.
This fusion of voices speaks for a psychological identification between the lovers,
although manipulation of the feminine voice is more visibly the effect of such fusion.

In number 11, the self mourns over his loss and waits anxiously as the seasons
evolve.[19] One is tempted to suggest that the self is lamenting here just like a
woman, but as the convention so demands, it is difficult not to sense the nuanced
difference between a man's romantic lamentation and that of a woman, as here, a
sense of control supersedes the compulsive fixation on mourning typical of the
boudoir woman confined in melancholia. Instead of hanging on emotional inertia, the text ends with two natural images, dissolving sorrow into the distance.
Nature, in an eternal cycle of birth and decay, opens up human anguish to a much
broader and not clearly defined space. This broadening of sentiment is scarce in the
lament proper, in which everything projects back to the woman an inconsolable
agony; she is caught up in a feminine mourning tending toward masochism,
deprived of both physical and mental mobility.

Du Fu's famous "Yueye" (Moonlit night) shares with Li Bo's series a fusion of boudoir lament and love theme—a rare example of boudoir sentiments, *gueqing,* from a poet who generally refrained from adopting the feminine mode.

> Tonight, the moon over Luzhou
> Is alas seen from the boudoir alone . . .
> Scented mist wets her dark hair of clouds
> In clear shimmer, her jade arms feel the chill.[20]

In a mode known for its fixation on woman and abandonment, the wife is presented with a touch of sensuality as Du writes from changing perspectives, transferring sorrow to the distant Other. The persistent masculine practice of voicing feminine plaints attests to the comprehension of the silence enshrouding women and, consequently, the urge to speak for the silenced. One only presumes to speak for an inferior or an invalid, certain that the pleasure of serving as a self-assigned deputy will not be denied him. This partially explains the rationale of the lament, when encompassing the silent feminine is perceived as a burden for the compassionate and a privilege for the vainglorious. Silence of the Other thus is incorporated into the building, the manifestation of masculine power.

Positioned at the end of the *Quan Tang shi* (Complete collection of Tang poets) are a group of poems by a particularly talented anonymous poet, which presents a unique rendering of giving voice to the silenced.[21] With artistic subtlety of details, the quiet sounds of the loved one are heard in deep, troubled silence.

> In green-feathered curtains, someone wakes up from her dream
> Sound of a jeweled hairpin falling on pillow case . . .
>
> Our hearts know each other's motion in silence:
> She mends beneath the lamp, I stroll with the moon.
> Coming to the stairs, I find her awake
> In deep night, a pair of scissors gently put down.[22]

With great subtlety, the sounds of the silenced Other and their delicate effect on the lover are preserved in time. We hear echoing sounds of the deeply repressed feminine, as stifled voices are transformed into quiet, tiny sounds produced by intimate objects. The burden of silence stands heavy when again, no speech is granted woman.

Women are hence made to receive the masculine gaze and a voice/sound tailored for the feminine. Deprived of self-expression, they serve as the blank surface projecting back the images of male desires. The need to hinge measureless longings on the feminine, the confusion as well as clearly defined gendered expressions presented by the lament mode, beg one question. What constitutes the necessity for the invention of a feminine persona saturated in melancholia? A handicapped feminine desire, a devoted soul that imprisons the female body, these are ardently fancied female conditions that guarantee the comfort of masculine desires. We would be seriously mistaken to underestimate the power of such discourse and the extent to which it forges female consciousness. The machinery of the field of discourse is invincible and detrimental to female subjectivity; it reaches deep into the feminine psyche and strikes it, demanding it to take shape. The physical confinement of the female body works hand in hand with this education of the soul, until women are cast into a state of paralysis in the prison house of language and in their self-perceptions.

*   *   *

The wife's symbolic position inside assigns her the role as a center that holds, an emblem of the ultimate home.[23] If this seems a contradiction to the alienated position of women in the prose stories discussed in the preceding chapters, it is because the narratives have excluded in one stroke domestic wives. In literary discourse in which ethical demands recede to the background, these Confucian wives receive rather limited, humble profiles. As they are presented in lyrical compositions, there is nothing flattering about the wives' position as the center, imprisoned in an eternal waiting in life as in death. Witness the following quatrain, "Longxi xing" (Ballad of Longxi) famous for its end couplet:

> Sworn to wipe out the Jurchens, forsaking themselves
> Five thousand warring coats perished in barbarian dust.
> Commiserate—white bones by the No-calm River bank
> Are yet quickened in sweet dreams of spring boudoir.[24]

A shocking parallel presents itself: the bones of the dead and the dreams of the young wives contrast each other to bring out the brutality of war. As the bones of the warriors are laid bare on the battlefield, the soldiers' wives, ignorant of these deaths, still have sweet, even erotic dreams about them.[25] Women, the locus of desire, become the lyrical stasis and reflective center in death. Their innocently obstinate dreams are the ultimate vessels that receive the dead, that reject death. The soldiers at the frontiers are tied to a center that holds, and as they move further and further away and finally into their deaths, that bond remains tied.

The subtly erotic tone of the term *chungui* (spring boudoir) in juxtaposition to the bones of the dead has a perturbing quality almost to the point of being gruesome. This unintentional sarcasm, issued from an irony of fate, exposes female bodies as eternal vessels of male desires. The young wives' dreams of the dead, although meant to convey a sense of the tragic, are tainted with a sensibility that eroticizes the feminine. The amorous dreams are held up against the reality principle, and again woman is assigned the role of the flesh that forever desires, the ultimate weapon against death.

A DOUBLE ABSENCE

Both Li He's short life and his genius are exceptions to the Chinese literary tradition. Born an aristocrat, Li indulged himself in sensuous enjoyments and turned that sensuality into something terrifying. Endowed with a taste for the grotesque and the excessive, he resurrected palace poetry from its near oblivion in the middle Tang and initiated an aesthetic consciousness that combined the historical and the erotic to create a sublime mode of sensuality. This paved the way for a full-fledged resurgence of an indulgence in poetic exuberance in the late Tang.

The transformation of the boudoir motif in Li He is significant. Li has written a good number of laments in palace style, releasing its masochistic tension by ascribing a sense of carpe diem to the courtesans' quarters. At Li He's best, the two poles of pleasure and sorrow are inevitably intermingled, alternating just as the courtesans alternate between the arrival and departure of guests: "New guests descend their horses, old guests depart/Green cicada hair and fine black brows brushed and combed anew."[26] In Li He's hands, the boudoir theme is shifted to an atmospheric mode without the voyeuristic eroticism of the Southern Dynasties, and the melancholic sentiment is often transported to a keen awareness of temporal mutations.

Caught in the trafficking of desires, courtesans and entertainers served as the peripheral site of pleasure in lyrics. This is prominent in the vibrant lines of Li's famous "Jiangjinjiu" (Bring in the wine):

> Lapis lazuli goblet
> Thick as the amber.
> From the wine-cask drip crimson pearls.
> Boiling dragon and roasting phoenix, weeping jades of fat.
> Silk screens and embroidered curtains enclose the scented breeze.
> Blow the dragon flute
> Beat the lizard-skin drum
> Sing the white teeth
> And dance the slender waists—
> It is spring and near day's end
> Peach blossoms scatter like red rain.
> Come: let us be drunk all day and night
> For wine does not reach the earth on Liu Ling's grave.[27]

Dancers and singing girls spin the sensuous surface of a world of abandonment, and a consciousness of transience is bluntly stated as the drumming and dancing accelerate under the threat of death.

Identified with the realm of the senses, the presence of courtesans helps the elite to defy anxiety over impermanence, and together with the wine, the elixir of forgetfulness, they offer a temporary harbor from realities. As the semiotic sign of sen-

suality, they also embody the locus of anxiety over ontological absence. Witness
Li's "Su Xiaoxiao mu" (The grave of little Su):

> Dew on the dark orchid
> Shines like a crying eye
> Nothing to bind the heart to:
> Misted flowers, too thin to be cut.
> Grass her cushions
> Pines her parasol
> The wind is her skirt
> The water, a tinkling pendant.
> A coach with lacquered sides
> Waits at dusk.
> Cold green candle-flames
> Labor aluster.
> Under the West Mound
> The wind blows the rain.[28]

Built on a ballad allegedly composed by the courtesan Su Xiaoxiao, Li He's text
fixates on a dead woman's hovering desires. A courtesan delimited by the pleasure
principle retains that condition in death in the collective unconscious, and Li He's
piece is not an isolated case, as poems inscribed on a courtesan's tomb are common
practices. The alluring presence of Su is transmitted to surrounding objects: dew
her tears and grass her bedding. Such animation has a ghostly tinge, as absence is
translated into presence in a perpetual longing, and the phantasmal presence of the
coach is frozen in an unbearable stance of waiting. The desire of a departed soul
marks a double lack, and Su becomes an omnipresence of mourning and desiring,
transforming the wind and the rain into something unsettling.

This image identifies a feminine soul (scented soul as it is named) as the locus of
lack, to the same extent that boudoir lament is an externalization of a sense of
absence hinged on the site of the mourning woman, who becomes the figure of
language defined by and operating within lack.[29] In the ultimate sense, the lament
mode is a linguistic act that arises out of a desire delimited by absence and at the
same time substantiates the very nature of language as motivated and supported by
that absence. In this sense, this lyrical mode may be considered symbolic of the
essence of language itself.

The identification between woman and lack is further complicated by the original ballad attributed to Su:

> I ride a coach with lacquered sides
> My love rides a dark piebald horse.
> Where shall we bind our hearts into one?
> On the West Mound, beneath the pines and cypresses.[30]

The lighthearted lover in the original is transformed into a despondent soul, both by death and by Li's poetic imagination. If there is a certain continuity between Li's poem and Su's ballad, the textual dispute of the latter creates a further problem. The double absence of the desire of a ghost could well be reverberated by a third absence: the absence of Su in a usurpation of her voice. Thus the lover Su in the ballad is already overtaken by an all-encompassing male desire, rendering the amorous courtesan a reflective object of eros.

MYTHICAL SOLITUDE

We have seen the domestication of divine women in the narrative; in the lyrics, the goddesses are again tamed by boudoir lamentation. Through Li He's talent for the fantastic, mythical women acquire as it were a melancholic sentiment in the piece entitled "Beigong furen" (The goddess of the seashell palace).

> Her slender brows freeze in green powder for a thousand years
> Serenely, she suffers time by the lone phoenix.
> In autumn, her skin touched by the cool jade-robe
> Heavenly light translucent, watery the sky. (*LH,* 292)

Calmly facing her reflection in the mirror (while the widowed phoenix danced until he died before his solitary image), the goddess feels the autumn chill, a metaphor for solitude. The subtle juxtaposition of immortality with the fleeting world presents the goddess as imprisoned in an eternity marked by a terrifying calm. The force of such calm and a huge desolation are equally present, and the goddess balances dangerously between these states. The closure points to a smooth sky and an equally smooth body of water, images of expansion and emptiness. Loneliness, so pervasive in the boudoir women, steals in to characterize the sea goddess. Such transportation of the earthly to the divine makes one wonder if the habit of presenting woman in a perpetual state of longing has not imperceptibly reshaped the poetic conception of the divine woman, who appears to be so dignifiedly elusive in the rhymed prose.

The poem below, entitled "Shenxian biequ" (Another tune for the magic strings), provides an eerie portrait of a goddess returning from a journey to the mundane.

> Daughter of Mt. Wu takes leave beyond the clouds
> Spring wind blows away pine blossoms on the hills.
> Her green parasol returns alone, crossing scented paths
> White horses and flower poles lead the way, magnificent.
> Shu River—light wind over a silky water
> Orchids are falling—who would sail by here?

On the south mountain, cinnamon tree dies for you
Cloud-robe taints flora of crimson rouge. (*LH*, 286)

Perceived from the perspective of the human, the goddess ascends to her mythical realm after revealing herself to the devotees. Moving through mountains not trespassed by mankind, the goddess changes the scenery as she moves. Her entourage is strikingly picturesque, and her contaminating force is vibrant: the tree dies for her in ecstasy. The magic force of the goddess points to a life-giving as well as death-commanding omnipotence, felt acutely in the dying of the cinnamon tree.[31] A vague sense of alienation is felt in the word "alone" and the strange, unpolluted landscape.

The gift of death is both sublime and diabolic, and if the goddess's presence is enough to create excessive responses from the natural world, her separation from them is also transparent. As the trees and flowers rejoice over her passage, we sense an inhuman might and a comfort too costly. Her touch of immortality lies heavy with the plants; like the Midas touch, it transforms things into blissful oblivion and at the same time seals the unbridgeable distance between herself and the mundane world.

Traveling between the world of humans and the divine mountains, with her poles hiding and revealing, the goddess's solitude is slowly conveyed, and although what holds the solitude is something sublime, its echo of as well as contrast to the boudoir sentiment, however faint, should not go unnoticed. The goddess of Mt. Wu, moving terrifyingly through space and time, is presented as shielding an eternal solitude within herself. Seen in this light, the unmitigated sense of lack as symbolized by the feminine finally finds its home in the changing signs of the supernatural feminine.

CODA: RETURN OF THE VOYEUR

Echoing the dissemination of desires in the narrative, poetry composed in the late Tang, following the lead of Li He, acquired a sharpened aesthetic consciousness that submits to an immersion in the poetic present perceived as sensuality. With an indulgence in the extravagant surface of the poetic language, asserting with aggressiveness the value of eroticism per se, Wen Tingyun, chief among poets of the era, followed the example of Li He in shifting the focus from depictions of sentiments to an elaborate description of sensuous details with an emphatic touch of voyeurism.

With the reputation of a hedonist loafer, topped with his reputedly homely physiognomy, Wen writes with ease some of the most picturesque and dainty poems and holds a significant position in the transition between poetry and song lyrics.[32] For a number of modern critics, Wen's achievement in the lyrics supersedes that of his poetry, and his compositions, together with the collection *Huajian ji* (Among the flowers), constitute an important corpus in the genre. The sentiment of the lyric below, "Pusaman," both harks back to the Southern Dynasties palace poetry with its subtle eroticism and anticipates later lyrics characterized by a delicate evanescence.

> Double hill-brows, dark gold forehead
> Hair clouds fall across her scented cheeks of snow.
> Lazily she rises up and paints her moth-eyebrows
> Putting on rouge, she prepares herself languidly.
> Glancing at the flowers in the front and the back mirrors
> The flowers and her fair face light up each other.
> Newly stitched on embroidered silk gown:
> Two by two, golden partridges.[33]

A gaze is fixed on a woman doing her morning toilet; the modal words "lazy" and "languid," together with the image of the harmonious pair of partridges (a stock conceit delivering a latent sense of bereavement), suggest the embedded lament mode. A subtly suggested loneliness pervades the woman, while the sensual details reflect an obsession with her body exposed under a voyeuristic gaze. With economy, the poem presents a woman alone. Composed of a mere aesthetic surface registering stock sentiments, what directs our attention here is the text's rendition by singers in the entertainment parlors. Although many of the laments and quatrains were sung at the entertainers' quarters, the song lyrics, composed according to set tunes, were written with their rendition into songs in mind. With all its convoluted consciousness and usurping sentiment, the lament is eventually put in a woman's mouth. The problems of androgyny and confusion of voices are resolved in this technical reality, and the process of transference is complete.

The personification of the feminine practiced in the lament is complicated by this performative rendition. The usurped female voice will now be given back to, or rather, imposed upon a woman presenting it as her own. The double delivery of female anguish, first by the lyricist and then by the singer, hinges on the culturally constructed figure of a woman in mourning. What the singers will be singing, then, is something sculpted by male desires, and once put into their mouths, the fabricated feminine sentiment acquires seeming authenticity. Of course, the singer could always adopt an ironic gesture and present the lyric as her comment on the received conception of feminine existence, thereby distancing herself from the enfeebled female persona. But when entertainers were but exchangeable commodities, such a critical position was unlikely to have been entertained.

The problem of the complex network between the voices of the poet, the persona, and the singer should be dealt with in an extended study of the song lyrics. For our purpose here, it leads to a series of questions essential for our discussions of Tang women poets, many of them versatile courtesans, and probes for the condition and presupposed bylaws under which women composed their verses. How do women's definitions of their sexuality differ from male canons, and how is that difference reverberated in the ways they endured their predestined positions? When the impersonated women begin to speak for themselves, do they speak as subjects, or as mere mimicking objects, the sculpted icons of the Other? These questions should be studied together with the problem of the usurpation of feminine voice and its effects on reading: in other words, do we read differently with the knowledge of the author's gender? When both are expressing amorous thoughts, what sets of codes and reading habits differentiate the male voice from the female? We return to these questions in part 4.

Chapter 11

Literati in Love:

The Case of Li Shangyin

Story of the Literati

Since they did not believe that the weaker sex could express themselves well with words, through their collective effort, the literati invented a mode of mourning in female persona. In this mode, women, every single one of them, are devoted lovers frozen in perpetual waiting in their chambers saturated with scent. The literati had cast this mask for so long and so well, when women ventured to pick up the brush with a sudden urge to write, they inadvertently took up this mask modeled for them. Because of this persona, amorous sorrow had acquired a feminine name, and when men were driven to express their own pains, they realized that it had become impossible, for people would take their lament, which held up their misery like a holy vessel, to be that of a mourning woman. Thus the literati were deprived of their own expressions of the sorrow of love, and the feminine mask grew deep into their faces.

However, they took comfort in having this mask of the weak, so that when they wished to cry, they could hide behind the mask and cry from its two eyes shamelessly, and people would say: "See how he cries, see how jade-white the tears are—he has truly learned the art of feminine sorrow."

The complex problem of boudoir lament and its confusion with political allegory is best exemplified in the figure of Li Shangyin, arguably the most refined and difficult poet in the Chinese lyrical tradition. Li suffered repeated political failures; through his own indiscretion, he was sacrificed in an intense factional agon between his powerful father-in-law and his patron. Topical interpretations of his works were developed in the Qing Dynasty (1644–1911), when commentators vehemently read his political life into his enigmatic works, and as a consequence, his image as a poet was soured to a regrettable degree.[1] The sexualized metaphors for the lord-minister relationship, which constitute the critical basis of allegorical reading, return with a vengeance in Li, as this interpretive strain comes full circle and threatens to undermine the poet's subjectivity. With Li, a foremost poet on the theme of eros, the destructive force of this hermeneutic tradition is fully delivered.

Li Shangyin's poetry embodies a sharpened focus of the aesthetic of *qing,* which becomes the shaping force for later song lyrics. The concept of *qing* (feeling, sentiment, affection, passion), specific to Chinese sensibility, differs from the word *love,* for it embodies a whole spectrum of emotions, at the center of which is a cosmic empathy.[2] Similar to the concept of *se,* which draws a vague and much larger contour around the central act of sex, *qing* tends to be an "oozing" emotion, a quietly overflowing sentiment. This notion of *qing* is so specific to the Chinese way of loving, indeed, that when the word *love* is used in the context of Li's poetry, one hastens to qualify it with care.

For Li Shangyin, *qing* is inherently marked by an ontological vision, and an inverted empathy, working through a process of transference, can be qualified as Li's poetics. The mutual exchange of sympathy among natural beings, the shedding of tears by the orioles, reverberates movingly in Li's lyrics and serves as the registers of the intense feelings of the self. His "love" poems, derivative of boudoir laments, reveal the necessary fact that the persistent impersonation of the feminine voice has fashioned eros or *qing* into a permanent feminine cast, to the extent that when a man expresses his amorous feelings, he has to resort to the lament mode. The confusion of voices we experienced in Li Bo's series now reaches another height when, through a sustained cultural practice, the masculine self has lost its own amorous expression.

The problematics of Li Shangyin's love poems are threefold. In the first place, with the substitution function of lament, the reader's tendency is to take Li's romantic verses as a woman's lament. The gender confusion Li's commentators read into his verses is disturbing, and it exposes the urgency of the problems of the politics of cross-dressing. Second, Li's hermetic and infamously enigmatic works are couched conveniently in political interpretations. His traumatic relationships with his patron and his powerful father-in-law are utilized to legitimize such allegorical readings. Finally, the feminine mode of Li's love poems points to the question of androgyny, which lurks underneath the very construct of the lament and begs for careful extrapolation. The poet's negative capability supported by a formulaic mode notwithstanding, it is essentially an androgynous capacity, working hand in hand with a profound empathy, that enables him to write persuasively as a woman. While in various versions of lament the feminine persona points to a playfully androgynous voyeur, in Li's verse, the masculine self moves dangerously close to an identification with the woman it tries to capture in its amorous imagination.

Western feminists have argued that gender traits beyond biological endowments are socially constructed, and various qualities are arbitrarily attributed to genders to maintain sexual stratification. Feminist theory tries to move beyond the binary opposition of the masculine and the feminine by proposing an androgynous existence, thereby transcending the preconceived conceptions of genders. For French feminists who are concerned with establishing a theory of *écriture féminine,* androgyny comes to characterize the styles of women writers who encompass "another bisexuality" that transgresses gender confines.[3] By claiming this bisexuality, the repression of the feminine and, more importantly, that of human consciousness, it is hoped, will be expelled.

Evidence in sociocultural discourse shows that traditionally, androgyny is programmed to further empower men, whereas androgyny in women is deemed dangerous.[4] Similarly, in the convention of boudoir lament, by impersonating woman, the poet finds a channel for his own drive; through pitying the weaker sex, his strength is confirmed. As the alternative to being abandoned, he stands safely as one who pities—such is his self-definition.[5] Thus androgyny not only makes man larger than woman, it also makes him, through careful control of the linguistic surface and the programmed movement of desires, larger than himself. It is precisely these long-standing conceits that make the feminist countermove of claiming androgyny for women essential, when androgyny no longer means the usurpation of and imposition on the Other, but a brave adventure into the uncharted realm of the self.

While it is futile to decipher whether women and men experience the anguish of love differently, literary conventions and cultural censorship clearly dictate a gendered division.[6] Through supervised practices, men and women learn their self-presentations by following prescribed formulas, deviating thus from the natural bent of their emotional needs. It is particularly enlightening to discern the truth of the insinuating fabrication of the feminine persona that spread out across epochs like an epidemic. The modern understanding that life imitates fiction is unmistakably affirmed in this phenomenon, when the act of writing, as well as the expectation and perception of human behavior, are imperceptibly shaped by this fictional posture.

In some telling moments, the very ambiguity of the lyrical voice exposes the dubious nature of this practice. As the feminine trope is used strategically in poetic writings, a certain degree of androgyny is assumed for the impersonation to be convincing. In the case of Li Shangyin, the function of androgyny is seen in the coexistence of dual voices marked by an urgent meaning, emanating a confusion of identities that is unique. As if suffering from an inner split, or more precisely, multiplied points of view that lead to a murky field of vision, the self is caught in a deranged expression of intense emotions. Two sets of voices lash out simultaneously, and the result is a vague, indiscernible sound of anguish.

Below is the most renowned of all the untitled poems on amorous pain by Li:

> Difficult when together, difficult still to part
> East wind failing, all the flowers fade.
> Spring, silkworm spins its silk till death
> Tears flow until all the candles are burned to ashes.
> In the morning mirror, sad at the changing temples,
> Citing at night, the cold moon sets upon you.
> The road to Mt. Peng is not long—
> Bluebird, quick, go seek her out for me[7]

In his typical approach of turning sorrow into a poetic epiphany and thereby conveying the meaning of *qing* afresh, Li imbues the sense of transience with an ultimate rupture between human and divine worlds. The will to reach Mt. Peng, the mythical dwelling of immortals in the Taoist cult, defies in a nutshell human ephemerality. The anxiety over love is quickly exalted to an urge for transcendence, projected through the messenger of a legendary bluebird. As if by an act of defiance, the frustration of love is transported to a higher realm.

To interpret the allusion of Mt. Peng as alluding to the lover's Taoist priestess identity, or simply as conflating her unattainable beauty with immortals, would betray Li's intense imagination. The forceful description of the detrimental force of love in the images of burning candle and silkworm leaps abruptly to the pathetic will to transcend human destiny. In the end, one cannot talk about love without bringing to the fore the truth of human existence as transient. The anxiety over changing temples is intermingled with the lovers' sorrow—in the shadow of death, love quivers and is all the more quickened. With this we have moved away from the lament mode, which in general stops short of probing the ontological basis of love, and entered a new aesthetic intensity that will become the principle for later song lyrics.

The residue of boudoir lament in this poem should not be overlooked: with the imagery of mirror and temples clouded with hair, and the imagined female sentiment, its genealogy is evident. However, a fusion of perspectives rather than impersonation works as the controlling principle here. What sets the text further apart from the lament is the expression of sorrow that exceeds the intensity of stylized feminine mourning. Li Shangyin's extensive compositions on eros, together with his intense sentiments, have dangerously removed the safety barricade of the mannered difference between the ways woman and man mourn for love's defeat. The subtle nuance we examined between the genders' expressions in Li Bo's series breaks down with Li Shangyin, bringing a sea change to Chinese lyrical expression.

If the "Untitled" manages to retain an amorous voice not necessarily cast in feminine terms, "Yantai" (The terrace of Yan), a much more difficult piece, presents a radical confusion of genders.

> The winged visitor of honeycombs is of a feminine heart
> Flirting with all wanton leaves and loose twigs . . .
> In sorrow, an iron net is cast to enmesh the corals
> The sea is wide, heaven vast—all the clues are lost . . .
> Heaven does not recognize a faithful heart—
> A celestial prison should lock up all the wronged souls.
> Lined gown put away in the chest, light silk reappear
> Scented skin sets off cold, tinkling pendants. (Spring)[8]

Shrouded in deliberate ambiguity, concealing all telling circumstances, the poem defies interpretation. The bitter contrast between a honeybee familiar with all the flirtatious flowers and a faithful soul lost in expanded space is acute. A sharpened sorrow is brought out by the image of the iron net as a desperate effort to catch whatever has been lost, and the wish to guard all the wronged souls alludes to an exasperating discontent. From these shocking emotions the poem turns to a quiet couplet of changing seasons and the image of pendants, alluding to the absent woman.

The ambiguity is created by concealing the identity of the voice(s) and by alternating between the lovers' viewpoints, causing the various commentaries to find absolutely no agreement on the lyrical self's identity. The tone of yearning goes beyond the decorum of the lament, and more than "Untitled," it puts on the front line the enigma of sexual difference. For lack of a proper channel, the masculine self wanders in the labyrinth of lament, shielding its passion in deliberate ambiguity. Witness the third poem in the series:

> Mica screen stands still, sheltering lonely knit brows
> At the west chamber, wind chimes blown hard all night.
> To weave garland of love for one far away:
> All day long, yearning yet resenting.
> One can only hear the Dipper turning away
> Unseen, Milky Way's water runs clear.
> A goldfish locks up the red cassia
> Ancient dust fills cushion of mandarin ducks . . .
> Startled by night frost, a parrot on the curtain-hook
> Woke up southern clouds over the Cloud-Dream Marshes.
> A pair of tinkling earrings attached to white silk
> Records River Xiang of our first encounter.
> Singing lips are forever seen through rains
> Alas, fragrance dies from the hands. (Autumn)

The mourning continues into the fall, when the moon takes center stage. Again, the knit brows and the weaving of garlands identify the woman, while the parrot, a boudoir pet, disturbs her amorous dream. The goldfish lock sunders spring/eros, and on the bedding of love dust prevails. The last couplet identifies the woman as a singing girl and can be read from two perspectives. Closer to the previous couplet, it may denote the woman reading the letter through tears, while the scent fades in her hands; in a more conclusive note, the self realizes that it will always remember her through tears, when the fragrance fades with time.

Preoccupied with absence and change, the poem follows its own logic, laden with mythical barriers and markers of time. The transformation of metaphors also prevails: the turning of the Dipper is heard rather than seen—through a function of synaesthesia, the norm of perception is shifted. This move is endorsed by a series of crossings of spatial and temporal barriers, and a final projection into the future. Yet what controls the crossing here are the interchanged voices of the lovers. When even a letter attached with a feminine object could not point with certainty to the gender of the voice, when with a feminine synecdoche (singing lips) the lyrical subject still cannot be identified due to syntactic ambiguity, the boundary between masculine and feminine selves has also been transgressed.

What problematizes the poem's otherwise rather unlikely identity as a boudoir lament is its sustained intensity, even violence, of anguish over an absence. The interchange of two voices is so complex that it is futile to try to differentiate them. Ultimately we have to accept the fusion of the lovers' voices, with the lyrical self speaking both for and as the lover and as himself. It is no longer probable to decipher whether the self is lamenting, or pretending to lament like a woman, for a profound empathy has united the two in a wrenching union.

This group of four poems, arguably the most intricate of Li Shangyin's corpus, has a singular intertext in his lyrical series "Liuzhi" (Willow twig), whose preface recounts how Li's neighbor Liuzhi, an eccentric maiden, overheard his cousin reciting "The Terrace of Yan" and, surprised by its beauty, tried to arrange a rendezvous with the young poet.[9] Liuzhi's urgent questions—"Who has such sentiments? Who wrote these lines?"—show the poetic power of stirring a woman to desire the poet behind it. With this, the situation becomes intriguing: the maiden is excited by a poem intricate with feminine sentiments. The circularity of the reception of lament by women readers, such readership, and its self-referentiality are important problems that are dealt with in the next chapter. Suffice it to say here that the personification of the feminine voice seems to strike home in a woman reader who, like Liuzhi, is susceptible to its saturating force. The transport of the literati-feminine into women's consciousness, then, is conceivably a smooth task.

The maiden reader's enthusiasm could also be directed at the unusual passion of the lyrical self, which releases an extraordinary sentiment of the masculine eros. If such is the case, we may interpret Liuzhi's response as a female desire that finally finds its satisfaction in a genuine, full-fledged expression of romantic sentiment by a man. Hence Liuzhi's urgent tone of questioning. For lack of documentation, we cannot conjecture what dynastic women expected from male expressions of love, or if they had been discontent with the poets' faltering utterances. Without the leeway to offer a counterdiscourse that would balance the insipid literati-feminine, women might be forced to accept whatever was presented. Yet again, it is a mistake to underestimate anyone whose opinions and power, out of a historical injustice, were gravely deprived of them.

We need to consider the problematic of making the feminine the emblematic vehicle of mourning. Has such practice given mourning a feminine accent, or is mourning a "feminine" sentiment in itself? In the Chinese context, the lament mode is such a convoluted convention that a self in amorous mourning automatically triggers the image of a woman craving for an absent lover, or an effeminate minister whining over an ill falling out. The latter is precisely the obsession of Li Shangyin's commentators since the Qing, and their readings of "The Terrace of Yan," its title an allusion to a life as the secretary of high officials, transform it into a political allegory. The glosses on the "Untitled" also transform it into a self-humiliating plea for recommendation into the Bureau of Literature.[10] Similar readings of Li's other works render a plaintive love poem a self-degrading exercise, a humble request for the restoration of favor. For instance, Zhang Caitian reads a group of four untitled poems by Li as the expressions of an old maid's forlorn state, and his elusive patron as the exalted lover.[11] The intense amorous agony, when transformed into a confessional plea to a prominent patron, becomes self-abasing and is offensive to modern sensibility, and such readings paint a rather dark picture of Li's image as a poet. When a poet could not express himself without being subjected to such extraliterary curiosity, when it was generally accepted that a man should plead through humiliating decorum, the cultural implications of the lament mode strike home somberly.

It is through Li Shangyin that we understand best the damaging consequence of the coinage of the female persona and its allegorical reading. With the entrenched lament, literati were deprived of the expression of amorous frustrations in their own terms. In other words, because of the lyrical convention and, perhaps more importantly, because of the social stratification between genders *and* among women, it was difficult and in all likelihood inhibited for literati to speak about love as we know it today. When women were either respectable wives or sensuous objects of desire, when they were cast in an enveloping silence, and when by a collective conceit women were cast into petrified figures of mourning, Tang literati resorted to a deviate way of venting their unfocused passions.

The particular roundabout way of their romantic expressions presents a mind either unable to love or unable to express that love with straightforward honesty. In juxtaposition to the narrative replete with affairs with the supernatural feminine, and in direct contrast to the blunt utterance of love in folk tradition, literati's aversion from or disguise of their private emotions is culturally indicative. The inability to express one's most private feelings further suggests a repressed psyche truncated by social and self censorship and is, in truth, psychologically gruesome.

The convention of lament gained autonomy as it developed with intertextual variations; with each text falling back on and commenting on previous texts, the lament acquired a meaning to itself and grew on itself. Just as poets writing on Jinling could not discard the literary Jinling created by the lyrical imagination, poets composing a lament could neither remove nor ignore the giant shadow of this convention and the enormous body of works it had produced.[12] The sorrow of love experienced in reality then became confused with, if not replaced by, the lament expressed in literature, and the lyrical convention gained momentum until it reached a rebellious point with Li Shangyin. Then, it became clear that after lamenting for centuries in female persona, man's capacities and needs for amorous mourning were seriously denied him, and the mask of feminine mourning, with all its innocence and gentle submission, grew vindictive.

Part Four

Resurrected Voices

Chapter 12

The Shaping of Female Tradition

The Woman Who Ate Books

A woman dreamed that she was eating crispy pages from a torn book. Night after night she tried hard to swallow papers written over with black calligraphy, papers brittle and yellowish from time. In dreams she continued to engage in this act of difficult consumption and hence was not able to enjoy a good night's sleep. Sometimes her aged father would hear her conversing in her dreams with dead masters on esoteric subjects such as those dark religious cults and metaphysics. It turned out that she was to become extremely learned and brilliant in composing rhymed prose; by day she would be studying the most difficult classics, and by night deep in debate with famous men of antiquity. She continued to have dreams of eating books every night, until she was no longer able to consume real foods prepared by the servants.

No men had such demanding dreams, for their dreams were short and quick, and their books were transformed into pearls or many-colored brushes. The woman realized her unique destiny through these dreams, and finally she gave up fighting. Her body became thin and transparent, filled with the strange taste of dusty papers and dried ink, and perfumed words came out of her mouth beyond her control. People came from all over the empire to observe her lantern-body, to hear her fragrant speech that rose high above their foreheads. Thus she continued to produce texts that few understood and was eventually summoned to the emperor's court to heed an audience.

The Son of Heaven saw a woman with sorrowful countenance and hollowed eyes of strange colors, her transparent body filled with masculine calligraphy and unfathomable scripts that piled up like those great ruins. The emperor leaned toward the woman and asked: "How is it with your dreams of eating the books?" The woman cast down her eyes and answered: "I am now on the last chapter of the *Classic of Apparition,*" a book lost to time and of which people had little knowledge. The emperor said: "I sometimes swallow in dreams ashes of the classics—they taste burned." The woman smiled imperceptibly: "Mine are tasteless—sometimes the pages cut my throat as I try to swallow them." The whole time the emperor was gazing at the woman's inside, trying to figure out the jumbled characters in oracle bone styles that posed as a mystery.

At the age of twenty-seven, the woman died. She had not eaten grains for three years, and she could no longer swallow any more of those books that had filled up every conceivable inch of her tormented body.

179

In *The Complete Collection of Tang Poets* compiled in the early Qing, women poets are positioned between Buddhist and Taoist adepts and anonymous poets, with the latter marking the end of this comprehensive anthology. Such an arrangement is well within our expectation, when both monks and women were socially marginalized. Often referred to by their fathers' or husbands' surnames, premodern Chinese women lived the collective existence of the anonymous, deprived of names that in the scholars' minds were essential for the establishment of the self.

Although modern readers may be disappointed by these female texts, whose artistic achievement is incompatible with the brilliance of their counterparts by male poets, there is something profoundly tragic in their simplicity and humble gestures that needs to be recognized. Reminiscent of the literati-feminine mode of the lament, these circumscribed writings should be understood as expressions tied in with a suppressed life. That the anthology was compiled by late imperial scholars upon royal order poses another problem in the forefront: the quality and quantity as well as the kinds of works by women that have withstood time are by and large predetermined by cultural prescriptions fraught with gender politics.[1] In reading these meager works in juxtaposition to the huge corpus by Tang men, one feels repugnant toward the tyrannic erasure of history. However one may be left unsatisfied with these texts, and however female self-representations seem to conform with the literati-feminine, our destiny—the destiny of these poets' female descendants—is to invite the texts to speak again, stripped of the masks imposed on them, subverting canonical decrees.

From a critical perspective, the subjectivity of a woman who writes is subject to scrutiny, since a woman writing is already a woman written by cultural definitions, and what she writes is prescribed by patriarchal norms. This apprehension is essential for our reading here, for the contrived images of the feminine prevail in women's own writings, honoring the logic of the lament mode. To expel the sense of frustration, strategic readings of prominent works and lives must be undertaken, with commentaries on their works discussed in conjunction with the texts. Other than exposing the critic-as-voyeur, this strategy is necessary when contextual anecdotes are often the only information we have concerning these poets. Through an erotics of editing, woman is made legendary, transported both by her words and the incredible anecdotes wrapped around them. Such a rendition makes the fetishistic reading of these women's lives equally present as that of the texts, until these intertexts shape the reception of one another. As a result, the verse is denied independence but is read as an oddity, a metonym that projects back to the woman whose life comes down in truncated fragments.

CONDITIONS OF THE FEMALE TRADITION

The Tang was the first era to witness a large number of female poets (including some professional ones) who wrote with stifled voices, bearing the stigma imprinted by their fathers. In the works of over one hundred women that come down to us,

an intimation of male desires (itself an appropriation of female
itself. The recurrent amorous anxiety attests not so much to a castrated imag
but rather to an obsession with the mourning feminine on the part of the editors.
The function of this erotics of editing weighs down these female texts, giving them
shapes that can only be regrettable distortions.

From the earliest collection of poems, *The Classics of Poetry,* women were associated with the theme of abandonment, which became a persistent theme that per-
meated Chinese verses. The writing on woman and abandonment is a complex issue,
for the coinage of the female persona in Han literati folk songs, *yuefu,* suggests that
anxiety over abandonment was as much a social reality as it was male posturing. Two
of the most famous poems on female abandonment, Zhuo Wenjun's "Baitou yin"
(Song of white hair), and Consort Ban's "Yuange xing" (Ballad of forlorn), have
questionable authorship, and modern scholars agree that these texts are male inventions pegged to historical women famous for their plight.[2] Strictly speaking, the Chinese female literary tradition suffers seriously from insinuating forgeries, for male
interventions have delineated its contours from an early stage.[3] As a consequence,
the lament mode and a dubious female tradition worked hand in hand, one to dictate, the other to coach as an internalized truth, signaling to women to recognize
themselves in the personified, ideal woman of amorous captivity. Under this condition, women of the Tang were to write within a strictured poetic tradition.

A psychological sanction further suppressed their writings, when woman and the
act of writing were cast into mutual alienation from each other. A late Tang anecdote tells of a woman who burned her poems under the judgment that "talents and
ideas do not befit woman"; another gives a forbidding warning with the story of a
talented woman who became a prostitute as a result of her transgressing conduct
and later hanged herself, leaving hundreds of poems behind.[4] By this time literary
authority, held first by low-ranking aristocratic (*shi*) in the Zhou, then by the imperial houses at the Six Dynasties and early Tang, had gradually shifted into the hands
of the literati who emerged as a new class. As the Tang weakened, a purification
of territory from female transgressors was in effect. The phenomenal success of
the palace official and poet Shangguan Waner in the early Tang, together with the
Song sisters of the middle Tang who wielded considerable influence among imperial ladies-in-waiting throughout the reigns of five emperors, was drastically contrasted by the late Tang sentiment embodied by these tales, which reflect the general decline of women's status.

While poetry composition was considered unwomanly, a peculiar relation
between woman and poetry was conjured up in the masculine imagination. Presented
in conjunction with these female texts are such curious anecdotes as the following. A
palace maid sewed a poem into a winter jacket sent to the frontier and was later given
to the soldier who received her poem-in-the-jacket. A poem written on a fallen leaf
drifted out of the forbidden city, and the man who picked it up was given the dismissed palace woman, poet of the leaf-poem, years later.[5] These wishful intertexts
provide an extraliterary interest that compensates for the otherwise meager texts, and

they display an acute fascination with the plight of palace women, pointing further to a latent association of women's verse with their bodies. The maidens' poems left the palace, their virtual prison, and reached the men, who received both their plaintive poems and the women themselves. Such ending is less a compassionate wish fulfillment and more a fetishism that fancies women's words as the manifestation of female desires and extension of their physical beings.

Encapsulated in these intertexts, in the erotics of editing, and conditioned by the lament mode, the majority of Tang women's poetry thus frustrates inquiring modern minds. It is hence to the more substantial corpus of the courtesans that we must turn. Writing from the ethical fringes, courtesans embodied a female psyche with telling intricacies. A large portion of our discussion focuses on two of the most recognized women poets of the Tang: Xue Tao of the middle Tang and Yu Xuanji of the late Tang, with their works and lives as integrated intertexts weighed against each other. Yu Xuanji, a deserted concubine turned Taoist priestess, succumbed to the role of courtesan through associations with famous men of her time. Xue Tao, an official courtesan of the Shu province, was under the patronage of local officials and socialized widely with the elite circle. Their extant works are gathered from various anthologies and suffer textual discrepancies. Since these works are a handicapped rendering of their poetic achievement, the degree to which they are fair representations of the women's complete corpus is hard to decipher.[6]

THE EATING OF BOOKS

From the numerous tombstone inscriptions written for gentry wives, one gathers the impression that Tang women of higher standing were prone to absorb themselves in diligent readings that went beyond ethical or religious texts. Song Ruozhao, second of the five versatile Song sisters and a respected scholar in the palace, was named the author of "Niu Su nü" (Niu Su's daughter), a biography of Niu Yingzhen, who was initiated into the classics through supernatural provisions.

> [Niu] wrote over hundreds of compositions. Later she exhausted the teachings of the three religions and was comprehensive in her scholarship. Every night in her sleep, she conversed with scholars who were renowned since antiquity. She answered and cross-examined them, calling them by the names of Wang Bi, Zheng Xuan, Wang Yan and Lu Ji, and the debates were sometimes heated and often lasted for several nights. The subjects were either literature or philosophy.
>
> She died at the age of twenty-four. At first, Yingzhen dreamed that she tore up books and ate them. After having dreamt of eating over dozens of books, her literary style was transformed, and this continued for a while until she became well-versed in rhymed prose and odes. Her literary collection was titled *Remained Fragrance*.[7]

In the *Taiping guangji* (Comprehensive collection of the strange), Niu's tale stands as a mystical account of a brilliant woman scholar. Among other tales of supernatural initiation into literature, this is the only one with a woman protagonist and is carefully detailed in comparison.

The cult of literary worship had induced various accounts of the obtaining of words through the wish-fulfillment machine of dreams. In one anecdote, Emperor Xizong dreamed of swallowing the ashes of *Qijing* (Classic of chess). Other tales recount the poet Jiang Yan who received and then lost a many-colored brush; a man who swallowed a pearl; another whose chest was cut open with a book placed inside.[8] Among these tales, Niu Yingzhen's dreams of eating torn books is unique, suggesting a woman's unconventional way of aspiring to possess words. It is through the slow process of internalization, through actually swallowing and digesting the words, the tale seems to suggest, that a woman becomes one with language from which she is exiled. This obsessive act is not readily seen in men, and of all initiating dreams, the act of eating the classics seems the most direct, hence the most difficult—a painful deliberation of labor. The verbs used in separate cases of these dreams: *shi* (eat) and *tun* (swallow) relate one, to the act of eating for survival, and the other, to hasty consumption. In addition, the ashes' difference from raw papers is comparable to that between raw and cooked food, rendering the eating of papers a more primitive act.

This biography of a woman of unusual dispositions first appeared in *Jiwen* (Records of hearsays) by Niu Su, father of Yingzhen, who was himself productive in tales of the strange. Due to its biographical character, the text can be read as a father's testimony of the short life of a talented and very likely obstinate daughter, bringing in the intriguing problem of the confusion of realities with fiction. The attachment of Song Ruozhao's name to the text takes us to another dimension. The most erudite of the five sisters, Ruozhao chose to stay single, dedicating herself to a literary career. While her sisters received Emperor Dezong's (779–805) sexual patronage, Ruozhao declined it. Impressed by her single-minded dedication, Emperor Muzong (820–824) offered her the highest post among palace officials, *shanggong,* in charge of literature with the royal members as her pupils.[9] It is hence not accidental that Song was named the author of this unusual biography of Niu, when she herself was an exceptional woman of letters in her own right. The self-conscious bonds between women and language, and among women themselves, are miraculously manifested in this tale.

This unique text suggests that, exiled from language, the only way for woman to acquire it is through radical transformation, through literally absorbing the words with the body. Inscription "within" the body is urgent precisely for the dispossessed, and the agon between women and language induces the desperate desire to devour the words. Niu's body remains an exotic site containing indigestible characters, which, in a metaphorical reading, induced her premature death. Compared with the dreams of sudden enlightenment, these lengthy, continuous dreams of acquiring the classics differentiate themselves as detrimental dreams of the willful feminine.

This physical and internalized relation with language is in direct juxtaposition to the fetishization of woman's words, which ignores the painful and deliberate process behind a woman writing. The conflation of woman with words is most blatant in two poems in the section "Fairies' Poems" in *The Complete Collection of Tang Poets,* which are attributed separately to a dream beauty and a woman singer on the painted screen.[10] The beauty who sang and danced in a man's dream left a poem in his sleeves upon his awakening, while the woman on the screen was summoned to sing by a Taoist adept. The confusion of woman and verse, or more precisely, of woman and illusion here, produces these tales in which the woman and the lyrics from her lips, equally fetishized, are identified, and the illusive dream beauty is transfigured into a tangible piece of paper inscribed with verse. By a strange conceit, the female body turns into icons of words.

Composition of verse is considered morally contaminating for women precisely because of this metonymical relation between the corporeal and written words. This fancy for woman's rhymes is prevalent in the general curiosity about courtesans' lives; when poems are considered metonyms of a woman poet, capricious readers are tempted to trace to the physical and psychic depth of the woman whose poetic charm promises further gratification. In the case of Yu Xuanji, her violent death and the legal dispute that preceded it have been heatedly debated. Buried in half-baked truths, Yu's life and death as equivocal texts form an important substratum of her prosody, while her translucent verse that brought her fame might have also brought her disastrous end. Possession of language for woman proved to be perilous, and the circulation of her verses exposed Yu to gazes that penetrated into unwelcome territories.

The eroticizing of women's words presents itself as symptomatic of the male psyche, and such eroticism is both anticipated and refuted by the unconscious in Niu Yingzhen's dreams. Commanding language through the painful act of eating, through slowly consuming it with the body, a woman remains physically bound to words. And as the laborious dreams suggest, there is nothing frivolous in the relation between woman and language, when a sense of despair, marked by the suicidal swallowing of congealed books, lies beneath the effort with which woman strives to obtain the words of the father that hasten to alienate her. The body, rather than an eroticized reserve of her words, is in fact the factory in which language is absorbed, purified, and transformed through an agonizing process.

In arguing for a metaphorical relationship between woman and words as presented in Niu's dreams, we also note the danger of placing woman in such kinetic relation with language, which enacts the priggish dualistic practice of associating the feminine with nature and irrationality. In this regard, the text has multilayered meanings that move beyond a facile, one-dimensional reading. In the last analysis, we have to accept the precarious condition of woman's existence and her alienation from language as the fabric of the unconscious that produced such dreams. Daughter of a writer obsessed with the fantastic, Niu Yingzhen might have left us with psychologically the most profound dreams of the collective feminine that, more than all the verses put together, expose the ambivalent bondage between woman and writing.

THE ANTI-SUN MYTH OF THE MOON

In the categorical correspondence upheld in the *Book of Changes* and further developed by the Han *yin-yang* school, the moon embodies the feminine principle. It is put under the same category with water, another metaphor for the feminine in Taoist terminology. In the Tang custom, juxtaposed to the eclipse of the sun, the eclipse of the moon was to be countered by women beating their bronze mirrors to chase away the Heavenly Hound said to be devouring the feminine moon, *yueyin.* Thus at the eclipse, women of the empire beat their mirrors hard in an effort to rescue the moon, symbol of feminine energy.[11] A more regular ritual was moon worship; at the rising crescent women exerted reverence to the Moon Goddess in their separate courtyards. Underlying the cult was an anxiety over waning youth, a comprehension that time, with its threat of impermanence, worked defiantly against them.

The Moon Goddess Chang E, a preferred poetic subject, received transformed meanings in the hands of Tang women. In traditional lyrical conceit, she embodies cosmic solitude, as two famous lines on her, penned by Li Shangyin, run thus: "Chang E regrets her stealing the elixir/An emerald sea, a blue heaven, hangs forever a lonely heart."[12] Such intense solitude coupled with a sense of regret have long been injected into Chang E, whose legendary husband Yi shot down nine of the ten scorching suns and brought the untamed heaven to a peaceable cycle of day and night, while Chang E stole his elixir and took flight to the moon.[13] In these (a)symmetrical myths, order was restored and a new territory conquered. An unmistakable dichotomy of masculinity versus femininity is thus fashioned. The shooting of the circling suns was the feat for a man of divine order, whereas the cool sphere of the moon and its changing forms came to be dominated by a capricious woman. In mythical beginnings, woman was compelled to exile herself to cultivate her sphere beyond patriarchal confines. Angered by this bold move, patriarchy condemned it as devious usurpation, and Chang E was punished with a sense of regret that erodes the glory of her eternity. To make her victory empty, a victory eaten away by a solitude the dimension of which stood beyond imagination, this punishment was delivered time and again by various male poets, writers, and critics who refused to see Chang E as other than repentant and solitary.

With our interpretation of Chang E's flight as a defiance against masculine order, the cult of moon worship receives transformed meaning. Underlying the ritual was an identification with Chang E, as Tang women envisioned her in very different ways, breaking away from the prison constructed for her in male consciousness. However, another captivity of consciousness was taking shape—below is an excerpt from a piece entitled "Bai xinyue" (Bow to the new moon):

Bow to the moon, grief overtakes me.
Flowers in the courtyard, dew crystallized in the wind.

The moon ascends as we grow old:
The ever renewed moon moves into the sky.

Grandmother of east door bows to the moon
Each bow with a mournful cry, her voices sundered . . .
Turning to behold others bow to the crescent
She remembers the red chamber, her days of youth.[14]

Identical in sentiment is the piece below by Chang Hao, identified as a courtesan in *Tangshi jishi* (Anecdotes of Tang poetry):

The fair one treasures her beauty
And fears that it should fade, chasing scented flowers.
At sunset she left the painted hall
Descended the stairs and bowed to the crescent.
If words were spoken to the crescent
How would others know?
Returning, she cast herself on jade pillow
And let tears—so white—hang down slow.[15]

These expressions of sorrow, in line with the lament mode, are much less mediated when women confront the moon coming to a renewed cycle. Face to face with their past, two socially stratified women—a gentry wife and a courtesan—mirror each other's dejection and that of others. An inexplicable sadness reverberates among these women, exhibiting a psyche with its habitual fragility.

The picture may indeed be haunting: in the courtyards across the empire, women of various backgrounds and ages bowed to a faint crescent, which had seen generations of women observing the time-honored ritual. Both poems describe professedly the agony of another: the objectivity to which the texts resort cautions us of the fact that female perspectives are inherently conditioned. When both their lives and lyrical creations were under masculine surveillance, women were prone to subject unconsciously other women under that same gaze, that same melancholy in which the boudoir woman was cast. The turning of others into tearful beings reveals for us how lyrical convention has imperceptibly shaped women's ways of seeing and provided them with a prescribed mode of (self-)representation. The trope of woman in mourning has gained such momentum that the real woman recedes, and in her place stands, as if a haunting apparition, the woman of sorrow.

The prevalent distress stirred by the moon should partially be construed by an absolute value attached to youthful beauty, when women were in principle sexualized objects, whatever else the ethics might demand. The Confucian emphasis on female virtues has always been under the shadow of the instinctive craving for sex and beauty, and women fell victim to such moral weakness. Although mourning over change, a prominent literary theme, is universal, the unusual intensity here comes from a female consciousness instilled by fear. This excessive anxiety over impermanence embodied by the changing moon is incongruous with what the Moon Goddess symbolizes, pointing thus to a collective fall from grace, as Chang E's earthly sisters were trapped in the conception of their physiognomy as their most valuable possession, forsaking the glorious height of the eternal promised by their mystical predecessor.

The distance between the daring Chang E who defected to claim her territory and her weakened progeny, then, appears to be radical. However, the burden of the fear over physical deterioration was counterbalanced by moments of consolation, when women found in Chang E sources of inspiration that transported them to a realm of permanence within change, shattering all corporeal limits. A piece by Xue Tao in a tri-set entitled "Trying on Clothes Newly Tailored" bears this out.

> From divine palace I received a red piece of silk:
> Vague is the mythical mist, away from the sea.
> The frosty hare's fur so cold, ice cocoon, so pure.
> Chang E laughs and points to the bridge across Milky Way.[16]

Through the image of a laughing Chang E dominating the heavenly bodies with stars underneath her fingertips, all clichés of her imprisonment in chilling immensity are dispersed. Solitude gives way to interactions with the planets under her command, while the frosty fur of the moon hare and the ice cocoon of many-colored silk weave a subtle texture of sensuality. Such intimate details, when juxtaposed to her laughter, unfold a triumphant goddess embodying transcendental *jouissance*.

The text reveals that woman, through her mythical communion with the goddess, is unintimidated in her imagination by the inhuman habitat of the moon. Xue Tao's freshly tailored robes of extravagance provoked in her a sense of union with the divine, and her portrayal of Chang E made her a secret sharer of the goddess's laughter. A Tang poet once imagined that in the inner palace of some divine king, his women regretted that Chang E had stolen the elixir of immortality ahead of them: "Had Chang E not stolen the numinous medicine/A struggle remains for eternity on the moon."[17] The moon and the elixir, then, had come to be affiliated with women, who would ascend the moon and dominate the night. The ritual of moon worship, when coded with mythical connotations, renders Chang E, in defiance of the patriarchal order, the prototype and ultimate precursor for the feminine.[18]

GAZE OF THE BRONZE MIRROR

The importance of the bronze mirror for Tang women can be seen in the practice of divination by mirror, *jingting,* which involves praying to the stove god, rubbing the mirror in a secluded place, and walking anxiously on the street with a mirror concealed beneath one's robe, listening to the chance-encountered first words and capturing the image of a distant husband.[19] The mirror that belonged to the bridal dowry now became the vessel through which the whereabouts of a drifting husband would be detected. The utterly helpless situation of women was exposed in this peculiar form of divination, and the mirror that reflected their changing visages to them was also the miraculous instrument that would cast an omen and bring back the wayward man.

The bond between woman and mirror is further contested in the tale of Yao Yuehua, who once dreamed that a moon fell on her bronze mirror and since then she became enlightened.[20] The mirror, the metonymical extension of a woman, received the moon from the sky, and metaphorically, the woman was also impregnated. In this episode, the moon and the mirror, two principal feminine objects, collide to form the mystical source of inspiration. The most intimate item in the boudoir and through which secret instructions were sought, the mirror presented a significant element in Tang women's daily existence.

The priestess-courtesan Li Ye, who preceded Xue Tao and Yu Xuanji and had received higher praise than both by past critics, is regrettably underrepresented by the small size of her oeuvre. Through her extant eighteen poems, the lofty temperament of a Taoist priestess who associated with the high monk Jiao Ran and the hermit Lu Yu (author of the famous *The Classic of Tea*) could be appropriated. Yet like other women poets, Li vacillated between a sense of pride and a profound self-degradation. At a late point in her career, Li Ye was summoned to the court owing to her literary reputation, upon which she composed the following.

> Talentless and ill, I resigned myself to age and decline.
> Unexpected, my overblown name reached the Son of Heaven.
> Abashed, I dust the cap to put on my white hair
> With shame I brush the mirror to paint on a faded face.
> Unleashing my heart from the palace gate, I will follow scented grass
> And exhaust my gaze toward the South Mountain, over old hilltops.[21]

Paradoxically, the diffidence over a weathered visage stands out in a poem in which a hermit's life is the professed intent of the self. In Tang women's lyrics, we encounter often a woman looking into her bronze mirror to meet the judgmental gaze of the Other: such a gaze is very much with Li Ye at this exciting moment of her life. For a religious woman no longer young, whose intent is to live in quietude, her reflection in the mirror forces her to face two sets of values: one of spiritual fulfillment, the other a tribunal of mundane lives. The self's insufficiency under the judgment of the second is received with remorse, a feeling not forthcoming in the exalted standard of the first. For lack of a better term, I call this a feminine symptom of inner split, which describes a self that rises up to meet a standard in direct contrast with its own principle and in spite of itself, a face that learns to examine itself in ways coached by the Other. The specificity of this feminine tribulation lies in the reality that the powers of the female self and masculine command are radically disproportionate. The fetishism with a woman poet's beauty dictates that the accomplished poet past her prime undertakes a humiliating self-examination.

In a similar fashion, Xue Tao looked at herself critically in this apology:

Languid, how could I bear to meet my lord?
Scattered flowers, frail beauty, resent the east wind so.
My heart yet thought that youth was with me
Blushed, I gaze at my disheveled hair in the stone mirror.[22]

These four lines spell out the trials of an official courtesan whose job was to entertain; Xue's face, something approaching a public possession, was not free to retrieve itself at will. In this apology for being sick/absent, Xue is sensitive to the necessity of appealing for her vulnerability, with the expense of this self-deprecation as a misshapen woman magnified in the huge stone mirror. By judging herself harshly from the viewpoint of a disappointed patron, Xue retreated from the humiliation of public gaze. Parenthetically, Xue Tao's poems underwent stylistic changes, and her mature works exhibit a markedly different attitude toward others as well as toward herself. One may suggest that her earlier compositions, possibly including this one, adopt more regularly the strategy of humility, the assigned position of the feminine.

Numerous women had looked into their mirrors and found the penetrating gaze of the masculine. The following shows an acute consciousness of such a plight, although the text and its context, taken from *Yunxi youyi* (Conversations from the cloud stream), a miscellaneous collection of anecdotes, have considerable textual problems.

About to touch down the brush
I grab the jeweled mirror to observe—
Already my countenance has been desolate
Lately my temples too have withered.
Tearful eyes are easy to sketch
Agonized mood yet hard to portray.
I fear that you have forsaken me—
Pray, unfold this portrait to behold.[23]

Like many other female texts, this one has a curious intertext. It recounts how one Nan Chucai, favored by a local magistrate who offered him his daughter's hand, sent for his zither and books and was on the point of abandoning his wife, Xue Yuan, upon which Xue took up her brush and produced the poem along with her self-portrait. The ubiquitous gaze of the patriarch here has a double function: it dominates not only the self's reaction to its reflection, but the way it renders itself in pigments. The purpose of the self-portrait predetermined, its production is closely supervised by a desire to appeal. The portrait will eventually be scrutinized by the betraying husband, and painting itself from a reflection, the self passes down twice the pending judgment of the Other. The "agonized mood" to which the pigments have difficulty doing justice is spelled out in the poem. A woman who came to her husband in a melancholic self-portrait and a mildly reproaching poem must have been difficult to swallow, and Nan returned promptly from the tempting path of betrayal, as we are told.

This anecdote has the familiar tinge of most tales with the abandonment motif, in which women resort to various expediencies to fight against their pending abandonment. As the folk song sings of Xue's portrait, "But for her pigments of red and blue/She would be left alone in an empty room," women rely dangerously on language, or in this case pigments, to change the course of their fate. In this sense language acquires a very different meaning, when it (as in the case of the leaf-poem) traverses through space as the deputy for one confined. Words as the physical extension of a woman, then, become vital; her bridge to the outside world, in more urgent moments they also become her feet and tongue and the only means to save herself.[24]

Did a medieval woman actually paint such a portrait and compose the poem to rescue herself? Given the precise information of all characters involved, the poem acquires a certain credibility, although like other texts of similar plots, its fictionality should be entertained. In any event, Xue Yuan's poem further exposes the hovering gaze of the masculine, powerful not only in its penetration, but also in its retrieval, which could mean a far more terrible fate for the object of that gaze, whose condition of being is defined by it. The self-portrait is an invitation to that vital gaze, just as Xue Tao's poem is a plea for its temporary suspension. In their cold bronze mirrors, Tang women repeatedly encountered or restructured the gaze of the patriarch, who stared out with forbidding eyes to pass down quiet commands.

In the end, nothing prepares us for these texts of such self-conscious humility. The mirroring diction of self-abasement entails not only an accepted decorum of feminine speech, but also a perceived image of the feminine as utterly vulnerable. Here the dividing line between the courtesans and the lawful wives is obliterated, when both are subject to the patriarchs' changing wills. After all, women did write differently from the literati-feminine, in the sense that they had been made absolutely humble. The textual problem of Xue Yuan's poem exposes further the intrinsic problematics of the female tradition, when texts composed either by or for women echo each other, until it is impossible to tell one from the other. Consequently, female consciousness embodied in writings is so much impregnated by masculine ideologies that its truth is dreadfully blurred.

* * *

In the context of Xue Yuan's painting and the importance of words as an instrument for self-preservation, embroidery as a prominent domestic skill among dynastic women should be considered. In traditional China until the very recent period,

Textile with phoenix pattern by Tang women.

weaving was the principal form of female labor that consumed the lives of numerous women; the weaving machine with its many crude wooden stalks stood like a miniature factory in the household, exacting female energy by day and by night. Together with weaving, the practice of embroidery, a quintessential feminine art, was mandatory in female education; it was also the art form through which women with no other means for self-expression achieved the highest perceivable accomplishment.[25] Since it was essential for women to perfect this skill, another important female ritual at the Tang was the annual prayer to the Weaver Girl at the seventh day of the Seventh Month for better embroidery techniques.[26]

In a funeral inscription, Liu Zongyuan recounts a young girl named Ma Leiwu's impressive talent: "Leiwu was born with extremely rare artistry, and all her embroideries are otherworldly—when I saw them I was absolutely at awe." The girl, before her death at the age of fifteen, had requested: "I heard that his lord Liu used to praise my craft and my intelligence, now, gravely I am to die, how could I have his lord write my tombstone inscription?"[27] A quiet pride of embroidery as her art could be felt in Ma's plea, and Liu, in recognition of this pride, consented to write an inscription unusual for a virgin.

While language played a fatal role for women, it was weaving and embroidery that occupied women's attentions and demanded much of their time. Although like paintings, it is another form of self-expression, from the scant records of embroidery as an art, it seems that this craft, accomplished by women in their separate chambers through measureless labors, had not established itself as a recognized channel for female creativity, and it was lost to history.

A COUNTER DIALECTIC

In a particular philosophical debate, the logic of issuing verdicts upon female appearance is refuted from the ground up. The biography of Niu Yingzhen cites one of Niu's rhymed prose pieces that centers on a debate between the self's ghost and its shadow, composed while Niu was seriously ill. The ghost *wangliang* accuses the shadow of letting itself deteriorate to such bony deformity without partaking of the self-regenerating cycle of nature and rejoicing in the arrival of spring. The shadow argues that, dependent on the contingency of light and darkness and the changing body, it could not be held accountable for its state of deterioration.

> I heard that the essence of the ultimate Tao is harmonious and unfathomable, and its extremity dark and silent. Men of virtue transcend the anxiety over the length of their lives, and gentlemen follow the changing destinies; neither regret nor plight could engulf them, nor could glory confuse them; a loss is not considered a loss, and a gain is not deemed a gain. Why then are you angry about my not enjoying the fragrant spring, or cherishing those glittering adornments? Besides, my principle and my virtues—how could they be within the reach of your wisdom? (*TPGJ*, 271.2135)

In the spirit of philosophical Taoism, the shadow argues eloquently that it remains unaffected by the deteriorating body; emulating those sages in harmony with their fate, it remains one with the cosmic movement.

This unusual text by Niu Yingzhen is a strong female text that not only over-turns the weight placed on appearances and adornments but claims that the (female) shadow's virtues are beyond common wisdom.[28] In a symbolic symmetry, we may identify the ghost and its spirituality as representing the masculine principle with its propensity to dictate, and the shadow as representing the feminine principle with its corporeal proximity to the body and its shining adornments. Their debate, then, symbolizes the struggle between a domineering patriarch bent on feminine charms, and an eloquent woman of her own mind, shattering thus all preconceived ideas of feminine values and giving precedence to what is essential. Developed from Zhuang Zi's renowned passage of a ghost chiding the self-tormenting form, Niu's text is a counterattack that allows the shadow, the form's extension, to manifest its unwavered intent. Transcending the judgmental gaze and patriarchal values, the shadow exorcises once and for all the ghost of feminine mourning over physical impermanence.

However, attributed to a woman claimed to have conversed with ancient schol-ars, the text's tone wears the expository veil of the masculine. One is invited to consider that when a woman speaks, not identified as one but conforming to and interacting with a master discourse, she has more freedom to break away from the feminine shackles of the lament. Yet the Taoist transcendence of physical existence might have been too conveniently applied by this text to make the argument truly pertain to female consciousness. Furthermore, with the exception of a few femi-nine references, the female identity is suspended in the text. The confidence that Niu was capable of bravely transcending prescriptive values, however dearly sought for, must be qualified by this paradoxical situation.

With this, we arrive at the difficult problem of *écriture féminine*. As an insightful coinage of the feminist dilemma puts it: when all discourses are male discourses, how can we claim an unadulterated female discourse?[29] How is it possible to speak as a woman, especially in the context of a towering state and a truncated female tradition? Niu Yingzhen's text, like her dreams, poses complicated problems for us, and ultimately we need to answer the critique on essentialism: strictly speaking, no differences between genders are not socially constructed. The effort to locate a fem-ininity against masculinity, namely, to define what constitutes woman's subjectiv-ity or what delineates her voice, then, is essentially futile.

Our discontent with this strong female text forces us to think hard about female tradition, when on the one hand a fabricated female voice shapes the normative mode, and on the other hand woman either approximates a voice fashioned by the literati-feminine or mimics the masculine mode of speech and simply approximates man. At either axis, we reach a dead end. One thing remains certain: Niu's text, however entrenched in male discourse, sheds light on the possibility of escaping the position of the prescribed weak feminine, *ruoyin*. That it was when her health was deteriorating that Niu wrote this piece unique in the female repertoire, and that she spoke with pride and defiance, shattering all clichés of the humble feminine, is enough to demonstrate that having absorbed the words of the father, a woman was capable of speaking with precision and strength. The existence of the text, despite its textual problems and its proximity to masculine discourse, is miraculous, and one wonders whether, if not for the erotics of editing, a drastically different female tradition would have emerged to chastise the impression of a collective state of feminine paralysis.

LA FEMME ÉCRITURE

The concern for their female neighbors among Tang women seemed persistent. Besides observing each other during rituals of moon worship, often they described in lingering details the charms and talents of other women. Yu Xuanji particularly was compelled to compose elegies for total strangers. This sense of communion was extended to their ill-fated female ancestors: the following piece, "Tongque tai" (The terrace of the bronze peacock), laments the fate of the Wei emperor Cao Cao's consorts confined at his preponderant mound.

> Singing fans unfolded towards his mound
> Sacrifices offered in jade cups.
> As they danced, swallows paraded in the sky
> In their dreams, a cloud quietly entered.
> Enchanting moonlight induced but remorse
> Sound of sweeping pines evermore embittering.
> Who would pity these undying consorts?
> Raising wet sleeves, they descended the bronze terrace. (*QTSG*, 71:145)

Composed by Liang Qiong, whose life is unknown to us, this unusually artistic poem conveys a pathos for consorts enclosed in a death-in-life sacrifice to an emperor's unappeased soul; its sense of immediacy presents an acute historical imagination. Obsession with abandoned women and exiled consorts was prevalent in Tang women poets, who convey a shared sense of fate in their dirges for the dead.

Female literary circles, a late Ming and Qing phenomenon, were not yet established in the Tang; exchanges between women seemed not all that uncommon nonetheless, and the following is a response by Yu Xuanji to three sisters' draped rhymes.

> In their chambers they watch the parrot in rhymes
> By the green screens they embroider phoenixes.
> Red fragrance fills the courtyard, they plucked at random

Green liquor to the brim, they drink in turns . . .
As long as they could make rain to their hearts' content
The affair with the flutist would not matter.
Their mother chides them for conversing beneath the blossoms
The handsome Pan An once entered their dreams.
Holding their slender lines my soul is about to break
Die content I would after seeing their fair faces.
Forlornly I gaze away—where are the fair ones?
The traveling clouds turn to the north, then to the south.[30]

Yu's composition follows closely the rhyme characters of the original. Such exact observation bespeaks a desire to bring herself to the sisters' presence; by repeating the rhyme words, Yu joined the lyrical play of the sisters and made her identity their double. The admiration for these strangers is excessively expressed in her desire to die in the blissful moment of witnessing their visages.

It should be noted that women poets often appreciated each other with the eroticizing impulse of the male gaze, and their depictions of other women often are not readily separated from those written by a literatus. Amorous yearnings as the controlling feminine sentiment surface toward the end of Yu's poem: fallen under the dictate of poetic conventions, the feminine gaze insists on exacting desires from women, and a subtle homoeroticism emerges. In a similar function, a sensuous poem attributed to Yang Yuhuan, "Zeng Zhang Yunrong wu" (For Zhang Yunrong's dance), renders the dancer objectified:

Silk sleeves transport the scent, endless
Red lotuses elegant in autumn mist.
Light clouds on the hills—wind stirs suddenly
Willows gently touch the water.

Writing (possibly through a ghost writer) to a dancer wonderful at the many-colored-robes dance with which she herself was well acquainted, Yang's narcissistic instinct to praise the other as a flattering reflection of the self is evident. This reminds one of the doubling of Yu's text, through which she approaches the sisters whose talents and beauty are apt reflections of her own.

Such homoeroticism reaches a climax in Jiang Yun's poem to a certain woman entertainer:

Slender fingers pluck on the zither
To break the hearts of youths at her door.
Her smile opens up a rouged face
In the east garden, peach blossoms die . . .
Lifting up her silk robe, fragrance fills the room
Blowing off the candle, alas, nights are far too short.[31]

The unabashed allusion to sex and the belief in the fatal power of feminine beauty move simultaneously toward a faintheartedness and an uncanny femininity bordering on the supernatural. Self-absorbed in her beauty, the woman is placed in a sensuous atmosphere that enhances her mysterious charm. At the same time lifting the woman into a supernatural realm and rendering her trapped in perpetual desires, the text demonstrates the unsteady (self-)presentation of woman.

Strictured by a handicapped existence, dynastic women created a shared sphere through composing verses to transcend physical confines.[32] The homoeroticism of Yu, if so named, is a spiritual one, and the lyrical union among these four women is an emblem of the special role verse played for the feminine. Lacking a collegiate environment, they resorted to building a community by observing the women next door, by mourning for deceased strangers and ancient women, and by continuing the rhymes of distant sisters. Thus women sought out each other through words that moved across time and space to bear witness to a truncated life, fragmentary words that are memories of their unfocused existence. And harking back on each others' words, women moved toward shaping a female tradition out of the great ruins of their deprived condition.

Below are a few couplets from the original by the three sisters; fragmented by their method of composition, they echo a general inertia.

Embroidered bed, fear of rousing the black dragon's cry
Embroidered words, bluebird carries away in sorrow (Pou)

Hate to have time thrown away by my window—
Laughing bitterly, I understood the world's lovers (Pou)

A fossil has a heart difficult to tame—
I am content to be the amorous clouds (Wei)[33]

From the casual rhyme character, "three," a series of words multiply themselves: shirt, hold, man, ashamed, whisper, hairpin, contained, dark, and meditation. It would be strenuous to argue that, guided by the principle of association maneuvered by the unconscious, these rhyme words have distinctive feminine connotations. It would be equally negligent to deny this proposition without giving the group of words due consideration. Suffice it to say that these rhyme characters, when put in context, convey a mental paralysis and a vacuity that characterize the large body of Tang women's poetry. Compared with Yu's imagination of their lively activities, the sisters' original verses are shadowed by a much darker mood. This discrepancy is telling; while Yu had made the image of the three sisters a mirror image of herself, erasing thus the inherent gap between women's different modes of being, the sisters' lives and their self-representations suffer possibly from yet another inner split.

With this, we return to the question of the authenticity of the female tradition. We need to consider here the variance between a woman's life and its rendition dictated by an internalized voice of the literati feminine. The self-representations of the sisters may simply be adopted personae echoing predominant lyrical modes, for as we have seen, the crowning of the feminine persona has made real women obsolete, until in their unconscious, in the deeply ossified lyrical mode, they become the other women, the women of ennui.

In a preface to a piece entitled "In Sorrow and in Anguish," Li Nongyu describes her happy life with her female companions while still a maiden, how they sojourned in lofty sites while time passed by unnoticed.[34] This unusual account tells us that communities among women were not unique, and in less suppressed regions, Tang women had enjoyed themselves beyond common perceptions. This collective *jouissance* among women, however, is disrupted in the poem that follows, which states the sorrow of a widow and returns all too quickly to the prescribed mode of feminine verse. The field of discourse as the machinery of power is undeniable, when the unique preface and the poem pose as two contradictory strains, offering opposed sentiments. While resorting to less clearly defined prose, Li reveals the rich layers of her life; while composing heavily coded verse, she picks up the voice molded for women and loses the complexity as well as the authenticity of an original life. Thus the celebration of a joyous maidenhood is replaced by the drifting existence of a widow, and the weight of a husband returns.

These intertexts and their problematics disclose for us the interaction between fiction and reality, reality and lyrical norm. If the lament creates a woman frail in flesh and mind, texts such as Yu's poem on the sisters, Xue Tao's image of Chang E, and Li Nongyu's preface create images of women beyond public sanctions. Literary discourse as the site of power struggles inscribes an urgent condition, for as the shaping instrument of consciousness, who has control over it has fatal consequences. The general female texts from the Tang expose the peculiar condition that women succumb to to speak as the Other, even as their own negative image, when their subjectivity is lost in silence and in a double mimicry: the mimicry of the mimicry of the feminine.

It is in this sense that a profoundly tragic sense is inherent in their works, when they place themselves under an erasure, and offer up the faithful mirror image of male desires. It is not accidental that the majority of these female texts are artistically meager, and a certain naiveté in terms of the poverty of style and diction is further reinstated by a weakened consciousness. As they speak from behind the masks fashioned for them, the void in language consigned to the feminine is exposed, for the mournful, monotonous mimicry shows the extent to which women are exiled from language. As they speak, they are not in possession of words, for it is from the vacuum of an emptied-out feminine self that they utter stifled sounds of anguish.

Our search for the shape of female tradition ends with this discovery of what has been gravely violated and wears the stigma of male consciousness.[35] Deeply truncated, like the fragmentary bodies of those chaste women, these female texts present more than anything else the effect of a total curfew on women's collective existence. We would be greatly misled to try to map out the lives of Tang women by reading these troubled texts, which are curiously unfaithful (self-)representations and, as discussed earlier, pose as a contradiction to other representations of Tang women. In the remaining space, we turn to Tang courtesans' works, for positioned at ethical peripheries, at some culminating moments, they have reinvented the feminine self and present their descendants with brave new texts.

Chapter 13

Against Boudoir Lament

Amid the general frenzy over embellished words, Tang courtesans, adopting the lyrical modes together with the aesthetics and lifestyles of the rising literati, shared with the socially marginalized Taoist and Buddhist adepts a process of "literatization."[1] Well-versed in the art of conversations, these courtesans, many of them intelligent women of letters, were counterparts to the growing literati, just as the palace officials counterbalanced the large body of court ministers. But of course, these counterparts were marked by a gross imbalance, and the courtesans' effort at approaching the elite, as we have seen, was often self-destructive.

Unlike gentry women whose relation to language was defined by a negativity, the courtesans' profession exacted much more complex demands on their association with words. When a woman, whose position in relation to language was both metonymical and subordinate, was exchanged together with the words and as part of the words, what she might have written underwent a similar function of objectification, when it was read among the patrons with acute fetishism, reducing both the verse and the poet to obscure objects of pleasure.

A female voice that had unlearned the literati-feminine mask, that denied the pleasure of the inquisitive voyeur, then, must rise up to break away from this general passivity that had entrapped women poets. If the literati were wont to translate the courtesans' words into flesh, our readings that try to approach their minds mark a countermove that is essential: for in truth, the mind was precisely what was denied to these women of letters.

POLITICAL ALLEGORY OF THE FEMININE

At a low point in her career, Xue Tao was exiled to the frontiers for having offended General Wei, her foremost mentor. Several poems were produced to plead her case, and the humility of the tone conveys the plight of a further marginalized courtesan. The couplet "Abashed, I sing songs of the sensuous banquets/To soldiers at the frontiers" shows that the difficulty lies not in the alienating locale, but in the awkward slippage of her identity, which enlightened Xue to the specificity of her role as a courtesan. Placed in the harsh environment of the military, the assailable truth of her role as one designed to please in a more compromised climate was embarrassingly exposed.

Below are two of Xue's couplets composed at this time:

A firefly at the wilderness, a moon over the sky
How could a firefly reach the moon-disk's brim?

If only your child is allowed to return
I vow never to gaze at the painted screens.[2]

The extremity of Xue's marginalization is evident: the lofty moon, symbol of the privileged official, pits the firefly to utter obscurity. The self-reference "your child," *er,* although not uncommon for dynastic women, is unique in courtesans' writings and marks further degradation from the standard female self-reference, *qie* (concubine), indicating thus thorough submission.[3] Such diction well suits the image of a courtesan whose value was no higher than that of a horse or a poem; yet as we shall see, even in self-degrading pieces, Xue did not stay long within the confines of humility.

The series of "Shili shi" (Ten partings) attributed to Xue Tao has long been a text of dispute; critical scholars question its authenticity, whereas others doggedly look for proofs for its authorship.[4] Judging from its forced parallel and increasingly strained metaphors, most probably it was composed by a literatus who harbored an obsessive fascination with the theme of abandonment. The ideologies behind the critics' judgment intersect with predefined concepts and point to a complex network of gender politics. To understand fully the peculiar rationale of the series, we set them against the exegesis of the literati's lament as political allegory to examine the courtesan's version of abandonment.

"Quan li zhu" (A dog parted from the master)
    Tamed inside the red gate for years
    Cherished for its fragrant fur and dainty feet.
    By chance it bit an intimate guest
    And is forever exiled from the red silk carpet.

"Yingwu li long" (A parrot parted from the cage)
    West of the desert, one solitary figure
    Flying adrift, perching atop the brocade bedding.
    All because of her inconvenient words
    Now she no longer calls out from the cage.

"Zhu li zhang" (A pearl parted from the palm)
    Bright and round, translucent to the core

Brilliant as the crystal palace's light.
Simply for one fleck of dirt
No longer held through the night in his palm.

"Ying li gou" (A falcon parted from the gauntlet)
 Talons sharp as knife, eyes bulge like rings
 Catching hares on the plains to please a high mind.
 Suddenly it bolts beyond the huge blue clouds
 No more to perch on his majesty's arms.[5]

The problematic of the series is self-evident: with the falcon, the parting shifts from a sense of remorse to that of liberation. The parrot leaving its cage is ambivalent: the cage locks up the tamed existence of an exotic bird that, kept in the inner quarters, is metonymically associated with women, and its parroting (a truncated expression of language) makes it a special companion in the boudoir. In this context, its offense is a rebellious utterance of "inconvenient words," no longer parroting to please. This defiance is more visible in the falcon poem, with "blue clouds" suggesting an expanded space. The exile from the lord's arms seems self-chosen, and the "no more" receives a transformed meaning, giving the series an ironic twist.

 The prepossessing virtue of the pearl produces an impression of its being beyond reproach, and for it to be discarded over a trifle is an irony directed against the master. This is exactly the implied intent of the series: to plead guilty and not guilty, and to reclaim the lost favor. However, such pleas undergo subtle transfigurations until the parting becomes a state unconsciously willed by the discarded objects. Both the nature of parting per se and the reasons that induced it have been sufficiently transformed as the series unfolds, moving from a disenfranchised pet wishing to be reinstated to a far more intricate conflict within a self suffering from an inner split.

 To push the argument further, the perceived author/courtesan is presented as rethinking her role through the ten poems. In her most self-abasing pose of a pet dog, an opposite emotion rises up and conjures the metaphor of the falcon. Unassuming objects come to embody the discarded courtesan who must plead, not as a woman, but as deserted objects; such an unpleasant personification can only be challenged by the actual complexity of the series as it turns on the theme until the abandoned object obtains a different sense of purpose. Suffice it to say that one so obsessed with the theme of abandonment eventually transforms it into something beyond the original intention. In the end, the political allegory of this specific text loses its allegorical edge when the ideological center of humility ceases to hold.

 One psychological ground for arguing for Xue Tao's authorship of the text is that only a woman, and especially a courtesan at her patron's mercy, could have composed with such humility. In the political allegories of the lament, ousted ministers resort to female personification as a humble gesture for pleading; it is beyond common expectations that men should go further to adopt less dignified objects as emblems of their pleading voice. The logic behind this line of reasoning is clear: while a man lowers himself by adopting a feminine mask, a woman in turn lowers herself further by identifying with obscure pet objects. While a man petitioning as a vulnerable woman has been established as a literary convention, the feminine version of political allegory exemplified by the ten partings presents another mode prescribed by the master discourse. Apparently, the literati have usurped the feminine voice so thoroughly that, when a woman writes, she is forced to pick a predefined and much narrower path.

These arguments, however probing, could be easily defeated by precisely the same function of female personification. To put words in a woman's mouth has long been the literati's privilege, and the imagined pathos of a deserted courtesan may well have triggered the belabored series. If we can trust the *Youxuan ji* (Collections of more obscurities) (which carries the first of the partings under Xue Tao's name), a man with curious taste might have followed its lead and continued the series to its estranged conclusion, sustained by a culturally poignant preoccupation with female tribulations. In this regard, identifying the poet's gender on the grounds of the specificity of the female plight is paradoxically misleading, when such identification and its supporting arguments are both the results *and* the sources of the expressions of such a plight.

With this, we return to the problematic of the female tradition, when texts of this dubious sensibility are slipped under the name of a woman poet, transgressing the domain of female writings. This preconceived idea of feminine writings and the pathetically circumscribed sphere allotted to women poets has the effect of undermining female writings from the ground up, and it presents more than anything else a contorted masculine consciousness.

IN MASCULINE VOICE

While gentry women wrote from the depths of their boudoirs, Tang courtesans wrote under public surveillance and were conscious of their self-presentations. Their lyrics composed upon solicitation picked up promptly the standard discourse in either feminine or masculine mode to work their ways into the circle. In the courtesans' quarters, the masculine pose as the patron's peer, together with a coquettish gesture of the wife/mistress, composed the counterparts of a courtesan's lyrical roles. Such dual voices are found in all three major women poets of the Tang, and a radical polarization of the two stances is most notable in Xue Tao.

Xue composed several occasional poems of farewell in the lament mode; at times, the excessive intimacy of a courtesan addressing a patron-husband deflates this convention, depriving it of all sincerity. This effect, in all likelihood unintentional, constitutes the courtesans' occasional lament as an anti-lament that feeds on an outmoded, hyperbolic convention. The smoothness of its empty mannerism shows the collapse of this subgenre in its extended application in the hands of courtesans. It has evidently become a parody, a ventriloquism that neither the speaker nor the receiver could take at face value.

On the other hand, the success of Xue's adaptations of the masculine mode must have been tremendous, for the Ming scholar Hu Zhenheng commented: "[Xue] is devoid of the voice of the feminine, which certainly is the sign of longevity."[6] This is perhaps the highest possible compliment for a courtesan, and both Xue Tao's triumphant career and her tranquil old age support the verdict.[7] Thus a courtesan enjoys, according to Hu's judgment, prosperity through an absence of her gender qualities—in other words, by being not fully herself. For a woman's poetry to enjoy longevity, Hu also seems to be insinuating, she must conform to the dominant mode of the masculine. The capacity for playing the patriarchal games, a survival skill for women, must have been perfected by Xue. This faculty not only promises an entrance to the elite circle, it is in effect a camouflage, a culturalization for the otherwise sexualized profession of courtesanship.

With the complex logic of gendered discourses, a masculine voice in a courtesan necessarily carries different weight from the feminine mask of the lament, for to write like a man was to succumb to the dominant discourse, whereas male appropriation of the feminine insidiously constituted the normative force of female discourse. The androgynous voice in courtesans' verses, if so named, was demanded by a social contract that was unaware of its own contradiction. With their bodies inscribed with erotic scripts and their words, both spoken and written, floating around as exchange icons in conjunction with the flesh, courtesans, coerced by the literati, nevertheless were driven to express themselves in the masculine mode.

Other than adaptations of masculine allusions, what differentiates male speech from preconceived female speech may be described as reflective interactions with the environment and with the addressee. Such compartmentalization of gendered speech is particularly evident in the lament, in which the absence of the weight of a subjectivity, hence the absence of the composure of male speech, embodies a prescribed lack in the feminine. It is often in adopting the masculine mode that a woman moves with assurance toward self-expression, as is illustrated in the following two poems by Xue Tao:

"Ji Zhang Yuanfu" (Sent to Zhang Yuanfu)
    Alone I stroll by the creek and wander
    Egrets recognize this red robe and do not stir.
    Tell me, a quiet contrition is in our world:
    Bo Ya's strings finished, a deadly silence descends. (*XTSQ*, 29)

"Zeng Su Shisan zhongcheng" (For Minister Su the Thirteenth)
    The road to Luoyang buries the cart wheels' energies
    You chase across the autumnal sky to snatch flying falcons.

Today the purple ink seals an imperial summons—
You shall yet realize a frosty solemnity beyond. (*XTSQ*, 33)

Xue approaches the addressees from different positions: to Zhang Yuanfu, a talented secretary at an ambassador's office, Xue speaks as either one who has lost a sympathetic listener or one who awaits the music from the great zither player.[8] To Minister Su, Xue praises the man's awesome solemnity and his potential to strike high. The latter piece follows more of the tone of exchange between ministers, whereas the former, that between spiritual equals.

The reference to Bo Ya entails the concept of *zhiyin,* literally one who knows the self's music, a concept essential in the elite's consciousness. Although possibly a solicitation for correspondence, the piece's laconic nature allows deeper interpretations. When a woman expresses this rather luxurious concern for either being known or for cosmic listening, she removes herself from the subordinate position of passivity. If we take the last line as referring to a sense of spiritual solitude, the subjectivity of the self is intensified in its abandoning of the world that knows not itself. In this reading, the poetic reversal is considerable, for from a congealed passivity, the self becomes the one who abandons on a grand scale. All this, however, is overshadowed by the deliberate neutral tone of the piece that appropriates male speech, undermining thus its feminine identity.

In the second poem, the faultless masculine diction fits into the dominant discourse seamlessly. Composition like this shows Xue's understanding of the expectation of poetic conventions, and her competence in handling masculine images challenges the forced division between gendered speech. Her relation to language, in direct contrast to being the receiver of male inscriptions, is brilliantly transformed through this self-assured possession of male discourse.

The masculine quality in courtesans' poetry, together with the lament mode, deconstructs the dichotomy of femininity versus masculinity in linguistic expressions, when gender differences are bypassed through a conscious mimicking of the other. The literati-feminine approaches femininity from a privileged position and is fundamentally an imposition on female consciousness overwrought with politics. Ultimately the two stances share the same function of transgression: The lament is a pragmatic casting of the feminine, whereas the courtesan-literatus is another polemic absorption of the masculine. Ironically, the socially advantaged personify themselves as the deprived to achieve certain aims; likewise the alienated learn to utilize the voice of the master. Their practices intersect each other like a cross in an anguished quest that takes each away from itself, at the same time missing the other in its drive toward its self-deceiving aim.

In the end, we must return to the inevitable question: what is culturally defined, and what is essentially different between the genders' self-expressions? The difficulty in defining the courtesans' androgynous writing as such discloses the intricacy of cultural sanctions. It also points to the erasure of the female self. When courtesans write cross-dressed, we are not certain, due to a basic inequity, if they are asserting an androgynous faculty or are simply mimicking the master discourse out of dire necessity. The adaptation of masculine voice is a way for courtesans to chastise the enfeebled feminine and to side with the upstart literati, a self-preserving strategy for the socially deprived. In short, in the engulfing abyss of patriarchal discourse, women are deprived of the right to go androgynous: the preferred mask of the Other becomes for them a fate and an imposition.[9]

With this, we have returned to the double bind of feminine voice. On the one hand is its usurpation by the literati, and on the other is its need to stifle itself to attain the mode of the masculine. Under the circumstance, the analysis of Tang women's writings is infinitely complicated by the usurpation of female voice and its need to conform. The problematics of Niu Yingzhen's dreams return to haunt us, when the classics consumed by the female body come out as the voice of the master, and we no longer know how a woman could speak as herself.[10] When a Tang woman writes like a man, it is irksome to decide if hers is an acquired self, a courtesan-literatus comparable to the literati-feminine, or if, against all odds, she is stealing man's language to forge a new definition for woman. In order to be herself, in order to be not like the boudoir woman of the lament, a woman must shed her sexualized stance and don a masculine mask. In the liberal climate the Tang was known for, a courtesan had to write both as a woman and as a man—or in truth, she could be neither herself nor the Other. Trapped between a betrayed female tradition and an annihilating discourse of the father, between a feminine voice condemned as frivolous and a masculine voice used as survival skill, these women poets had to forge an alternative that would finally let their own voices break through.

A WOMAN ALONE: AGAINST BOUDOIR LAMENT

Both Xue Tao and Yu Xuanji in their amorous writings refer to the lover as one who knows the self's music, reaching for an understanding that is luxurious at a time when women deemed their lovers as lords and life-givers in a perilously tilted relationship. The following is taken from a series by Xue Tao entitled "Chunwang ci" (Spring gazing lyrics), with ramifications of Su Xiaoxiao's ballad:

Flowers bloom, no one to enjoy them
Flowers fall, no one to share the pain.
Wherein lies the thought of longing?
When flowers bloom, and when they fade.

I gather the grass to tie a knotted heart
And send it to one who knows my soul's music.
Spring sorrow is just breaking
Spring birds cry with mourning. (*XTSQ*, 3)

Encapsulated in clichés of spring sorrows, the sense of a void is nonetheless genuine, and the poems display a heightened intensity, moving away from the camp of the literati-feminine with its enslaved eros.[11] With its restrained tones and strangely naive gestures, with its rhythmic repetitions of a subdued frustration, it formulates a lyrical mode not readily present either in the literati-feminine or in the dominant poetic modes. Possibly modeled on the Midnight Songs, *ziye ge,* quatrains by women of the Southern Dynasties famous for their daring eros, these lyrics exemplify a conscious following of a tradition in which female desires found less mediated expressions.

To understand fully the tenor of the feminine voice, we need to put things in context. The transformation of the female tradition after *The Classic of Poetry* is evident; the early songs sung by women working in the open fields register a liberal sentiment, without either the self-effacement of the Han imitation folk songs or the erotic tinge of the Midnight Songs. Even in plaints of abandoned wives, indignation, anguish, and steadfast devotion are set off against each other to draw a complex psychological picture. Since the Han *yuefu,* with the onset of lament by the literati-feminine, the female voice came to be dominated increasingly by an eradicating sorrow wrapped in profound humility. By the time of the Tang, the exuberant voices of women in the fields all but disappeared.[12] Unlike the early folk songs that proclaim amorous emotions outright, Xue's series here presents a much less focused longing, with an ineffable sense of absence at the core of this feminine desire. This absence echoes faintly the image of the boudoir woman as the symbol of lack, and it makes us question whether this languid feminine eros is after all something acquired. With this unsettling doubt, we need to return to the fundamental problem of *écriture féminine.*

While recognizing the fundamental impasse of the inherent condition that all discourses are male discourses, that women must write under the tyranny of the Logos, the upward movement of the father, French feminists propose the indispensable—however challenged—concept of *écriture féminine,* proposing styles such as fluidity, fragmentation, and "another bisexuality," among others, as the qualities that define women's writings. In their search for a mode of writing that is presemiotic and prediscursive (even counterdiscursive), metaphors of the primal sea and the white milk of the mother are enlisted to delineate its unique contour. Although not without their own contradiction or idiosyncrasy, these proposals are invaluable in the effort toward structuring a great female tradition, which is essential for breaking away from the law of the father, the masculinizing civilization.

Due to their prescribed nature and enfeebled voice, it would be strenuous to discuss Tang women's writings in the light of these definitions. Rather, we have to resort to another strategy by taking the presence of female consciousness as a source of light that illuminates the texts, without trying to spell out a pertinent grammar for these writings. In terms of the present text by Xue Tao, suffice it to say that the unfocused desires in these lyrics, sustained by delicate turnings and redoubling, quiet questioning and wondering, are not a programmed, purposely obsessive mourning, but an eros evolving in correspondence with natural cycles, delineating something that may shed light on the essentially feminine, however fraught with problematics and difficult to define it may be.

Yu Xuanji has composed a piece similar in motif but much bolder in conclusion, entitled "Zeng linnü" (For the maiden next door):

Shy at the sun, a fair face covered with silky sleeves
Mourning the spring, too lazy for makeup.
It is easy to earn priceless treasures
Yet hard to find a man with a true heart.
On the pillow your tears hang down slowly
Among the flowers, secretly, an agonized body.
Come now—you could peep at the handsome Song Yu
Why then resent so the lofty Wang Chang? (*TNSR*, 96)

On these lines Zhong Xing, the commentator of the *Mingyuan shigui* (Collected poetry by famous women), writes: "Only with someone who had both talents and beauty, could such [delicacy and passion] be achieved," which exhibits the curious association between a woman's writing and her physical endowments. The complaint on the scarcity of true men has become the popular parameter of Yu's temperament, leading to an unjustified verdict on her frivolity. The maiden next door alludes to Song Yu's "Ode on Master Dengtu's Erotic Drive," in which the court poet professes his virtue to the Chu king by stating his rejection of a presumptuous neighbor girl. In contrast to the talented Song Yu, Wang Chang, the popular object of female desires (as the folk song goes: "What's the hope for gold and fortune/I can't wed that eastern Wang tomorrow morning"), may be emblematic for any frivolous man of status. Yu's poem, whether a playful parody on the original or actually addressed to a neighbor, turns abruptly from amorous melancholy to a daring resolution. Since Song Yu's creation, the girl next door has become the embodiment of feminine yearnings; this identity is further explored here until the lyric ends with a unexpected turn. Indeed it has never been suggested that a woman could pursue any talented man without being pacified by a lost cause; the table has been turned, and a woman is advised, not without a touch of ironic twist, to disentangle herself from the passivity fashioned for her. The seductress invented to serve a rhetorical purpose has acquired a life of her own: with an autonomous gaze, she is free to turn away from the frozen mirror to choose new objects of desire. Yu's neighbor is invited to live up to her reputation, since every woman next door is already the peeping woman threatening male chastity. The blade is now reversed, and a famous rhetorical trope is transfigured to serve the purpose of female desires. Usurpation of male discourses is never more blatant as in this text, which is a rare antidote to the general inertia of female writings.

* * *

A brief biographical account of this defiant courtesan is in order. As Li Yi"s youthful concubine, Yu was pursued relentlessly by a jealous wife, until Li sent her to a Taoist belvedere. Gradually, Yu's literary name became known among the elite, and her identity as a priestess-courtesan evolved. Because of her untimely death at the age of twenty-seven, Yu's works lack the refined self-assurance of Xue Tao, and like the young Xue, she relies heavily on the formulaic conceit of a vulnerable courtesan and assumed intimacy with elusive patrons. These professional gestures are often counterbalanced by her religious self-definition, sometimes with an eerie, if not self-defeating effect.

Yu's early piece, "Qingshu ji Li Zi'an" (Love letter to Li Zi'an), stages a fusion of lament with the austere sentiment of a priestess:

> Feeding on ice and bitter herb, I vow to be non-striving.
> River Jin and the Hu Pass are in my dreams . . .
> By the well, dryandra leaves sound the autumn rain
> At the window, a silver lamp dimmed in the morning breeze.
> Your letter has not arrived, whither could I ask?
> All day I hold the fish poll, an empty river blue. (*TNSR*, 103)

With the expanding image of the river and the hope for letters (sent in fish-shaped cases), the text separates itself from the claustrophobic lament. Cast in an ascetic waiting, the controlled expression of an absence manages to shed off the formulaic sense of impasse in the boudoir. Without referential descriptions of the feminine and replete with Taoist inclinations, the text appropriates the mode of the elite, citing the allusion "drinking ice" from Bo Juyi's account of his rigorous career as an official.

In a telling moment, Zhong Xing's commentary compares Yu's talent in depicting amorous sensuality to that of Li Shangyin. While the lament has molded yearnings in a feminine cast and rendered romantic mourning of men suspicious, female appropriations of the elite's lyrical mode are equally liable to put a masculine mask over feminine sorrow and create a strange hybrid. The literatus in love and the courtesan-priestess wearing a masculine veil move incessantly toward the line of demarcation, fusing the voice of the opposite sex to offer up a complex sensual prosody of eros. Have lyrical modes so shaped the genders' voices that they create problematics for simple utterances of desires? Or perhaps a hybrid of gender/genre indicates all literary rules as superfluous? However we may choose to phrase this question, with the instilling of a pervasive discursive mode, writing per se cannot escape its expectations, and reading likewise is seriously conditioned. This creates the impression of a Li Shangyin writing like a woman and a Yu Xuanji writing like a literatus in their most private expressions. Ultimately, we need to expose the embedded ideologies and try to read women and men as they are, before language—in other words, before language has assigned each their separate definitions.

Consider Yu's "Dongyei ji Wen Feiqing" (Sent to Wen Feiqing on a wintry night):

> In anguish, I search for verse and read by the lamp:
> Long nights of insomnia, I fear the cold bedding.

Pale leaves cover the yard, cold wind blows
Transparent window screens—there, a sinking moon.
My wish to be at ease is at last not granted
Rising and declining, in vain a primordial heart.
Don't pick a quiet dwelling on dryandra tree:
Swallows chirp and hover above the woods at dusk. (*TNSR*, 107)

Sent to the voyeur-poet Wen Tingyun, the piece speaks of a *benxin* (primordial heart) with a philosophical overtone of an unadulterated mind that gravitates toward the origin of all things. Balanced on a manifest intent and its partial failure, the self resorts to a humble identification with unassuming sparrows, renouncing the dryandra tree, lofty dwelling for the legendary phoenix.

Composed by a priestess-courtesan, this communication of a plain heart and its plight in a desolate night may arouse a suspicion, albeit a rather ungenerous one, that this is another pose to elicit sympathy. Strangely dissatisfied with a heart unchanged, the self sends out messages that are somewhat confusing. If the wish to be at ease from which the priestess deviates is due to her role as a courtesan, the inner conflict of a priestess-courtesan bolsters the somber tone of the text. We may extend from this conjecture and propose that the most extravagant role for Tang women, the priestess-courtesan, is in effect an existence that induces a cleavage within the feminine self, who is denied the choice between a reclusive life and a public livelihood, between a steadfast mind and a sexualized body. The retreat from the dryandra tree, then, bespeaks a gesture of self-abandonment.

At a more confident and less self-searching moment, Yu wrote the following piece, entitled "Daohuai" (Directing my sentiments):

Unbound, I enjoy myself as I wish
Sojourning alone in wind and shimmering light
Sundered clouds and moon lie above the river
The rope untied, a boat adrift on the sea . . .
Bamboo woods fare well as my companion
A rock makes a faithful friend.
Swallows and sparrows seek fortune in vain
Gold and silver are not my intent.
A cup of spring wine to the brim
Facing the moon, my night zither darkly sounds.
I circle around to trace the clear blue pond
My hairpin pulled, reflections on the slender stream.
Reclining on my book-laden bed
Half drunk, I get up to comb my hair. (*TNSR*, 121–22)

Starting with precisely what the previous poem declares to be an unfulfilled wish, the text elaborates on the meaning of being at ease. The self is in harmony with itself: for the first time we see a woman wandering alone out in the open space, observing not herself in melancholia, but the expanse of nature and her inner landscape. The two feminine images, hairpin and hair combing, are transformed by extraordinary contexts: the latter is done half-drunk, hardly appropriate for a woman, while the hairpin is pulled from the coiffure, a symbolic act of liberation reflected on streaming water. In line with the well-known reclusive allusions of pillowing the stream and rinsing mouth with the rocks, this image lacks the sensuous overtone commensurate with feminine adornment and receives rather the charm of eremitic poetry.

And the bed, one object that invites immediate sexual associations, is transformed into a study. In another piece by Yu, it acquires indeed a lofty stature: "The pearled curtain curled up/I moved the bed to sleep against the hills."[13] Both the privacy and sexualization of the female body are removed when it defines itself against high mountains, declaring thus a spiritual sublimation. Elsewhere Yu has described her book-laden bed: "The sounds of seniors' carts outside my gate/Taoist scrolls scattered by my pillow" ("Qiusi," Autumn thoughts) (*TNSR,* 112); and robes: "My silk dress long embraces disordered piles of books" ("Xiari shanju," Summer mountain dwelling) (*TNSR,* 124). The self-consciousness of reading here is significant: a woman reading, like a woman writing, is already a woman read by cultural constructs, subsumed under the censorious gaze of the patriarchs. Yet when a woman stresses the fact that her bed (a sexualized site) and robe (with closest affinity to her body) are overcome by books, such emphatic envisioning of the self transcends preconceived norms and recreates the image of a woman reading.

In many ways, this is a magnificent reversal of the feminine under the voyeuristic gaze, when a woman is transported by her self-contained solitude to a lofty realm. The reader no longer controls the zoom; the presentation of the self moves in perspectives, shifts in angles, a far cry from the penetrating close-up of the boudoir. In short, the confining boudoir and the melancholic woman disappear together with the voyeur's stealthy lens. This is what happens when a woman writes, one is tempted to say, when a woman true to herself writes, against the deadly weight of the lament that threatens to annihilate her. That it is a freedom won by overcoming the many struggles within the self, breaking through continuous self-doubts and defeats, makes it ever more triumphant.

DEATH OF A COURTESAN

The dialectic of repression and resistance is unrelenting, exacting measureless sacrifices along its evolving motions. There is a strange plot involved in the short life of Yu, even a master plot, enacted by the merciless will of this evolving axis.

Exiled to the frontier of language as its negativity, while at the same time moving closely among the literati who were products of a new ethics, Tang courtesans, themselves talented women of letters, had ambivalent feelings about the exam from which they were categorically excluded. Below is a poem by Yu on this exclusion:

> Cloud-peaks permeate my eyes, a spring sun returns.
> Bright are the silver hooks given birth by slender fingers.
> I resent this silk robe that conceals my poetry—
> Gazing up, I envy the names on the wall in despair.[14]

It was not until the Ming and the Qing that cross-dressed women who attended the state examinations and enjoyed great political success began to emerge in the female imagination. In the Tang, the above lamentation is the only extant female complaint on this iniquity. Against an imposing array of masculine names in refined calligraphy, another feminine symptom of psychological split is inflicted: the feminine dress and the poet inside it are in disharmony, and a woman is made to regret her gender at this bitter initiation. By common conceptions, woman and poetry (in terms of their mutual glorification) are alienated from each other, the text seems to suggest, and the burden of the latter causes a sense of despair.

Yet the woman also knows that her dress hides a true poet. This self-celebration did not escape others. Zhong Xing's comment reads: "Wanton and beguiling, Yu associated with the literati widely; it is thus only appropriate that her words are weighted and self-congratulating."[15] Lamenting that its name is missing from the list, the self is in truth asserting its rightful place. The insurmountable distance between the names on the board and the woman underneath it is overcome instantaneously by the secret union of the poet inside the woman, a bliss (and curse) unknown to others. This subtly disguised confidence of a woman poet is echoed in the following piece by Xue Tao:

> Lines and mannered tones—anyone could have them
> I alone know the nuanced subtlety of nature.
> Singing of flowers under the moon, I pity their frailty
> And I write of willows at rainy dawn—they slant so low.
> I long had Green Jade hidden away in deep chamber
> And always write as I please on scarlet slips.
> Aged now, can't gather all my works and tidy up
> So I send you these, as if shown to teach a boy.[16]

Presented to Yuan Zhen, the confidence in the piece reveals a Xue Tao at the farthest remove from the young courtesan in exile. Ten years Xue's junior, Yuan was nonetheless a renowned poet in his own right; it was certainly unprecedented for a woman to teach an established elite the art of versification. Xue's time-honored self-assurance had prompted this peculiar introduction to her compilation of poems, and an aged Xue tailoring scarlet poem-slips became part of the legend of a courtesan with blessed longevity.[17]

The fate of Yu Xuanji is in direct contrast to such a rarefied end. The priestess who enjoyed solitude might have overdone it in her rejection of an admirer's request, a request that discloses the burden on a woman with ambiguous identity:

Why should a handsome lad, searching for verse
Come knocking on my door with jade-stone rhymes? . . .
You need not desire to see me so:
Where pine vines rise high, the mountains stand.[18]

The self prefers to leave the mundane world and its affected admirer, who is mocked by the allusion to secluded mountains, the dwelling of hermits whom he should seek instead. In another poem Yu describes her unswept path in waiting for the one "who knows her music." The persistent allusions to an untrammeled mode of being sketch a portrait of a woman who chose to be alone with the selected few, or with her unperturbed self. The inexplicable lack within the boudoir woman is thus dismantled by a self-sufficiency, an emotional independence denied of the feminine. The demand that woman open up a wound in herself as a safe haven for man is faced with blunt rejection when a woman refuses to accept the lack inscribed within her. As such, she poses a threat.

In direct contrast to the woman who refutes the world of vanities and prefers seclusion is a Yu Xuanji who, according to one scholar, is "the most licentious of the three [Tang women poets], her poetic manner likewise is decadent and frag-ile."[19] In traditional critics' consensus, Yu's achievement is the lowest of the three, her voice the most flippant. Counterbalancing such critique is Zhong Xing's high praise: "After all, for the talented and passionate, nothing is impossible. Xuanji is indeed the poet divine of all women poets."[20] A poet divine and a licentious woman—this is curiously the double personality perceived of an unusually talented and daring priestess-courtesan.

If one wonders about the truth of Yu, the verdict has already been cast. In the *Sanshui xiaodu* (Petty correspondence from the three waters) Huangfu Mei recounts with embellished fabrications the events that led to the death of Yu Xuanji. One day Yu returned home and was informed that a guest had just left; Yu suspected that the maid had had compromising relations with him.

> At night, candles were lit and windows shut, and Luqiao was summoned into the bed-room to be questioned. The maid answered: "Since I served you, I have restrained myself and avoided mistakes that may anger you. . . . As for love, it has not been in my thoughts for years. . . ." Yu was ever more furious—she stripped Luqiao naked and gave her over a hundred lashes, yet the maid still denied the accusation. When her spirit was giving way, Luqiao asked for a cup of water and made libation to the earth: "My mistress wishes for the Way of Immortality of the Three Deities, and yet can not forget sensual pleasure. . . . I will surely die in your hands today. If there is no heaven, there will be no place to tell my wrong; if there is, none could stop my soul. I vow not to be quiet in the underworld and let you enjoy your licentious endeavors." Thus she died on the ground. Yu was afraid and buried the body in the

backyard, thinking that no one would know. It was the first month of spring in the Xiantong era.[21]

Framed by fragments of Yu's lyrics, the text presents a fallen woman whose indulgence in erotic pleasures is contrasted to her maid's jealously guarded chastity. The death of the maiden is a harsh cry against promiscuity, and her resurrected body testifies to a just heaven. To keep women within bounds, a virginal token is installed to deprave excessive female desires.

The fictional quality of the text notwithstanding, according to various accounts, the accusation of beating her maid to death was indeed the legal suit against Yu that had brought her capital sentence.[22] Suspicious of the injustice of Yu's trial and supported by evidence from *Clustered Words from Northern Dreams* and *Comprehensive Collection of the Strange,* Tan Zhengbi suggests that Wen Zhang, the legal official renowned for his cruelty, might have tortured Yu into confessing to a framed crime.[23] Without further information to help us bring the truth to light, we can only make our judgment based on the self-images presented by Yu, the general injustice of the feudal legal system, and the vulnerability of a priestess-courtesan. The voluptuous Yu projected in the story points to a basic aversion from exuberant female desires, and in all likelihood, this may be Yu's only crime against the tyranny of the father. Whatever happened is lost to history, and we are left with the brutal termination of possibly one of the most self-liberating, and certainly the most outspoken, of all the women poets of the Tang.

Three deaths thus converge in the abysmal nadir of women's relationship with words. Metaphorically, we may consider Niu Yingzhen's death as the result of an ill consumption of the words of the masters, and that of Yu Xuanji, the inevitable end of a dangerous transgression. Li Ye, who was executed by Emperor Dezong for presenting a poem to the rebel general Zhu Ci, received death as punishment for a single linguistic act. The echoing deaths of these women who moved too close to words are ominous: while Niu Yingzhen's death cautions us to cleanse our bodies of the clustered words of the fathers, those of Li Ye and Yu Xuanji are far more forbidding. The perilous relation between women and language is made clear, and for a woman whose relation with words is both metonymically and metaphorically defined, her control over writing is gravely strictured. The laws commanding the limits of feminine writings are severe indeed, and Li and Yu, generations apart and equally talented, suffered brutal ends for failing to adhere to this masculine decree.

The hard-earned triumph of Xue Tao, the defiance against the mundane world and against the logic of the masculine of Yu Xuanji—all these are solemnly effaced by the execution of our courtesan-poets. The master plot is unambiguous after all: a woman transgressing the boundary is subjected to a timely erasure. The death of the courtesans marks the victory of the dialectics of repression, and just when the power of resistance was gaining strength, the inevitable end was waiting like a ubiquitous predator. This dialectic will continue, with the repressive mechanism building up in the late Tang and gaining momentum throughout late imperial China, reaching for sacrifices on a much more grandiose scale.

Epilogue

These women are to be pitied. . . . We should hold a great memorial service for them. After mourning for the dead, we must swear to be more intelligent, brave, aspiring and progressive. We must tear off every mask. We must do away with all the stupidity and tyranny in the world which injure others as well as ourselves.

Lu Xun

It is perhaps inevitable that we should end this study on gender politics in the Tang on this dark note, which inadvertently serves as an apt prelude to the oppressive ages for women that were to come. One fatal invention that savagely undermined women's strength, foot-binding, has a legendary origin in the court of the Last Emperor of the Chen in the Five Dynasties (907–960), the turbulent period of division that lasted for half a century following the fall of the Tang. With the introduction of this sexually oriented invention, which gained widening practice from the late Song onward, the fate of Chinese women was decidedly transformed.

The images of Tang women riding on horseback in extravagant costumes along the high roads of Chang'an and Luoyang were gradually replaced by those of women in layers of silk garments that concealed their slender bodies, who walked in willowy fashion on deformed feet that rendered them infinitely confined. Female jealousy lost much of its urgency after the Tang; instead, gruesome self-mutilations were conjured up by women who were eager to testify to their increasingly valued chastity. Variations on boudoir lament continued with enriched virtuosity, and the shifting aesthetic of feminine beauty erased the voluptuous female bodies of the Tang to promote the image of the boudoir woman, a fragile figure easily invaded by the wind.

The development in the Song was crucial for the oppression of women both in terms of their declining social standing and tightening ethical codification. In the burgeoning commercialization of the times, the neo-Confucian efforts at strengthening moral fiber worked side by side with more rigid demands on female chastity. Suppressions of women's literary creativity and claims to property rights registered a further mental and economic curfew on the already physically handicapped existence of women. In their concern for cosmic-moral principles pursued through painstaking introspection and philosophical speculations, the neo-Confucians placed

215

high demands on self-discipline—a sharp contrast to the relatively uninhibited sensibility of the Tang literati. In the vigorous exercise of the moral requirement, loyalty was intensely demanded of the gentry. In this regard, the tightening of the chastity code was but one facet of the closing in of moral requisition in the era.

The expansion of learning and of the population of the educated elite through the implementation of local academies should have provided a historical chance for female advancement, and indeed Li Qingzhao, considered by many as the most established woman poet in traditional China, appeared in this period. However, in the neo-Confucians' inclination for (male) inner cultivation, the threat of female desires was epitomized, and as stated above, the expansion of the elite brought a countermovement in the decline of women's value. The surge of women's intellectual communities hence had to wait until the late Ming, when the onset of a counterculture that celebrated eccentric lifestyles provided women with better opportunities.

In late imperial China, the vibrant literary communities of women brought forth various anthologies of women writers whose works include poetry, *tanci* (storytelling rhymes), and drama. Alongside this cultural advancement for upper-class women, fierce models of chaste widows and female suicides in much cruder manners are widely recorded, and a growing number of chastity tablets were installed on the winding streets of the empire. In exchange for the cold stones inscribed with their austere lives, women were coerced to forsake their natural drives and become icons of chastity. The flesh and blood of female bodies were metamorphosed into the stiff-faced tablets that arched over the streets where people crossed under, shuddering with a sense of awe.

It was due to such drastic transformations that the Tang became the legendary era when women enjoyed luxurious freedom, when their plump, healthy bodies were transported by gallant horses, and this dazzling empire was looked upon with nostalgia by later epochs. Yet, as I show at the beginning, it is dangerous to pit the Tang against its descendants to argue for a steady descent from grace. The era itself, especially since the fall of Empress Wei, had sown the seeds for the gradual decline of women's status. The tightening of ethical codes for the princesses was but one of the parameters that determined the further historical fall of women, countering the entrenchment of the examination system that guaranteed the rise of the elite and the institutionalization of minds. While studying the apparatus of gender politics, we cannot afford to miss this important fact: with growing complications of rules and decrees, human civilizations impose increasing sanctions on women under the masculine logic of progress. Furthermore, it is when the state is losing its grip, when it senses an impending peril, and most significantly, when it is wrecked by an acute sense of diffidence, that its hold on women tightens.

This study aims at revealing the undercurrent of confinement of Tang women and at exposing their liberal lives as a partial myth. In an era when poetry was worshipped, leaving behind a huge corpus of the literati's compositions, the extreme scarcity of women's writings alone is enough to testify to a stupendous injustice.

We must therefore read between the lines and resurrect voices from behind the acquired masks, and this has been my strategy throughout the preceding two chapters. If more works by Tang women had survived . . . but one should not ask hypothetical questions, however critical they may be.

In this study, I have also aimed at revealing the profound damages such sexual stratification caused men. The significance of feminism, I believe, lies in its critique of a civilization inflicted with a disease of self-destruction through its subjugation of one sex under the other, making the exalted sex bear inconceived-of, hurtful burdens. The problematics of male sexuality, as we have seen above, force us to think hard on this absurd asymmetry and instruct us to finally deliver ourselves from this unfortunate syndrome.

* * *

The loss of cultural vitality has been a cause for urgent and often desperate calls for cultural transformation from modern Chinese intellectuals. The symptom is derived partially from the chasm between the congealed present and its creative origins and partially from the pervasive constraint on women, a situation for which the Tang shared some responsibility. When half of the empire's population was placed under oppression from all fronts, one can hardly expect that empire to remain standing on firm and fertile ground. This is another paradox: by subsuming women under merciless sanctions to create an illusion of order and to safeguard masculine power, the civilization renowned for its many inventions, dignified rites, and high cultures suffered an increasing failure of strength, both militarily and culturally, until its bitter fall in modern history.

The collective rethinking of Chinese traditions continues into the end of the twentieth century, without bringing much insight into the plight of this once proud empire that stands today with its open wounds. Much of the discontent with the traditions and with the subservient character of the people, when placed in feminist perspective, gains fresh meanings and possible outlets. We begin to see the injuries an ancient patriarchy inflicted on its subjects through a peculiar mechanism that deployed the sexes to the effect of squandering their vitality, self-respect, and capacities for loving. If we are to understand a culture through the women and men it creates, Chinese culture presents itself, in all honesty, rather somberly.

Against my own expectations, the truth of this much admired dynasty emerges with its dark secrets, manifesting that our present burdens have complex layers of memories that go back a long way. We have expected dynastic women to suffer tremendous self-annihilation, but that men too should suffer a psychological split with dogged patience—this speaks for all the unhappy aspects of this civilization. All civilizations have exacted sacrifices by imposing oppressions through intricate mechanisms, and our focus here, the epitome of one of the world's ancient civilizations, presents us with its unique version of the tyranny of the patriarchs.

Chinese women and men will continue to carry this burden with the patience they are known for through the turn of the twentieth century, which witnessed twice the assassination of the fathers by the revolutionary sons and daughters, assassinations that, to our great regret, were aborted by the resurgence of the vibrant patriarchs of the modern state. Amid a continued impasse and self-deluding downfall, with the obstinate resurgence of the oppression and commercialization of women, it is left to the offspring of these daring daughters to direct this unfinished endeavor back onto its right track. For the enlightened and the undaunted, this remains the modern project that will lead us bravely into the twenty-first century. It is therefore my wish that this study of the past serve as a blueprint for this essential, this pressing project of the present. For, frankly and in the most profound sense, the past with all its barbarous persuasions is still very much with us.

Notes

INTRODUCTION

1. *Ennin's Diary: The Record of a Pilgrimage to China in Search of the Law.* The book was written in Chinese, bearing the Japanese title, *Nitto guho junrei gyoki.* Although somewhat less reliable as a historical source because of faulty transmission, the degree of authenticity of the text itself is unquestionable. For a discussion of the diary, see Edwin Reischauer's *Ennin's Travels in T'ang China* (New York: Ronald Press, 1955).

2. *Ennin's Diary,* trans. Edwin Reischauer (New York: Ronald Press, 1955), 214. Monjushiri is the bodhisattva of wisdom, often pictured riding on a lion on the left side of Shakyamuni.

3. *Ennin's Diary,* 148–49.

4. *Ennin's Diary,* 352–53. The building of the Taoist terrace is recorded in both the *Old Tang History* and *New Tang History* in Wuzong's annual.

5. *Ennin's Diary,* 345.

6. "Song Li Yuan gui Pangu xu" (Preface to seeing Li Yuan returning to the Pan Valley), translation mine (unless otherwise specified).

7. Xiao Gongquan, *Zhongguo zhengzhi sixiang shi* (History of Chinese political thoughts) (Taipei: Wenhua University Press, 1980), 410–12.

8. Xiao, *Zhongguo Zhengzhi,* 415–17.

9. *Histories of the Six Dynasties* and *Sui Shu* (The Sui history), compiled in the Tang, and *Old Tang History,* completed in the Five Dynasties (907–960) based on materials left by Tang historians, are all modeled after Ban.

10. It should be mentioned that by the time the civil service examinations were entrenched in the Tang, the mentality of the literati had pretty much settled into a much subdued state. This may be considered the consequence of the fusion of Confucianism and Legalism propagated by the Han scholar Dong Zhongshu.

11. We may entertain the neo-Confucian master Zhu Xi's comment: "The Tang originated from the barbarians, hence they don't take heed for improper behaviors within the boudoir." *Zhuzi yulei* (Records of Master Zhu's words) (Shanghai: Guji, 1992) 44. 735.

12. The An Lushan rebellion was quenched with help from the Uighur, with the Tang promising them gold and women in the capital. Later when the weakened empire engaged in prolonged battles with Tibet and Uighur, various tribal forces were assembled.

13. Such is the opinion of Jacques Gernet presented in his *A History of Chinese Civilization* (Cambridge: Cambridge University Press, 1972), 235.

14. Gernet, *Chinese Civilization,* 268–71. The process is a back-and-forth sort, and through the late eighth and much of the ninth centuries, the center's power was restored from its low point right after 755.

15. For the killing of the foreign merchants, see Gernet, *Chinese Civilization,* 292.

16. It is not hard to imagine the historical consequence of this change, which manifested itself most forcefully in the nineteenth century in the disastrous crash of the Qing empire with the West, when both the center and the marginal acquired radically transformed profiles and strengths, and frankly different, if not reversed, definitions. In the end, the dialectic of the center versus the periphery proves itself to be both obstinate and fearfully exacting.

17. Recent studies by David Johnson and Patricia Ebrey argue for continued aristocratic strength—including aristocratic success—in the examinations throughout the Tang. Dennis Twichet also questions the dividing line between the aristocratic bloc and the literati in *The Cambridge History of China,* vol. 3 (Cambridge: Cambridge University Press, 1979).

18. For a discussion of the historical effect of the civil service examinations on the literati, see Xu Fuguan, "Zhongguo zhishi fenzi de lishi xingge yu lishi mingyun" (Historical characters and historical destinies of Chinese intellectuals) in *Zhishi fenzi yu Zhongguo* (Intellectuals and China), ed. Zhou Yangshan (Taipei: Shibao Publisher, 1980), 201–20. Among modern writers, Lu Xun is the most vocal about the servile mentality of modern Chinese intellectuals.

19. Gong Pengcheng, "Lun Tangdai de wenxue chongbai yu wenxue shehue" (On literary worship and literary society in the Tang), in *Wan Tang de shehui yu wenhua* (Society and culture of the late Tang) (Taipei: Xuesheng Publisher, 1990), 1–98.

20. Patricia Ebrey, "Shifts in Marriage Finance from the Sixth to the Thirteenth Century," in *Marriage and Inequality in Chinese Society,* ed. Rubie Watson and Patricia Ebrey (Berkeley: University of California Press, 1991), 97–132. Ebrey does not suggest that devaluation of women was involved in the soaring dowry; her emphasis rather is on the devolution of property and possible female gains in this new phenomenon. It should be noted that the issue of dowry and its indication of women's status are extremely complicated. A woman's right to the possession of property may raise her status in her husband's family, thus counterbalancing the overall devaluation of women in the Song.

21. Here Hilda Smith's discussion on the study of women's history as something to be weighed carefully against that of men is instructive; see "Feminism and the Methodology of Women's History" in *Liberating Women's History,* ed. Berenice A. Carroll (Urbana: University of Illinois Press, 1976), 369–83. In another note, according to Lacan, women, positioned as the lack, constitute the Other in language. That in the case of the Tang the rise of the power of words should spell the further downfall for women serves as an intriguing counterpoint to Lacan's theory on the relation between women and language.

22. The Zen sect's transformation of Buddhism was a long process that involved important contributions of various figures, chief among them Shen Xiu of the northern sect and, more significantly, Hui Neng of the southern sect. *Zhongguo chanzong tongshi* (History of Chinese Zen Buddhism), by Du Jiwen and Wei Daoru (Jiangsu: Guji, 1993).

23. Li Zehou, *Zhongguo gudai sixiang shi lun* (Intellectual history of ancient China)(Beijing: Renmin, 1986), 212–23.

24. This renunciation of language is remotely echoed in the Song neo-Confucian's rejection of *wen,* literary embellishment, which was of vital consequence for intellectual development. Peter Bol, *"This Culture of Ours": Intellectual Transitions in T'ang and Sung China* (Palo Alto: Stanford University Press, 1992), 177.

25. Another contradictory evolution realized by Zen Buddhism was the invention of the *conglin* system by Baizhang huaihai (749–814), which practiced ascetic cultivation that involved mundane activities such as farming, in part triggered by the worsening economic situation of the postrebellion Tang. Yu Ying-shih, *Zhongguo jinshi zongjiao lunli yu shangren jingshen* (Religious ethics and mercantile spirit of late imperial China) (Taipei: Lianjing, 1987), 15–25.

26. "Words of Yixuan," from *Gu zunsu yulu* (Recorded sayings of ancient worthies), ed. Ze Zang (Shanghai: Guji, 1991), chap. 4.

27. For a discussion of Zen's physical treatment, see Feng Youlan, *A Short History of Chinese Philosophy* (New York: Free Press, 1948), 255–65.

28. During 713–756, over fifty thousand nuns resided in over two thousand Buddhist nunneries, about two-thirds of the monk's population. *Tang huiyao* (The Tang compendium), hereafter *THY* (Beijing: Zhonghua, 1955), chap. 49.

29. Rf. Patricia Ebrey, "Jealousy," in *The Inner Quarters: Marriage and the Lives of Chinese Women in the Sung Period* (Berkeley: University of California Press, 1993), 170–71. Although Ebrey's subject is Song women, it is reasonable to suspect a similar mechanism in the Tang; however, different social structures of the eras and the relatively liberated voice of Tang women warrant more careful judgment. For a discussion of Buddhism as a way out from sensual desires, see Li Yuzhen, *Tangdai de biqiuni* (Buddhist nuns of the Tang) (Taipei: Xuesheng Publisher, 1989).

30. Often, at the death of their masters, women were also sent to convents. In Heian Japan, the transformation of past mistresses of the lords into wandering nuns traveling from temple to temple, transcribing devoutly Buddhist sutras hundreds of times, is a parallel phenomenon with a somewhat different implication.

31. Rf. Mou Zhongjian, *Zhongguo zongjiao yu wenhua* (Chinese religions and cultures) (Chengdu: Bashu Publisher, 1989), 51–60.

32. *Jiu Tang shu* (Old Tang history), hereafter *JTS* (Beijing: Zhonghua Publisher, 1987), chap. 16, p. 504 (hereafter, chapter and page expressed as, e.g., 16.504); 18.1.610; 15.470–72.

33. The practice of internal alchemy developed in late Tang tends to sublimate this exercise to an attainment of spiritual immortality.

34. Song Shugong, *Zhongguo gudai fangshi yangsheng jiyao* (Collection of sexual yoga in ancient China) (Beijing: Medical Research Institute, 1991), 1–12.

35. The presentations of Tang women in literary writings involve much more complex facets and are discussed in part 3.

36. For a lengthy discussion of the problematics of human expressions and the instrumentalization of human lives and of language, see Shi Zuocheng, *Zhexue renleixue xushuo* (Preface to philosophical anthropology) (Taipei: Yangzhe, 1988).

37. We cannot discuss here the consequences of Tang military policies, or the An Lushan rebellion and its far-reaching effects, although these noncultural factors were instrumental to the changing social structures that followed, which in turn changed the cultural climate, of which the expansion and localization of the Song literati is a case in point. Neo-Confucianism, especially Wang Yangming's School of the Minds, borrowing from Zen Buddhism an inward turn to the mind for an understanding of the cosmic principles and rejecting the preeminence of literary embellishment, is a move toward a more natural state of being. Yet the neo-Confucian interest in ethical teachings, its prohibitory rhetoric that contributed to female repression, and its fundamentally moral concerns make it less adequate a candidate for a heroics of cultural renaissance.

CHAPTER 1

1. "Bai guan zhi" (Documents on officials) in *Xin Tang shu* (New Tang history), compiled by Ouyang Xiu and Song Qi (Beijing: Zhonghua, 1975); hereafter *XTS,* 49.1285–86.

2. For a description of the court session and a day in the capital, see Cheng Qiang and

Dong Naibing's *Tang diguo de jingshen wenming* (Spiritual civilization of the Tang empire) (Beijing: Sheke Research Academy, 1996), 138–53.

3. *THY,* 62.1078–79.

4. *Tang lü shuyi* (Tang legal codes), ed. Zhangsun Wuji (Shanghai: Shangwu Publisher, 1927), 7.58.i2. The actual implementation of this law can be seen in the case of one musician who passed words for the palace women and was first sentenced to death and then exiled to distant regions. *THY,* 55.950.

5. Wang Dang, *Tang yulin jiaozheng* (Exegesis on forest of words from the Tang) (Beijing: Zhonghua Bookstore, 1987), 4.i570.

6. *Zizhi tongjian* (Comprehensive mirror for governing), hereafter *ZZTJ,* by Sima Guang (Taipei: Shangwu Publisher, 1966), 243.2.17. (Hereafter, these numbers represent chapter, section, and item number within the source.)

7. See the episode on Taizong, in Liu Su, *Sui-Tang jiahua* (Propitious anecdotes from Sui and Tang)(Beijing: Zhonghua Bookstore, 1979), middle section, 18.

8. For a discussion of the infusion of Legalism into Confucianism and its historical consequences, see Yu Yingshi, "Fanzhilun yu Zhongguo zhengzhi chuantong" (Anti-intellectualism and Chinese political tradition), in *Lishi yu sixiang* (History and thoughts) (Taipei: Lianjing, 1976), 1–46.

9. As an aristocrat, Qu Yuan's devotion to his king is understandable and should be considered as a complex that anticipated later contradictions facing the ministers.

10. In the case of Xu Jingzong, the name "faithful," *zhong,* capable of correcting oneself, finally overruled the name "absurd," *miu,* after heated debates, which designates a discrepancy between truth and appearance in the life of the dead minister. *JTS,* 82.2764.

11. *Offerings of Jade and Silk,* by Howard J. Wechsler (New Haven: Yale University Press, 1985), 142–60.

12. *JTS,* 71.2562. Wei's monument was reinstalled after Taizong's disastrous march to Korea, when the man's counsel was sincerely missed. Events concerning Wei Zheng, when not cited, can be found in the same chapter.

13. Infuriated by the insolent words He Xiangxian threw out on his way to his execution, the Emperor Zetian ordered the exhumation of his grandfather He Chujun, her old enemy whose funeral had been honored by Gaozong's generous gifts (*JTS,* 84.2801). The conceited Li Linpu, Xuanzong's influential chief minister, suffered the same fate when, slandered by Yang Guozhong, he was exhumed and the burial pearl was snatched from his mouth.

14. Various anecdotes describe how a magistrate tried to uphold ethical standards by punishing wayward women. The most famous example is about a woman who was lashed by Yan Zhenqing for having asked for a divorce. Fan Shu, *Yunxi youyi* (Conversations from the cloud stream), in *Tangdai congshu* (hereafter *TDCS*) (Shanghai: Saoshanfang, 1930), 3:4.

15. The importance of Han Fei in the transformation of Confucianism should not be underestimated, as Yu Ying-shi emphasizes. The master-disciple relation between Xun Zi and the Legalists Li Si and Han Fei is essential for an understanding of the complex network between the two schools.

16. *JTS,* 78.2705.

17. The *I Ching,* trans. Richard Wilhelm, rendered into English by Cary F. Baynes (Princeton: Princeton University Press, 1950), 11.

18. Wilhelm, *I Ching,* 361–62.

19. The convention of political allegory and the problematics of Qu Yuan's feminine pose are studied in part 3, chapter 10.

20. *JTS,* 1.18.

21. *JTS*, 74.2608.

22. *JTS*, 71.2549.

23. *XTS*, 105.4020.

24. In both the Han poet Sima Xiangru's and the Jin poet Tao Qian's diction, *fumei* is used to describe unusual beauty. It should be mentioned that at least in another Tang usage, the term is used to describe the plum blossom, when compared to a lord.

25. *JTS*, 71.2562. For a discussion of Wei Zheng, see *Mirror to the Son of Heaven: Wei Zheng at the Court of T'ang T'ai-tsung,* by Howard Wechsler (New Haven: Yale University Press, 1974).

26. *THY*, 62.1084–85.

27. *THY*, 57.977.

28. *JTS*, 77.2680.

29. Yang Yi, "Tanyuan" (Garden of conversations), quoted in *Li Shangyin xuanji* (Collected poetry of Li Shangyin), ed. Zhou Zhenfu (Shanghai: Guji Publisher, 1986), 289.

30. *Congshu jicheng xin bian* (Compiled series, new edition) (Taipei: Hsinwenfeng, 1986), 641. The fact that it was under a woman emperor that the book was compiled deserves more careful considerations. More on this in chapter 3.

31. See *THY*, 65.1132.

32. *JTS*, 71.2549. Ten years later, when a secretary of rites proposed that it was against propriety that ministers above third rank saluted imperial clans when their carriages met on the streets, Taizong retorted: "So you ministers take yourselves as lofty and wish to put down my offspring?" Again it was Wei who pointed out the dividing line in legal codes and the importance of keeping hierarchy among imperial personages. On this occasion Taizong, much pleased, unfastened his knife and bestowed it upon Wei. *JTS*, 71.2558–89.

33. *THY*, 55.954–55.

34. *THY*, 55.952; 30.552–53.

35. *JTS*, 7.147. On an imperial outing, officials above third rank were ordered to participate in a tug of war, and Ruizong and his women had a good laugh when the elderly ministers fell on the ground and could not regain themselves. Here, imperial women moved themselves above the ministers by sharing with the monarch hearty laughter (*ZZTJ*, 209. 2.3).

36. Pei Tingyu, *Dongguan zouji* (Records of memorials from Dongguan)(Beijing: Zhonghua Bookstore, 1994), 1.91.i14.

37. Pei, *Dongguan zouji*, 2.106.i33.

38. *THY*, 63.1102–03.

39. Tapering toward the end, one chapter is devoted to the in-laws, one to the eunuchs, four to legal officials (benign and cruel ones), three to men of virtues (filial piety and righteousness), two to famous scholars, three to literary talents, one to monks and priests, one to hermits, one to chaste women, and seven to the neighboring tribes that sit at the end.

40. The histories of the previous dynasties, compiled by Wei Zheng and others, present a similar structure and are apt reflections of Tang ministers' ideologies.

41. This flaw is corrected in another genre, the annalistic history epitomized by the *Comprehensive Mirror for Governing,* by the Song historian Sima Guang. Intended to serve as a guiding mirror for the ruler, the didactic function of the genre is self-evident.

42. The practice of keeping records of daily court activities left the Five Dynasties historians with plenty of materials drafted by their Tang predecessors, and in most cases, the judgments on bureaucrats and sovereigns were already cast by Tang historians.

43. *THY,* 63.1112–13.

44. *THY,* 63.1094–95.

45. *JTS,* 71.2557.

46. Women have been positioned next to the little men for over two centuries, sanctified by the famous indictment from Confucius: "Only women and the little men are impossible to raise. When you are close to them, they become insolent; when you keep a distance, they complain." *Lun Yu* (The analects), in *Sishu jizhu* (Collected annotations on the four classics) (Hong Kong: Taiping Publisher, 1964), 125–26.

47. It may be simplistic to place such cultural and social prejudices under the Confucian ideology alone, yet if we consider the School of Moism, whose members were lower-class people adhering to the doctrine of undifferentiated love, which tried to erase ethical boundaries; Taoism that distances itself from moral judgment and places priority on the feminine principle; and the Logicians who concerned themselves with abstract debates, only Legalism, the many doctrines of which the Confucians had absorbed, is left to share the blame. Yet the Legalist theory and practice concentrate more on governing through laws and punishment than through education, rites, and ethical codification, which are the stock of Confucian teachings and its principal constituents of ideology. However, one should also note that Confucianism, as it stands today, is very much a hybrid with elements derived from Taoism and Legalism; even Buddhism has its contribution since neo-Confucianism. More importantly, there is a serious discrepancy between theory and practice, and it will only be fair to separate the actual teachings of the classics from their practices by the gentry, both among themselves and in the political arena.

48. One may compare this stress on responsibilities for others with the emphasis on a ruler's control of the self, in both the Confucian classics and in the Western imperial epochs. See *The Great Learning* (Daxue) and *Doctrine of the Means* (Zhongyong); also Michel Foucault, *The History of Sexuality,* vol. 3, *The Care of the Self* (New York: Vintage Books, 1988), 81–95.

CHAPTER 2

1. Claude Lévi Strauss, *The Elementary Structures of Kinship,* trans. James Bell (Boston: Beacon Press, 1969), chap. 5; Gayle Rubin, "The Traffic in Women," in *Toward an Anthropology of Women,* ed. Rayna Reiter (New York: Monthly Review Press, 1975), 157–210.

2. *XTS,* 83.3644.

3. An excellent example is the case of Zheng Hao, who long bore a bitter grudge against Bo Mingzhong for having recommended that he marry Princess Wanshou, daughter of X'uanzong, thus preventing him from uniting with the prominent Lu clan. *ZZTJ,* 249:8046.

4. Their gang included another royal couple, the Princess Baling and her husband Chai Lingwu. Fang Yiai was exiled, protected by his dead father, the Revered Minister Fang Xuanling. The father however was consequently dispelled from Taizong's sacrificial temple.

5. *THY,* 57.981.

6. After Xue's death, Wu Youji's wife was killed for him to marry Taiping.

7. The two were married soon after her husband's death.

8. *XTS,* 83.3654.

9. *XTS,* 34.878. Her request for the great Pond Kunming being rejected, Anle dug Pond Dingkun and seized one senior princess's mansion, destroying its neighboring dwellings.

10. *XTS*, 83.

11. In an amusing episode, a reluctant courtier was ordered to serve the elderly Azang, mother of Wu Zhao's male concubine Zhang Yizhi.

12. See *XTS*, 34.

13. Taiping was first ordained priestess to pray for the afterlife of her grandmother and then to avoid marriage with Tibet. Princess Wan'an too was ordained priestess to pray for the spirit of Ruizong during his mourning. According to Ruizong's defense of building the belvederes for the Princesses Yuzhen and Jinxian, it was for the blessings of his mother that they were ordained. Princess Huayang requested to enter the religious life on account of ill health, another prominent reason for ordination. Of these, the most unique may be the Princess Xinchang, who requested to join the order after the death of her husband. *ZZTJ*, 210.3.14; *THY*, 50.877.

14. Edward Schafer discusses the poems on Yuzhen and her famous belvedere in "The Princess Realized in Jade," in *T'ang Studies*, no. 3 (1985), 1–24. Poems that allude to their romantic liaison include Li Shangyin's controversial "Bi cheng" (Green City) and "Henei" (River region), which have been interpreted as critiques on the princesses' illicit conduct.

15. *THY*, 50.871–75.

16. Although historically, except during the reign of the Emperor Zetian, Buddhism held a lower status than Taoism for the royalty, its influence remained strong throughout the Tang.

17. *XTS*, 83.3676.

18. The Princess Hanyang cried inconsolably when taking leave to her betrothed's home; when asked if unsatisfied, she replied: "Just the thoughts of parting—I have no other regret."

19. Princess Jiaohe, daughter of a defected tribal leader, was made princess prior to her marriage to a Turkestan khan. This conceit backfired as the princess failed to exact respect from Tang officials at the border, which infuriated the sultan. The sultan however was a man of clever means, who later married a Tibetan and then a Turkish princess, making all three women principal wives. The value of a Tang princess was thus vastly downgraded. *ZZTJ*, 212.5.23; 213.1.19; 214.5.12.

20. Interestingly, at least in two incidents, men were exchanged: Wu Yanxiu (by Zetian's order) and a minister from Tibet (during Zhongzong's reign) were sent to wed the woman of the other party. *JTS*, 6.126; 7.148.

21. *ZZTJ*, 213.6.2.

22. Two years later, the princess requested a monument be installed at the Red Mount to mark the border between the Tang and Tibet; a monument was installed and peace was vouchsafed for a few years, until Tibet stopped its tribute and warred with the Tang until Jincheng's death. *ZZTJ*, 213.8.4; 214.7.14.

23. In a radical case, in her twenty-one years in Uighur, Princess Xian'an married first the khan, then his son, his grandson, and a minister, respectively, following the tribal custom when one man ascended the throne after another. Although the Tang did not in theory and in practice stress the code of chastity, such undiscriminating marriages within the family seems absurd even by liberal standards. *THY*, 6.77.

24. *XTS*, 83.3669.

25. For accounts of Taihe's turbulent career, see *XTS*, 83; *JTS*, 16; and *ZZTJ*, 241.3.16; 246.4.19, 5.19, 2.13; 247.1.1.

26. *THY*, 6.78.

27. *XTS*, 83.3675.

28. *ZZTJ,* 209.3.14; 213.2.6; 214.2.4.

29. *JTS,* 17.576.

30. *XTS,* 83.3672. 31. The change of climate had a decisive effect: X'uanzong's daughter, the Princess Guangde, demanded her own death after her husband was killed by the rebel Huang Chao and in the end took her own life. *ZZTJ,* 248.5.12.

CHAPTER 3

1. *ZZTJ,* 199.6.6.

2. After the Northern Zhou was overthrown by the Sui, over a thousand of its imperial consorts were placed in the Wanshan Buddhist Convent. *Tang liangjing chengfang kao* (Research on two capitals of the Tang), by Xu Song (Taipei: Shijie, 1963), 4, 18.

3. The notorious Xu Jingzong induced the exile of his son who continued to violate his favored maid-concubine. *JTS,* "Biography of Xu Jingzong," 82.2764.

4. See *JTS,* 5, "The Annals of Gaozong." The death of Gaozong was recorded with vivid details, which may bring us to a better understanding of the man who was condemned for bringing in the destructive force of Wu Zhao (111–12).

5. In the traditional conception, the most devious acts are associated with women, who stand in close vicinity with the treacherous "little men," and this furthers the inner palace's association with rumors of unspeakable malevolence.

6. The conspicuous case of Wu's killing her infant daughter to frame the Empress Wang is viewed with skepticism by modern scholars due to its fictitious quality, typical of the inner palace version of female vice. Two issues had led to the demise of Wang: first, she was without a son; second, she was accused of practicing witchcraft. The framing of murder, if true, did not contribute to her demise but had only a psychological effect on Gaozong. Wang was never formally accused of the crime, and the argument over the termination of her empresshood was steeped in the issue of propriety, leaving Gaozong without a stronger stance to push his will. In short, both the alleged murder and its effect remained shaky, beyond any possibility of proof.

7. *Da Tang xinyu* (New words from the great Tang), by Liu Su (Beijing: Zhonghua, 1984), 12.180–81; *JTS,* 51.2170.

8. From Li Hong's funeral inscription and the two edicts proclaiming his posthumous titles drafted by the mournful father, it is obvious that the heir had long suffered from tuberculosis. Modern scholars have argued strongly against this murder proclaimed in *XTS;* among Wu's many accused crimes, this is one that can be refuted with persuasive evidence. "Edict for the Crown Prince to Be Posthumously Titled Emperor Xiaojing" and "Edict for Posthumously Titled Xiaojing Emperor," in *Tang dazhaoling ji* (Compilation of Tang edicts), compiled by Song Shou and Song Minqiu (Shanghai: Shangwu, 1959), 26. *Wu Zetian zhuan* (Biography of Wu Zetian), by Hu Ji (Xi'an: San Qin Publisher, 1986), 47–52. Li Xian was possibly the son of Wu's widowed sister, the Lady Han-quo, conceived by Gaozong.

9. We should note here the binary opposition of a loving mother versus a rigid father.

10. Yan Zhiwei, who had failed his mission as an envoy to the Turks accompanying Wu Yanxiu, the bridegroom-to-be, surrendered to the latter, and when he was released to

return to the capital, a punishment of extraordinary brutality awaited him, enlisting all courtiers as onlookers. *ZZTJ*, 206.2.22.

11. Antonino Forte, *Political Propaganda and Ideology in China at the End of the Seventh Century* (Napoli: Instittuto Universitario Orientale, 1976), 263.

12. Forte, *Political Propaganda*, 269–70.

13. Forte, *Political Propaganda*, 161–62. For a detailed discussion on the Bright Hall, see Wechsler, "The Ming-tang," in *Offerings of Jade and Silk*, 195–211.

14. Forte, *Political Propaganda*, 268. Emphasis mine.

15. *JTS*, 6.133.

16. The theory of Wu Zhao's conscious increasing of the examination-recruited bureaucrats who provided the foundation of her government has been subject to criticism; similarly, Chen Yinke's theory of Wu's promoting the new faction to oppose the old Shandong bloc has been questioned by Twichet, for whom the dividing line is not so distinct (*Cambridge History of China*). In a memorial by Liu Xiangdao in 657, it was warned that Wu's policy had resulted in a wasteful swell of administration as well as lowering of standards. "Biography of Liu Xiangdao," *JTS*, 81. Such drastic expansion points to Wu's will to buy out the literati, whether or not for a strategic purpose of fending off the old bloc.

17. *JTS*, 89.2894. The "good man" Di recommended turned out to be Zhang Jianzhi, the prime minister who later brought Wu's downfall.

18. Wu had secured her own scholars while an empress. Under her instructions, the Northern Gate Scholars compiled *New Amendment for the Hundred Ministers, The Track for Ministers,* and *Biographies of Women,* among others. Gradually these scholars became Wu's wager against the chief ministers.

19. Li Shangyin, "Yidu neiren" (The Yidu palace maid), in *Fannan wenji xiangzhu,* in *Sibu Beiyao* (Beijing: Zhonghua, 1981), vol. 462, chap 8, 34–35.

20. *JTS*, One immediate example is the old nun under the patronage of Wu Zhao who was discovered to have indulged in a licentious lifestyle with her many disciples. *ZZTJ*, sections on Tang, 20.204.6498–550.

21. *ZZTJ*, 203.2.26. Whether the ascension of a woman sovereign had changed the landscape of the inner palace had not been recorded. Presumably palace women remained to serve the heir apparent.

22. *ZZTJ*, 205.4.3.

23. "Biography of Zhang Xingcheng," *JTS*, 78.2506–07.

24. The answer was: "This is precisely how I return your highness's kindness." *ZZTJ*, 207, 6.3, 585.

25. *JTS*, 7.143.

26. "Biography of Du Jingjian," *JTS*, 90.2912.

27. *ZZTJ*, 207.2.

28. By her fourth son, Emperor Ruizong, Wu was first stripped to her earlier title, the "Heavenly Empress," then honored as the "Great Divine Heavenly Empress," and finally as the "Heavenly Empress Divine Emperor." After the ascension of her grandson Xuanzong, a mere "Divine Empress" remained. There is some discrepancy between *Xin Tang shu, Tang huiyao,* and *Zizhi tongjian.* Sima Guang's record disagrees with the two in that he has made the conferment of honor an event after the ascension of Xuanzong, whereas in the other two it was clearly Ruizong's last doing, and the return to Divine Empress the first act by Xuanzong. *Jiu Tang shu* agrees with the two. At 716, the title "Empress Zetian" was in order;

at 749, together with other empresses, Wu was conferred as the "Devout Divine Empress Zetian."

29. "Annals of Zhongzong," *JTS*, 7.136–37; *ZZTJ*, 209.3; *ZZTJ*, 214.935.

30. *THY*, 37.675–78.

31. *XTS*, 132.4538–39.

32. Witness *Guoshi Dagang* (Outlines of a national history) (Shanghai: Shanghai Bookstore, 1989), by the renowned scholar Qian Mu, in which Wu is referred to throughout as Empress Wu, and a critique of her career is much in effect.

33. *Chaoye qianzai*, by Zhang Zhuo, (Beijing: Zhonghua, 1979) 5.117. Recounted by Sima Guang in *ZZTJ*.

34. *Songchuang zalu* (Miscellaneous from pine windows), by Li Rue, in *Shuofu Sanzhong* (Three collections of Shuofu)(Shanghai: Guji, 1988), 1:50.

CHAPTER 4

1. The ranks run like this: Under the empress are *fei* (four altogether), *bin, jieyu, meiren, cairen* (nine each), and *baolin, yunu, cainu* (twenty-seven each).

2. *ZZTJ*, 249.

3. Under the Twenty-four Divisions are Twenty-four Dian and Twenty-four Zhang, including *zhenggong, tongshi, nushi*, etc.

4. *JTS*, 7.149.

5. *XTS*, 207.5873.

6. *ZZTJ*, 218, 1.7, 1104–05. Rf. Paul Kroll, "The Flight from the Capital and the Death of Consort Yang," in *T'ang Studies*, no. 3 (1985), 25–54.

7. *Kaitian chuanxinji* (Collections of hearsay), by Zheng Qi, in *TDCS*, 3:2; *Minghuang Zalu* (Miscellaneous Records from Xuanzong) (Beijing: Zhonghua, 1994), 51.

8. *ZZTJ*, 216, 4.3, 1016.

9. *Tang guoshi bu* (Attachment to Tang history), by Li Zhao (Shanghai: Gudian wenxue, 1957), 18.

10. "Zi jing fu fengxian yonghuai wubai zi" (From the capital to Fengxian, five hundred words of sentiments), in *Dushi jingquan* (Mirror exegesis on Du Fu) (Taipei: Huazheng Publisher, 1978), 108–11.

11. *XTS*, 5.153.

CHAPTER 5

1. *Liji zhengyi* (Annotated book of rites) (Taipei: Shijie, 1963), chapter 18.

2. "Xinji xiongji shuyi" (Collection of rites on funerals and weddings), in *Dunhuang hunyin wenhua* (Marriage culture in Dunhuang), by Tan Chanxue (Gansu: Renmin Publisher, 1993), 12–16.

3. The symbolic meaning of Chang E's flight is discussed in part 4, chapter 12.

4. In a mother's admonition of her daughter, the lines read: "At home you are spoiled; now as Other's wife, entrust yourself to destiny. . . . Where you were born you are but a

guest; follow now your husband to your home." "Cuishi furen xunnü wen" (Lady Cui's admonition of daughters), in *Dunhuang hunyin*, Tan, 18–19.

5. *Tanglu Xintan* (New investigation on the Tang legal codes), by Wang Limin (Shanghai: Sheke Research Academy, 1993), 61–71.

6. "A lord as a lord, a minister as a minister, a father as a father, and a son as a son" (*The Analects*, 82).

7. Wang, *Tanglü xintan*, 1–4.

8. Exegesis on "Shi e" (Ten vices), in *Tanglü shuyi*, chap. 1.

9. *THY*, 39.712–13.

10. For the above legal codes, see Wang, *Tanglü xintan*, 13–14, 22–23.

11. In his attempt to guard against the rebels in the An Lushan faction, Zhang resorted to killing his concubine and serving her up to satiate the soldiers' hunger. Later, women in the city one by one were consumed to sustain the resistance; after them came the elderly and the children. *XTS*, 192.5534–41.

12. *ZZTJ*, 209, 680. *Chaoye Qianzai* (Records from the court and the people), by Zhang Zhuo (Beijing: Zhonghua, 1979), 5.117.

13. Rf. Li Yuzhen, 96.

14. Wang Dang, *Tang yulin*, 4.i603. Li Zhao, *Tang guoshi bu*, 2, 81.

15. A mother of the Annan bandits' leader severed her tie with her son, after her admonishments had failed, and insisted on living alone. In another case, a mother wept with joy at her son's arrest, proclaiming: "Now I would no longer be implicated and become a palace maid." Li Zhao, *Tang guoshi bu*,1.22.

16. A radical example of unconventional motherhood is presented in *New Words from the Great Tang*. A woman had sued her son for impiety and was not repentant when she was told to prepare his coffin. It was discovered that she had an affair with a Taoist priest, and the two schemed to be rid of the son who had been prohibitive of their tie. This unique tale, said to have happened at the Henan Province, facilitates one extreme example of female desire that rejects maternal bondage. *Da Tang xinyu*, 5.68.

17. For a taste of actual conjugal relationships in the Tang and Song, see *Bo-Kong liutie* (Six scrolls by Bo and Kong), by Bo Juyi and Kong Chuan (Shanghai: Guji, 1992), chapters on marriage.

18. *Nü xiaojing* (Classic of filial piety for women) (Shanghai: Guji, 1988), in *Shuofu sanzhong*, additional chapter 7:3288.

19. Rf. Michel Foucault, *Discipline and Punish* (New York: Vintage, 1991), 3–31.

20. *Women's Analects*, in *Zhuangyuan ge nu sishu* (The four classics for women from Zhuangyuange), Qing boxed edition, 2:13. In *Yishan zazuan* (Miscellaneous by Yishan), under the item for female education, singing is listed as a taboo. *TDCS*, 5.5. Although commonly taken to be by Li Shangyin, contemporary scholars conclude that it is actually by Li Jiujin with the same byname who wrote *Yishan Zazuan*.

21. "Yake xinfu wen," in *Dunhuang bianwen jiaozhu* (Exegesis on Dunhuang Buddhist narratives), ed. Huang Zheng et al. (Beijing: Zhonghua Publisher, 1997), 7, 1216.

22. In one rare case, a concubine Ma Shu had the honor of having her own funeral inscription. Although on rare occasions concubines are mentioned, it is mainly in the context of a list of the names of their children, while their own names are omitted. See *Liu Zongyuan ji* (Collected writings by Liu Zongyuan) (Taipei: Huazheng, 1990), 2:1349–58; 1:347. More often, the existence of concubines can only be conjectured by the extra num-

ber of children attached at the end of the list. Examples include inscriptions for Wei Dan, Li Ruan's wife Lady Xiguo, Li Weijian, Zheng Qun, in *Han Changli wenji* (Literary collections of Han Changli)(Shanghai: Guji, 1986), 380; 433; 465–66; 519.

23. In the miscellaneous records of the Tang from *Youyang zazu* (Miscellaneous notes from Youyang), by Duan Chengshi (Beijing: Zhonghua Bookstore, 1981), to *Duyang zabian,* (Miscellaneous notes from Duyang) by Su E, *TDCS,* anecdotes of female jealousy abound.

24. The mortality rate of young women seemed high in the Tang judging from the records of tombstone inscriptions. The remarriage rate among men hence also seems unusually high, following the deaths of sometimes more than one wife. If the Japanese Heian period is anything comparable, deaths from pregnancy complications might have been one cause for this high rate of premature deaths among women. According to Patricia Ebrey's findings, female death in childbirth was responsible for the disproportionately high rate of deaths for women before age forty in the Song. Ebrey, "Jealousy," 155. The remarriage rate for Tang gentry women is less easy to arrive at, there being far fewer funeral inscriptions for women.

25. *Zhongguo hunyin shigao* (Historical manuscripts of Chinese marriage), by Chen Peng (Beijing: Zhonghua, 1990), 712.

26. *Miscellaneous Writings of Yishan* mentions a man's plight of having to beat up a favored concubine to appease an angry wife, and his awkward position in facing a beloved concubine jealous of the wife. Under the item "Inconsolable" is the quarrel between couples over a maid, a rather vulgar situation. In *TDCS,* 5.1–4.

27. These are mere doctrines, and studies show that there were discrepancies in the actual practices of divorcing wives in different eras. Rf. *Tang qian hunyin* (Pre-Tang marriages), by Deng Weizhi (Shanghai: Wenyi, 1988), and Chen Peng, *Chinese Marriage,* 606–27.

28. *Suishu* (Sui history), by Wei Zheng (Shanghai: Zhonghua, 1936), "Biography of the Empresses," chap. 36.

29. Duan Chengsi, *Youyang zazu,* 132.

30. *Yuguanzi zhenlu* (True records by Yuguan zi), anonymous, in *Shuofu,* vol. 1, chap. 11.220.

31. Divorcing a wife on account of her jealousy seems to have decreased in later dynasties, under the influence of the conception that divorce is unethical. See Chen Peng, *Chinese Marriage,* 624–25.

32. *Chaoye Qianzai,* 4.91.

33. Sigmund Freud, "'Civilized' Sexual Morality and Modern Nervousness," in *Sexuality and the Psychology of Love* (New York: Collier Books, 1963), 32.

CHAPTER 6

1. Michel Foucault, following van Gulik's assessment, supposed that in ancient China, due to her competitive position in the polygamous society, a wife had the function of offering sexual pleasure to her mate. *The History of Sexuality* (New York: Vintage, 1988), 2:143–44. There seems to be a misunderstanding here, considering the broader social and ethical constructs and the tilted emphasis of Taoist sexual yoga on masculine gains.

2. Douglas Wile, *Art of the Bedchamber: The Chinese Sexual Yoga Classics* (New York: New York University Press, 1992), introduction.

3. Wile, *Art of the Bedchamber,* 12.

4. *Seeking Instruction on the Golden Elixir,* trans. Wile, in Wile, "Art of the Bed Chamber," 150.

5. trans. Wile, 13.

6. On the tension between the two social groups, see Chen Yenke, *Tangdai shehui zhengzhi shigao* (Manuscript of the Tang social and political history) (Chongqing: Shangwu, 1943), 38–93.

7. Things may work in reversed order, as in the case of Fei Yun who, shortly upon his engagement with the powerful Xiao Chu, passed the civil examination. In a counterexample, Li Pu returned his father-in-law's admonishment by stating that neither his passing the exam nor his official post were obtained through the latter's effort. Li's wife, whose jealousy was the cause of this dispute, died of anger after this. Wang Dang, *Tang Yulin*,7.i989, i965.

8. We will devote space to readings of these works in part 3.

9. *THY,* 83.

10. At the opposite end were women of poor families who, lacking financial and social attractions in the pedigree-wild Tang, often married late. One of the favored subjects for Tang poets was unwed maids in depleted surroundings.

11. Patricia Ebrey, *Marriage*, 97–132. The meaning of the change of dowry however is still subject to debate.

12. Ebrey, *Inner Quarters*, 1–9.

13. The change of intellectual structure in the Renaissance had the same effect of lifting men's intellectual level while simultaneously putting women in a much more disadvantaged position. Hilda Smith, in *Liberating Women's History,* 369–83.

14. Sexual metaphors are not readily conjured up in their pleas with the powerful—although in the political allegories, this is not a truism.

15. Luo Yin, who remained politically obscure most of his tormented life, complained bitterly about his ill fate as a result of his refusal to seek strong patrons.

16. *XTS,* 168.5134–36.

17. It is easy to perceive both Liu and Li's solitary existence as a necessary composite of their relative obscurity in the political arena. Wang Wei, however, was secretary on the right at Suzong's court, and possession of entertainers would only be natural if not for the Buddhist piety that steered him to a different course.

18. "Daowangji" (Mourning for my dead concubine), in *Huanhua ji* (Anthology of washing the flowers). Wang Dang, *Tang yulin,* 6.i843; Fan Shu, *Yunxi youyi, TDCS,* 3.8.

19. In one case, on account of his mother's displeasure with his wife, a man divorced her, stating: "One takes a wife for the purpose of serving the parents; now that she brings displeasure, how dare I keep her?" *Bai-Kong Liutie,* 30.3.272.

20. *Bo Juyi shiji* (Poetry anthology of Bo Juyi) (Shanghai: Guji, 1980), 28–29. In a social document, Yan Zhenqing is recorded to have punished a woman who sought divorce from her impoverished husband with thirty lashes; the man was rewarded with grains and silk. Fan Shu, *Yunxi youyi,* in *TDCS,* 3.4.

21. One extreme example is the killing of Yan Tingzhi's favorite concubine by his son, who was outraged by Yan's neglect of his mother. Yan was delighted by the youth's gallant act, a reaction that exposes further the nonvalue of a concubine. *Bo-Kong liutie,* 17.10.277.

22. When two sisters were entrusted to Sun Tai, out of righteousness he chose to marry the invalid elder; another man did not mind the extreme ugliness of his virtuous wife and advised his friend to feel likewise. *Tang zhi yan* (Gathered words of the Tang) (Taipei: Shijie Bookstore, 1959), 3.46. *Benshi shi (Anecdotes of poetry),* in *TDCS,* 7.3.

23. In poems addressed to courtesans in the convention of lament, more intense emo-

tions can be seen. The problematic of boudoir lament as love poem is discussed in part 3, chapter 10.

24. From the seventeenth-century *Liaozhai zhiyi* (Records of the strange from makeshift studio) to *Honglou meng* (Dream of the red chamber) and its critical readings, from Virgin Mary to Mary Magdalen, the idea of complementary women prevailed in the male imagination.

25. "Amorous rain clouds flew away, for two decades we were parted/Sleepless, I sought after dreams/Now with white heads we meet again/Back at the sumptuous banquet of the lord Xiang." *Benshi shi* (Anecdotes of poetry composition), in *TDCS*, 7.3–4.

26. Wang Dang, *Tang yulin*, 7.i900.

27. *Benshi shi*, in *TDCS*, 6.2.

28. *Beili zhi* (Record of Nothern Quarters), in *TDCS*, 6.5–7.

29. Gilles Deleuze and Felix Guatari, *Anti-Oedipus: Capitalism and Schizophrenia* (Minneapolis: University of Minnesota Press, 1983), 119.

30. Theodor Adorno, "Subject and Object," in *The Essential Frankfurt School Reader,* ed. A. Arato (New York: Continuum, 1994), 499.

31. Adorno, "Subject and Object," 508.

CHAPTER 7

1. There were far fewer professional women recorded in the Tang compared to the many diverse professions of European women in the Middle Ages. Foremost women entrepreneurs recorded in the Tang included wine sellers (often foreign women), at least one cargo-ship owner, and the controversial witches. Other professions included weaving and embroidery as home industry, manual labor, and gold mining.

2. Zhang Zhuo, *Chaoye qianzai*, in *TDCS*, 1.3.

3. Starting from the late Song, although officials could enjoy the courtesans' company at banquets, sexual relations with them were prohibited. This had the effect of creating a more widespread practice of adopting private entertainers. Wu Zhou, *Zhongguo jinü shenghuoshi* (History of Chinese courtesans) (Hunan: Wenyi Publisher, 1990), 192.

4. Such an argument is sustained by the Tang narratives, which are obsessed with the various fates of the courtesans, and by numerous poems on these women.

5. The frivolous Cui Ya, fond of ridiculing courtesans who feared his crude satires, once slandered Li Duanduan's appearance and brought an ill turn to her business; Li begged for mercy, and Cui produced another poem to the opposite effect. In Fan Shu, *Yunxi youyi, TDCS*, 3.1–2.

6. The Song entertainers, first official ones and then the more reputed city courtesans, were made to sell wines when the state pushed out its annual wine production. Official courtesans all but disappeared after the Yuan, and entertainers/prostitutes moved closer to the merchants and citizens of the cities when officials were banned from their quarters.

7. *Benshi shi*, in *TDCS*, 7.4, 7. Liu's poem runs: "A sight seen often by her master/Would yet break all of my hearts."

8. For a brief discussion of the terms used for courtesans, see Song Dexi, "Tangdai de jinü" (Tang courtesans), in *Zhongguo funu shi lunji xuji* (Collected essays on the history of Chinese women), second volume, ed. Bao Jialin (Taipei: Daoxiang, 1991), 67–70.

9. Sun Qi, *Beili zhi,* in *TDCS,* 6.4.

10. Typically, poems composed for courtesans are in the quatrain ("broken-off lines") or eight-line "regulated verse" format. Occasionally, there are also double regulated verses.

11. Wang Dang, *Tang yulin,* 3.i307.

12. *Beili zhi,* 6.3.

13. Finding it difficult to cope with the ennui of a kept woman, from her window Chu Er looked at passersby and sorted out her old acquaintances. The beatings she suffered from her military lord were as hard as her determination not to remain passive in this house that retained her. *Beili zhi,* in *TDCS,* 6.5–6.

14. Cui Lingxin, *Jiaofang ji* (Record of the entertainment bureaus), in *TDCS,* 7.2.

15. At the Zhide Belvedere, Xuanzong was outraged by the coquettish costumes and makeup of the priestesses and ordered them expelled. Wang Dang, *Tang yulin,* 1.i126.

16. The most infamous among the transgressors was an elderly nun at the Lingzhi Temple who called herself Vimalaprabha Bodhisattva, who was first patronized and then executed by Wu Zhao upon the discovery of her licentious conduct with her many disciples. *ZZTJ,* Tang 20, 6498–550. In a fantastic tale, a monk who traveled with three nuns had them put on makeup and dance, and as the nuns became more visibly tempting, they were wiped out by the monk, who revealed that they were mere broomsticks. Duan Chengsi, "Strange Skills," *Youyang zazu,* 54–55. An item in *Yishan zazuan* states that adulterous monks' and nuns' scolding of children who laughed at them is a short-lived vice. *TDCS,* 5.1.

17. *ZZTJ,* 256.

18. Wang Dang, *Tang yulin,* 1, i121; "Biographies of Empresses," *JTS; Chaoye Qianzai,* 3.63.

19. *THY,* 61.1071.

CHAPTER 8

1. The genre is associated with the middle Tang "ancient style" movement, a countermove to the then dominating decorative style of prose writing. Many of the movement's central figures, including Han Yu and Bo Juyi's circle, his brother Bo Xing jian and friend Yuan Zhen, have left important tales in their names.

2. For a discussion of the five types of *vraisemblance,* see Jonathan Culler, *Structuralist Poetics: Structuralism, Linguistics, and the Study of Literature* (Ithaca: Cornell University Press, 1975), 138–60.

3. In the section "The Five Elements" in official Tang histories, supernatural phenomena from blood rain to the Drought Goddess to metamorphosis of humans into tigers are recorded. *XTS,* 36.893, 954.

4. Jonathan Culler, *The Pursuit of Signs: Semiotics, Literature, Deconstruction* (Ithaca: Cornell University Press, 1981), 169–87.

5. Tzvetan Todorov defines the fantastic as a genre that enacts a reading that hesitates between naturalistic and supernatural explanations. *Introduction à la littérature fantastique* (Paris: Seuil, 1970).

6. Curtis P. Adkins, "The Hero in Tang Ch'uan-ch'i Tales," in *Critical Essays on Chinese Fiction,* ed. W. Yang (Hong Kong: Chinese University Press, 1980), 23.

7. Wang Ching–hsien, "Towards Defining a Chinese Heroism," in *Journal of the American Oriental Society* 95 (1975): 30.

8. E. D. Edwards, *Chinese Prose Literature of the Tang Period* (London: Arthur Probsthain, 1937), 2:23–26.

9. The most renowned of all, Jing Ke, was both an expert in swordsmanship and well versed in the classics.

10. Li Wai-yi, *Enchantment and Disenchantment* (Princeton: Princeton University Press, 1993), 13–14. Li analyzes the rhetorical functions and inward turning of feminine tropes in the genre, without somehow spelling out the cultural implications of this literary device. Ye Shuxian proposes that in its sequence, "Shennü fu" (Ode on the goddess), the previously willing goddess becomes didactic and is transfigured from a goddess of Eros to that of Beauty. "Gaotang shennü: Zhongguo de weinasi" (Goddess of Gaotang: A Chinese Venus), in *Huaxia nüxing zhi mi* (Myths of Chinese women) (Beijing: Sanlian, 1990), 53–75.

11. Ye, "Gaotang shennü," 74; following Foucault, *History of Sexuality,* 1:83.

12. Rf. Toril Moi's exposition of Julia Kristeva's view that women are positioned as marginal to the symbolic order and to society, and that the repression of the feminine is realized in terms of positionality rather than of essence. Moi, *Sexual/Textual Politics, Feminist Literary Theory* (New York: Methuen, 1985).

13. Steven Owen calls such craving for the emperor a function of the "family romance," as analogies between family and state are explicit in classical texts. This father-son metaphor for the emperor-subject relationship is not without erotic overtones. *Traditional Chinese Poetry and Poetics: Omen of the World* (Madison: University of Wisconsin Press, 1985), 259–61.

14. The courtier as a sexual plaything for the king has been suggested but not well supported by historical evidence. See Wen Yiduo, "Qu Yuan wenti" (The problem of Qu Yuan), in *Wen Yiduo quanji* (Complete works of Wen Yiduo), 4 vols. (Shanghai: Sanlian Bookstore, 1948), 1:245–58.

15. The text retrieved from Japan, "You xianku" (A sojourn into the goddess's cave), by Zhang Wencheng, is a lengthy recounting of an erotic encounter with a goddess; their sexually charged conversation, together with the setting, makes clear that it is actually an experience in the courtesans' quarter.

16. Translations mine unless otherwise specified.

17. Readers familiar with Fredric Jameson's *The Political Unconscious: Narrative as a Socially Symbolic Act* (Ithaca: Cornell University Press, 1981) will notice my debt to his critical theory concerning the political implications of the unconscious.

18. The literati's wishful portrayal of the courtesans is a good reminder here. In her critique of Freud's thesis on penis envy, Irigaray argues: "To castrate the woman is to inscribe her in the law of the *same* desire, of desire for the same." Elsewhere she argues that Western discourse is incapable of representing femininity other than as the negative of its own reflection, and that man is incapable of thinking outside of his specular structure. See Luce Irigaray, *Ce sexe qui n'en est pas un* (*This Sex Which Is Not One*), trans. Catherine Porter (Ithaca: Cornell University Press, 1985). Although in the context of Tang narrative the mirror image is more of the double rather than the negative of male desires, Irigaray's critique will bear more weight as we delve into the genre.

19. Tales with this theme include "Lu Ke," "Zhangsun Shaozhu," "Dugu Mu," "Wang Yuanzhi," "Cui shusheng," and with variations, "Liu canjun," among others.

20. Jean Laplanche, *Life and Death in Psychoanalysis* (Baltimore: Johns Hopkins University Press, 1970), 103–24.

21. Jacques Derrida, "Plato's Pharmacy," in *Dissemination,* trans. Barbara Johnson (Chicago: University of Chicago Press, 1982).

22. From *Taiping guangji* (Comprehensive collection of the strange), compiled by Li Fang and others (Beijing: Zhonghua, 1961), 452.3694. Hereafter *TPGJ.*

23. In Western romance, the union between the hero and the lady symbolizes the completion of natural cycles and promises fertility, thus the marriage is likewise not an end in itself, but the means to a higher goal. See Northrop Frye, *A Natural Perspective: The Development of Shakespearean Comedy and Romance* (New York: Columbia University Press, 1965).

24. Rf. Li Zehou, *A History of Beauty* (*Mei de licheng*) (Taipei: Yuanshen, 1986), 154.

25. The dreams of begetting literary talents are another prominent trend. In these dreams men swallowed brush or pearl, their bodies were dissected to receive books, and they woke up a literary genius. The obsession with words contributed to this special genre of dreams.

26. The relation between emperor and ministers, the sexual antagonism between father and son are discussed in part 1, chapter 1. The authorship of "Record of a Travel through Zhou-Qin" is ascribed to the prime minister Niu Sengru by members of his opposing faction, with the alleged intention of bringing him disaster through the presumptuous proposition in the text. The significance of this textual problem is its registration of an awareness of the coveting of imperial consorts as an act of usurpation.

CHAPTER 9

1. Rf. Yue Hengjun, *Gudian xiaoshuo sanlun* (Essays on classical fiction) (Taipei: Cunwenxue, 1976), 198.

2. In Freudian psychoanalysis, melancholia and hysteria are considered symptomatic of female patients. As seen from these narratives, the female propensity for intensified suffering is not specific to the West. In "Mourning and Melancholia," Freud defines the latter symptom as a result of an incomplete process of mourning, which makes the object internalized and hence the mourning perpetual. This is applicable to the presentation of women in the narrative (and in boudoir lament) who are caught in a perpetual mourning over a thwarted love.

3. Arthur Waley, trans., "The Story of Miss Li," in *Anthology of Chinese Literature,* ed. Cyril Birch (New York: Grove Press, 1965) 305–6.

4. See James Hightower, "Yuan Chen and 'The Story of Ying–ying,'" *Harvard Journal of Asiatic Studies,* (hereafter/*HJAS*) 33 (1973), 90–123.

5. Chen Yinke, "Yuan Weizhi daowangshi ji yanshi gianzheng," (Exegesis on Yuan Weizhi's mourning and erotic poems), in *Chen Yinke xiansheng wenshi lunji,* (*Chen Yinke: Studies in history and literature*) (Hong Kong: Wenwen Publications, 1973), 2:369–96.

6. "Yingying Zhuan," in *TPGJ,* 488.4014. Translation mine.

7. In "Surprising Fame: Renaissance Gender Ideologies and Women's Lyric," Ann Rosalind Jones discusses the association of women's bodies with their speech, and the link between loose language and loose living in the Renaissance ethics for court women. Her emphasis is on the mutual exclusiveness of fame and female chastity. In *The Poetics of Gender* (New York: Columbia University Press, 1986), 76–80.

8. The fact that the text is originally called "Encounter with a Goddess," when the term

goddess commonly referred to the courtesans, has led Chen Yinke to suggest that Cui was in fact a courtesan, which justified Zhang's act of desertion as socially acceptable.

9. Paul Rouzer argues that their understandings of conventions, defined by a gender division, are different, which creates the ambiguous figure of Cui. Whereas Zhang treats amorous communications as playful conventions, Cui treats them with seriousness. "Interpreting Sexual Difference in the 'Story of Yingying,'" unpublished manuscript, May 1992.

10. Translation by Hightower with modifications.

11. Rf. Hightower, "Yuan Chen and 'The Story of Ying–ying,'" 120.

12. For a proposal of the narrative as part of the presentations to the powerful, and the inclusion of various styles from the lyrical to the expository as derived from this practice, see Chen Yinke, "Exegesis," 405–06.

13. We should also entertain the critique that the narrator is an invented voice. See Hightower, "Yuan Chen and 'The Story of Ying–ying,'" 120–22.

14. In "The Conception of Engendering, the Erotics of Editing," Mary Ann Caws talks about the political implications of a man editing a dead woman's manuscripts (in *The Poetics of Gender,* 42–62). In the context of Confucian wives, the manipulated female images in different discourses illustrate the seriousness of this condition.

CHAPTER 10

1. The problems of the lack of female readership are brought out by Maureen Robertson in her discussion of the production of feminine voices from the Six Dynasties to the Qing. "Voicing the Feminine: Constructions of the Gendered Subject in Medieval and Late Imperial China," *Late Imperial China* 13:1 (June 1992): 63–110.

2. For a detailed description of the psychological depth presented in the laments of the palace mode, see Ann Birrell, "The Dusty Mirror: Courtly Portraits of Women in Southern Dynasties Love Poetry," in *Expressions of Self in Chinese Literature,* ed. Robert Hegel (New York: Columbia University Press, 1985), 33–69. That Birrell takes palace lament as love poetry without questioning its legitimacy as such points both to her aversion to adopting a more critical stance, and the problematics of the identity of these poems as either male impersonation of boudoir sorrow (hence a *woman* in love), or as a disguise of the poet's own sentiments.

3. For a comprehensive study of the poetry on abandoned women, see *Abandoned Women and Poetic Tradition,* by Lawrence Lipking (Chicago: University of Chicago Press, 1988). Lipking includes a discussion of poems by Li Bo and Cao Zhi.

4. For a discussion of the transformation of *yuefu* from the Han to the late Tang, see Joseph Roe Allen, "From Saint to Singing Girl: The Rewriting of Lo-fu Narrative in Chinese Literati Poetry," *HJAS* (December 1988): 321–61; Paul Rouzer, "Watching the Voyeurs: Palace Poetry and the *Yuefu* of Wen Tingyun," in *Chinese Literature: Essays, Articles, Reviews* 11 (1989): 13–34. For a definition of the two aesthetic moments of the Southern Dynasties and late Tang, see Yang Hsien-ching, "Beyond the Flowers: Wu Wenyin's Song Lyrics on Objects" (Ph.D. diss., Princeton University, 1987), chap. 1. Rouzer ("Watching the Voyeurs," 28) mentions the historical theme of "flourishing and fading" (*xing-shuai*) as a motif Wen Tingyun has adopted from Li He.

5. In the Western tradition, this theme is prominent in Dante and Petrarch. The latter's

Canzoniere, a collection of love poems for the elusive Laura, renders the metaphorical meaning of the beloved as one identified with worldly glory.

6. Pauline Yu argues for the latter persuasively in *The Reading of Imagery in the Chinese Poetic Tradition* (Princeton: Princeton University Press, 1987), 115–17. The influence of shamanism on Qu's female personification should be checked with the knowledge that in the *Nine Songs,* male shamans courting goddesses are also profuse.

7. A much quoted episode concerning Li Bo's career in the court recounts how the powerful eunuch Gao Lishi was made to undo the drunk poet's boots, showing Li's untamed temperament in this political setting.

8. *Li Taibai quanji* (Complete works of Li Taibai), hereafter *LTB* (Shanghai: Shanghai Bookstore, 1988), 74. Translations mine unless otherwise specified.

9. David Hawkes, *Songs of the South* (New York: Penguin, 1985), 68 modified.

10. *The Analects,* 1. Translation mine.

11. *LTB,* 257.

12. In *Poems of the High Tang* Steven Owen explains this literary practice. The radical social distance between Li and Pei may be the rationale for such a feminine gesture. However, Li Bo often flaunts such distinctions.

13. The transformation of virtue into feminine terms is another conceit of Qu Yuan, as he wears fragrant garlands of his unwavering principles.

14. Xuanzong printed on his palace women's arms the words *fengyue changxin* (ever fresh eros), after they had been presented to him sexually. This and the practice of the red lizard remind us of the inscription on a courtesan's body and women's metonymical relation with words.

15. According to the commentator Hu Zhenheng, this piece expresses the sense of loss of a "minister-concubine." *Li Changji shige Jizhu* (Li anthology of Changji), hereafter *LCJ,* ed. Wang Qi et al. (Shanghai: Renmin Publisher, 1977), 154.

16. "Zhiri qianxing jifeng beisheng jiugelao liangyuan guren ershou" (At solstice, assuaging my moods, two poems respectfully sent to old friends at the two departments of the old cabinet). *Du Gongbu shiji* (Poetry anthology of Du Gongbu) (Hong Kong: Zhonghua Publisher, 1972), hereafter *DGB,* 1:410–11.

17. Patricia Ebrey makes this important statement in the context of the cultural milieu of the Song dynasty in "Woman, Marriage and the Family" in *Heritage of China,* ed. Paul Ropp (Berkeley: University of California Press, 1990).

18. The conventional title *Daowang* (Mourning for the dead), first used by Pan Yue in the Six Dynasties, becomes the standard title for mourning for a deceased wife.

19. "Beauty" here does not refer to a lord, since political allegory tends not to take on such erotic undertones.

20. *DGB*, 1:380.

21. The group of poems also appears in Wei Hu's *Caidiao ji* (Shanghai: Guji, 1993).

22. Wuminshi, "Za shi" (Miscellaneous poems), in *Quan Tang shih gaoben* (Manuscript edition of complete Tang poetry), hereafter *QTSG,* ed. Qian Qianyi et al. (Taipei: Lianjing Publisher, 1979), 71:280–81.

23. Compare this to the symbolic values of women in Western discourse: simply put, they function as the womb and the tomb, the origin of life and finality of death. Hence the woman as mother presents one quintessential feminine role. For a discussion of motherhood

in Western discourse, see Julia Kristeva, "Stabat Mater," in *Tales of Love* (New York: Columbia University Press, 1987), 234–64.

24. By Chen Tao, in *Tangren jueju pingzhu* (Quatrains by Tang poets) (Hong Kong: Zhonghua, 1980), 250.

25. *Chungui*, spring boudoir, refers to a young woman with erotic connotation, for *chun* often conveys a tinge of awakening eros.

26. From "Yelai yue" (Music of night-coming), in *LCJ*, 344.

27. Translation mine with reference to A. C. Graham, *Poems of the Late T'ang* (New York: Penguin, 1965), 102. Liu Ling was one of the Seven Sages of the Bamboo Woods in the Six Dynasties and a famous drinker.

28. Translation mine; rf. Graham, *Poems of the Late T'ang*, 113.

29. Lacan suggests that language operates by designating an object in its absence, and a subject constituted through language is marked by such splitting. *Feminine Sexuality, Jacques Lacan and the école freudienne,* ed. Juiet Mitchell and Jacqueline Rose, trans. Jacqueline Rose (New York: Norton, 1982), 31–32.

30. Attributed to Su Xiaoxiao, ca. A.D. 500; trans. Graham, *Poems of the Late T'ang*, 113.

31. The commentator Wang Qi has it that the tree dies of ecstasy for having been brushed by the goddess, just as the people rejoice over the goddess's revelation. *LH,* 286–87.

32. For an extensive study of Wen Tingyun's poetry, see Paul Rouzer, *Writing Another's Dream: The Poetry of Wen Tingyun* (Palo Alto: Stanford University Press, 1993).

33. *Wen Tingyun shici xuan* (Anthology of poetry and lyrics by Wen Tingyun), ed. Liu Sihan (Hong Kong: Joint Publishing Company, 1986), 157.

CHAPTER 11

1. Steven Owen provides a note stating that the evolution of political interpretation of Li Shangyin is a rather late phenomenon in "Poetry and Its Historical Ground," *CLEAR* 12 (Dec. 1990): 115.

2. For a discussion of *qing* in Chinese literature, see Tang Junyi, *Zhongguo wenhua jingshen* (The spirit of Chinese cultures) (Taipei: Zhengzhong, 1953), 338–48.

3. Hélène Cixous, "The Laugh of the Medusa," trans. Keith and Paula Cohen, *Signs* 1 (summer 1976): 875–99.

4. Charlotte Furth discusses various cases of sexual transformation in late imperial China and proposes that while male androgyny is celebrated and utilized for sexual advances, female androgyny is deemed sexual deficiency and inauspicious. "Androgynous Males and Deficient Females: Biology and Gender Boundaries in Sixteenth– and Seventeenth–Century China," *Late Imperial China* (December 1988): 1–31. The problem is complicated by the folk story of Hua Mulan in which a woman impersonates her father as a soldier, and by other stories of female cross-dressing.

5. This is in fact a man's interpretation: see Lawrence Lipking, *Abandoned Women and Poetic Tradition.*

6. For a discussion of how cultures shape the different ways of genders' loving, see Nancy Chodorow, "Individuality and Difference in How Women and Men Love," in *Femininities, Masculinities, Sexualities: Freud and Beyond* (London: Free Association Press, 1994), 70–92.

7. *Li Shangyin xuanji* (Complete works of Li Shangyin), hereafter *LSY,* ed. Zhou Zhenfu (Shanghai: Guji Publisher, 1986), 198.

8. *LSY,* 63–67. Rf. James Liu, *The Poetry of Li Shangyin* (Chicago: University of Chicago Press, 1969), 68–77. Liu translated the subject as "she" throughout the series. I have refrained from using subject indicators here to retain the ambiguity in the original.

9. Due to circumstances, Li was forced to leave home and learned later that Liuzhi was carried off by a lord.

10. *LSY,* 67–68; 198–99.

11. *Yuxisheng nianpu huiqian* (The compiled commentaries on Yuxisheng) (Taipei: Zhonghua, 1984), 312–13.

12. Steven Owen, "Place: Meditation on the Past at Chin–ling," *HJAS* 50, no. 2 (Dec. 1990): 417–58.

CHAPTER 12

1. For a discussion on how the politics of male editing affects the contour of female tradition, see Jowen Tung, "Huoyan kaogu: Zhongguo nüxing wenxue chuantong yuanqi yu yinan" (Fire archaeology: Origin and problematics of Chinese female literary tradition), *Zhongguo wenhua* (Chinese culture) 15–16 (December 1997): 109–27.

2. "Song of White Hair" is an ultimatum to the versatile Sima Xiangru who was seeking a concubine, and "Ballad of Forlorn" speaks of a vivid fear of abandonment by the Han emperor.

3. Poems with unmistakable feminine voices from the great oral tradition of *The Classic of Poetry,* for lack of textual evidence, have not been established as the font of female tradition in many anthologies of women's writings. This seems to me an unfortunate decision, for it not only deprives the tradition an unrestrained voice but also subjects it to a rather suspicious beginning. Female plaints of abandonment from the collection constitute the earliest and the most forceful works on this theme; they are counterbalanced by poems charged with sexual energies, creating together a rich texture of female writings.

4. *Beimeng suoyan* (Clustered words from northern dreams), by Sun Guangxian (Shanghai: Guji, 1987), chap. 6.

5. The growing texts on similar themes suggest that some of them were fabricated in later dynasties.

6. In the case of Xue Tao, whose lost collection, *Jinjiang ji* (Brocade River poems), contains over five hundred poems, the ratio is less than one-fifth; Yu Xuanji has fifty-odd poems available, whereas Li Ye, reputedly the best among them, has only eighteen. Chen Wenhua, *Tang nüshiren ji sanzhong* (Three anthologies of Tang women poets) (Shanghai: Guji, 1984), hereafter *TNSR.*

7. Collected in *Jiwen* (Records of Hearsays) and later classified under the "Women of Talents" category in the *Comprehensive Collection of the Strange.* Niu Su is allegedly the author of a handful of narratives in the fantastic mode, and the verified identity of the father renders the biography of the daughter veritable. The authorship of Song Ruozhao, however, is debatable.

8. See *Taiping guangji* under the section of dreams and Fan Shu, *Yunxi youyi,* in *TDCS,* 3.7.

9. *Lidai funu zuzuo kao* (Research on dynastic women's writings) (Shanghai: Guji, 1985), 23.

10. Anonymous, "Mengzhong Meiren," Ying Qiqi, "Yangchun Qu," *QTSG*, 71.100.

11. *Kaiyuan Tianbao yishi* (Anecdotes from Kaiyuan and Tianbao), *TDCS*, 2.13.

12. Li Shangyin, "Chang Er," LSY, 299.

13. See *Shanhai Jing Jiaozhu* (Exegesis on the *Classic of Mountains and Seas*), by Yuan ke (Shanghai: Guji, 1985); and *Huainan zi,* "Lanming xun," Gao You annotated (Shanghai: Zhonghua, 1936). In the astronomical knowledge of the Tang, the sun and the moon are mutually dependent; that the moon is feeding on the light of the sun to make itself present was also acknowledged.

14. By Lady Zhang, wife of a secretary at the Finance Department. *QTSG*, 71.71–72.

15. "Zeng Lu furen" (For Lady Lu) (*QTSG*, 71:157).

16. "Shi xinfu caizhi chucheng," in *Xue Tao shiqian* (Annotated poems by Xue Tao) (hereafter *XTSQ*), ed. Zhang Pengzhou (Beijing: Renmin Publisher, 1983), 11.

17. Cao Tang, "Jiu shi ba shou" in (Eight old poems presented), Schafer, "The Princess Realized in Jade," 206. The association of the feminine with the moon may have contributed to the existence of the following anecdote:

> At the beginning of Lasting Felicity [A.D. 821] Yang Yin–chih looked up Retired Gentleman Tang, a man of the Way, and was detained there overnight. Although the room was dark, no lamp had been set out. Tang called his daughter and said, "Why don't you bring us a moon in its lower chord?" His daughter took a slip of paper, made the shape of a moon, and pasted it to the wall. She conjured it, "We have a vis-itor this evening and wish you would bestow light and illumination!" In a moment the entire room was brilliantly lit. (*Bo-Kong liutie,* 1:18b–19a. Trans. Edward Schafer, *Pacing the Void: T'ang Approaches to the Stars* [Berkeley: University of California Press, 1977], 185.)

18. Parenthetically, the goddess Nü Wa should have been the ultimate predecessor for Chinese women, who according to the myth created mankind and patched up Heaven with molten stones. In early carvings, her half human, half snake figure intertwines with that of Fu Xi, inventor of the hexagrams, and the two appear as equals. Nü Wa was gradually writ-ten out of the list of principal mythical heroes, and the myth of Pan Gu created at the period of the Three Kingdoms deprived Nü Wa her centrality in the creation myths. See Du Fangqin, *Nüxing guannian de yanbian* (Transformation of the concepts on women) (Henan: Renmin Publisher, 1988), 36–37.

19. Wang Jian, Li Kuo, "Jingting ci," quoted in Cheng Qiang, *Tang diguo,* 457–59.

20. Biographical notes on Yao, *QTSG*, 71.148.

21. "Enming zhuiru liubie Guangling guren" (Summoned to the court, taking leave of friends at Guangling), in *TNSR*, 13.

22. "Duan xiangguo you Wudansi bing bunengcong tiji" (Ambassador Duan visited the Wudan Temple; sick, I was unable to follow, so I wrote and sent this), *XTSQ*, 30.

23. "Xiezhen ji fu" (A self–portrait sent to my husband), *QTSG*, 71.69–70.

24. In an anecdote, Guo Shaolan is said to have composed a poem and had a swallow send it to her husband, a rich merchant doing business in the south. *Kaiyuan tianbao yishi* (Anecdotes from Kaiyuan and Tianbao), *TDCS*, 2.12. The intense emotion of "Answer to My Husband" (Dafu), by Zhangsun Zuozhuan's wife, also exhibits the weight of letter writ-ing for woman. *QTSG*, 71.84.

25. Renowned for her stunning expertise, Lu Meiniang was presented to the court and

sewed seven scrolls of Lotus Stura on one foot of silk. *Duyang zabian* (Miscellaneous notes from Duyang), *TDCS,* 1:7.

26. A woman named Xue Yaoyin was especially ingenious: she had her maids cut light silk into thousands of flowers, dyed them, and had them scattered in the wind and rise up to the sky, calling them auspicious flowers, thus pleading for embroidery crafts. *Zhuanglouji* (Records of the boudoir), by Zhang Mi, *TDCS,* 8.3. When Cai Niang prayed at one occasion, the goddess appeared, promising her expertise and, ironically, a future incarnation as man. In *Guiyuan congtan* (Conversations from the boudoir), by Feng Yi, *TDCS,* 2.6.

27. *Liu Zongyuan ji,* 349.

28. The authorship of the text could perhaps be decided by internal textual evidence. Judging from the text's various phrasings and parallels, which lack the steady assurance of masculine discourse, this text attributed to Niu Yingzhen may indeed be a woman's text.

29. Luce Irigaray, *This Sex Which Is Not One,* chap. 4.

30. "Guang Wei Pou jiemei sanren shao gu" (The three sisters Guang, Wei and Pou are orphaned since young), in *TNSR,* 134–35.

31. "Zeng Zhengnülang guyi" (For a girl named Zheng, in ancient style), *QTSG,* 71.259.

32. There are records showing the existence of women's communities in Dun Huang documents, which contain two social contracts of "Women's Community" drafted in the Five Dynasties, right after the Tang. *Dun huang yishu* (Manuscripts from Dun huang), S527, 3489. Quoted in *Tangdai funü* (Tang women), by Gao Shiyu (Xi'an: San Qin Publisher, 1988), 134–35.

33. *TNSR,* 136.

34. "Aifen shi bing xu" (Poem of anguish, with a preface), *QTSG,* 71.99.

35. In "Fire Archaeology," I offer the proposition that the literati-feminine be actually considered as part of the female tradition, both as an ironic twist and an apprehension of the particular position of the literati in state ideologies.

CHAPTER 13

1. Gong Pengcheng, "Lun Tangdai de wenxue chongbai yu wenxue shehue," 1–98. Gong's emphasis on the cult of literature in the Tang tends to override political and economic factors of determinacy, proposing the literati as the central force for social grounding in the era.

2. "Fa fubian shang Wei xianggong" (Exiled to the frontiers, submitted to Minister Wei), *XTSQ,* 14–15. Translation mine with reference to Jeanne Larsen, *Brocade River Poems* (Princeton: Princeton University Press, 1987), 47–48.

3. Another female self–reference, *nu* (slave), seems to be a later convention in Song times and is an apt indicator of the further decline of women's status.

4. In his seminal *Zhongguo funü wenxue shihua* (History of Chinese women's literature), for example, Tan Zhengbi criticizes the series' self–abasement and, based on the information given in *Tang zhiyan,* judges that it was written by a certain Secretary Xue under Yuan Zhen in Zhejiang province, a man thousands of miles from Xue Tao. Zhang Pengzhou in his *Xue Tao shiqian,* on the other hand, states that since the discovery of *Youxuan ji* edited by Wei Zhuang, which includes the first of the ten partings under Xue Tao, the authorship has become indisputable. Judging from the strained effort of the later partings in the series, the

possibility of forgery should not be dismissed. A more questionable proposal is offered by the editor of the Ming edition of Xue's anthology, who submits that it was written to Yuan Zhen after a falling out between the two. In conjunction with the exile poems, the first of the series is more likely addressed to a minister under a similar situation. Xue being Yuan's senior by ten years, it would be inconceivable for Xue to write with such slight manners, while their relationship, judging from Yuan's single extant poem to Xue which is marked by decorous praise and goodwill, probably has nothing romantic about it.

5. *TNSR,* 74–76.

6. *Tangyin guiqian* (Compilation of Tang voices), by Hu Zhenheng (Shanghai: Guji, 1981), 8.83.

7. A courtesan who retired and aged with grace is a rare blessing; both Li Ye and Yu Xuanji suffered brutal death by execution according to several accounts, and many anecdotes recount the utter poverty and pathetic decline of the once glamorous courtesans. Wei Zhuang's lengthy "Zhang Haohao shi" (Poem on Zhang Haohao) is one of them. The ill fate of women is seen also in Heian Japan, when the old wandering nuns bespeak of the radical impoverishment of the past mistresses of the aristocrats.

8. This alludes to the famous story of Bo ya, who quit his zither after the death of Zhong Zi Qi, a friend who comprehended his music to the minutest details.

9. The significance of the problem will be more prominent when put in the context of Western feminists' proposal of androgynous writing by Virginia Woolf, and a transcendental bisexuality by Hélène Cixous. For them, to write transcending sexual definitions is the ultimate way of writing for women. Seen in this light, the plight of the courtesan-literatus is fatal, for she cannot assert her own androgyny without qualifications.

10. The Foucauldian deconstruction of the self's subjectivity, although important in the postmodernist climate, constitutes a paradox for the feminist pursuit of the female subject and should not be used here against the rationale of such questioning—it would be self-defeating to the point of being sophisticatedly hypocritical.

11. The association between spring and feminine yearning is another cliché, to which the phrase *spring boudoir,* alluding to a young woman with erotic connotations, testifies. The Yuan dramatist Tang Xianzu's *Mudan ting* (The peony pavilion) is one work that places feminine desire and spring dejection as composites.

12. For a discussion of the transformation of Chinese female lyrical tradition, see Jowen Tung, "Fire Archaeology."

13. "Ti Yinwuting" (Inscribed on the Misty Pavilion), *TNSR,* 117.

14. "You Chongzhenguan nanlou du xinjidi timing chu" (Visiting the South Hall of the Chongzhen Temple I saw the list of new successful candidates), *TNSR,* 111.

15. *TNSR,* 112.

16. "Yuan Weizhi zeng Tao shi yin ji jiushi yuzhi" (Yuan Weizhi sent me his poems, so I sent my old poems in return), *XTSQ,* 39. Translation mine with reference to Jeanne Larsen, *Brocade River Poems,* 88.

17. Xue suffered a resurrection in the Ming collection *Jiandeng yuhua* (Leftover words from cutting the wick), by Li Zhen, in which her soul made itself available to a certain literatus, and the author showed off his poetic virtuosity under the pretext of a courtesan-poet's apparition. Thus Xue's myth after death continued, and both her body and her poetry were violated by a linguistic act.

18. "Heren ciyun" (Following someone's rhyme), *TNSR,* 133.

19. *Tangyin guiqian,* 83.

20. On "Ge Hanjiang ji zi'an" (To Zi'an from across the River Han), *TNSR*, 128.

21. *Sanshui xiaodu,* quoted in *TNSR*, 139–40.

22. Including *Beimong suoyan* and *Nanbu xinshu* (New book from the South), by Qian Yi (Beijing: Zhonghua, 1958).

23. Tan, Zhongguo funü wenxue, 159–60.

Glossary

Anle 安樂
An Lushan 安禄山
Annan 安南
Anxi 安西

Bai Minzong 白敏宗
Baitou yin 白頭吟
Baizhang huaihai 百丈懷海
Baling 巴陵
Ban Gu 班固
Ban Jieyu 班婕妤
Ban Zhao 班昭
baolin 寶林
Beili zhi 北里志
bianwen 變文
bin 儐
Bo Xingjian 白行簡
Bo Ya 伯牙
buyu 不遇

cainü 采女
cairen 才人
Cao Cao 曹操
Chai Lingwu 柴令武
Chai Niang 柴娘
Chang'an 長安
Chang E 嫦娥
Chang Hao 常浩
Changning 長寧
Chengqian 承乾
Chengui 臣軌
Chen Shuozhen 陳碩真

Chen Tao 陳陶
Chen Zi'ang 陳子昂
Chongguo 崇國
chuanqi 傳奇
Chu Er 楚兒
chungui 春閨
Chu Suiliang 褚遂良
Ci`en ta 慈恩塔
conglin 叢林
Cui Lingxin 崔令欣
Cui Ya 崔涯
Cui Yingying 崔鶯鶯

Danyang 丹陽
daowang 悼亡
Da Tang xinyu 大唐新語
Dayunjing 大雲經
Dezong 德宗
Di Renjie 狄仁杰
dianshi 殿試
Dingkun 定昆
Dong Zhongshu 董仲舒
Du Jingjian 杜景儉
Du You 杜佑
Duan Chengshi 段成式

Ennin 圓仁

fangqishu 放妻書
Fang Xuanling 房玄齡
Fang Yiai 房遺愛
Fan Shu 范攄

fanzhen 藩鎮
Fan Zuyu 范祖禹
fengsu shi 風俗使
fengyue changxin 風月常新
fumei 撫媚

Ganye 感業
Gaoguo 郜國
Gaotang fu 高唐賦
Gaozong 高宗
gongguan 宮官
gongren xie 宮人斜
gongti 宮体
Guangling 廣陵
guiqing 閨情
guiyuan 閨怨
Guoguo 虢國
Guo Shaolan 郭紹蘭

Han Fei 韓非
Han Peng fu 韓朋賦
Hanyang 漢陽
Han Yu 韓愈
He Chujun 賀楚俊
He Jingzong 賀敬宗
huaigu 怀古
Huang Chao 黄巢
Huangfu Mei 皇甫枚
Huayan 華嚴
Hui Neng 慧能
Huo Xiaoyu 霍小玉
Hu Zhenheng 胡震亨

Ji 妓
Ji` 姬
Jiang Yan 江淹
jiao 醮
Jiaofang ji 教坊記
Jiao Ran 皎然
jieyu 婕妤
Jincheng 金城
Jing Ke 荊軻
jingting 鏡听
Jingzong 敬宗
Jinxian 金仙
Jiwen 紀聞
jiyuan 寄遠

Kong Chuan 孔傳

Liang Qiong 梁瓊
Li Deyu 李德裕
Li Duanduan 李端端
Li Er 李耳
Li Fang 李昉
Li Gongzuo 李公佐
Li He 李賀
Li Hong 李弘
Li Jing 李靖
Li Linpu 李林甫
Li Longji 李隆基
Li Qingzhao 李清照
Lisao 离騷
Li Shangyin 李商隱
Li Shimin 李世民
Li Si 李斯
Liu Congjian 劉從諫
Liu Gongquan 柳公權
Liu Ling 劉伶
Liu Mi 劉汨
Liu Su 劉肅
Liu Xiangdao 劉祥道
Liu Xichu 劉栖楚
Liu Yiqing 劉義慶
Liu Yuxi 劉禹錫
Liu Zhiji 劉知己
Liuzhi 柳枝
Li Wa 李娃
Li Xian 李賢
Li X`ian 李顯
Li Ye 李冶
Li Yi 李益
Li Yi' 李億
Li Yuan 李淵

Li Zhangwu 李章武
Lu Ji 陸機
Lu Meiniang 廬媚娘
Luoyang 洛陽
Luo Yin 羅隱
Lu Yu 陸羽

Ma Leiwu 馬雷五
Mawei 馬嵬
mianshou 面首
mingjing 明經
Mingtang 明堂
Mingying zhuan 冥應傳
Monjushiri 文殊師利
Muzhou 睦州
Muzong 穆宗

Nan Chucai 南楚材
neiguan 内官
Nie Yingniang 聶影娘
Niu Sengru 牛僧儒
Niu Su nu 牛蕭女
Niu Yingzhen 牛應貞
Nongyu 弄玉
nüren she 女人社

Ouyang Xiu 歐陽修

Pan Yue 潘岳
Pei Shuying 裴淑英
Pingyang 平陽

Qian Qianyi 錢謙益
Qijing 棋經
Qiu Shiliang 仇士良
qucong 曲從
Qu Yuan 屈原

Ren An 任安
Ruizong 睿宗
ruoyin 弱陰
Ru Tang qiufa xunli xingji

(Nitto guho junrei gyoki)
入唐求法巡禮行記

Shangguan Waner 上官婉兒
Shangyang 上陽
shengling gaoxie 生靈膏血
Shen Jiji 沈既濟
shennü 神女
Shen Xiu 神秀
Shen Yazhi 沈亞之
shihao 謚號
Shishuo xinyu 世說新語
Shouwang 壽王
shuangxiu 雙修
Sima Guang 司馬光
Sima Qian 司馬遷
Sima Xiangru 司馬相如
Song Ruoshen 宋若莘
Song Ruozhao 宋若昭
Song Qi 宋祁
Song Yu 宋玉
Sun Qi 孫棨
Suzong 蕭宗

Taihe 太和
Taiping 太平
Taizong 太宗
Tao Qian 陶潛
Tianbao 天寶
Tian kehan 天可汗
Tiantai 天台
Tong Dian 通典
Tongquetai 銅雀台

Wan'an 万安
Wang Bi 王弼
Wang Chang 王昌
Wang Dang 王讜
wangliang 魍魎
Wang Qiang 王嬙
Wang Shuwen 王叔文
Wang Xizhi 王羲之

Wanshan 萬善
Wanshou 萬壽
Wei Zheng 魏徵
Wei Zhuang 韋庄
Wencheng 文成
Wendi 文帝
Wen Tingyun 溫庭筠
Wen Zhang 溫璋
Wenzong 文宗
Wu Chengsi 武承嗣
Wu Yanxiu 武延秀
Wu Youji 武攸暨
Wu Zhao 武曌
Wuzong 武宗

Xian'an 咸安
Xiangwang 襄王
Xiangyang 襄陽
Xianzong 憲宗
Xie Xiao`e 謝小娥
Xinchang 新昌
Xizong 僖宗
Xuanzong 玄宗
X'uanzong 宣宗
Xue Huaiyi 薛怀義
Xue Shao 薛紹
Xue Wanche 薛万徹
Xue Yaoyin 薛瑤茵
Xue Yuan 薛媛
Xu Jingzong 許敬宗

Yan'an 延安
Yang Guozhong 楊國忠
Yang Yuhuan 楊玉環
Yan Liben 閻立本
Yan Lide 閻立德
Yan Lingbin 顏令賓
yanqing 艷情
Yan Tingzhi 嚴挺之
Yan Zhenqing 顏真卿
Yan Zhiwei 閻知微
Yao Yuehua 姚月華

Yelai yue 夜來樂
Yicheng 宜城
Yidu neiren 宜都內人
Yili 儀禮
Yizhi hua 一支花
yongwu 詠物
youqing 幽情
Yuange xing 怨歌行
Yuan Zhen 元稹
yueyin 月陰
yunshi 詠史
yunü 御女
Yu Shinan 虞世南
Yu Xuanji 魚玄机
Yuzhen 玉真

Zengnei 贈內
Zetian 則天
Zhang Jianzhi 張柬之
Zhangsun Wuji 長孫無忌
Zhang Wencheng 張文誠
Zhang Xingcheng 張行成
Zhang Xun 張巡
Zhang Zhuzhu 張住住
Zhaozong 昭宗
Zheng Xuan 鄭玄
zhiji 知己
zhiyin 知音
zhongren 中人
Zhong Xing 鍾惺
Zhong Ziqi 鍾子祺
Zhongzong 中宗
Zhu Ci 朱泚
Zhuo Wenjun 卓文君
Zi dainei zeng 自代內贈
Ziye ge 子夜歌

Index

ancient style movement, 12
androgyny, 167, 170–71;
    in female poets, 170, 203, 204–05;
    in male poets, 152, 170
An Lushan, 78;
    rebellion, 1, 12, 76, 89, 157

Ban Gu, 7, 92
Ban Jieyu, 34
Ban Zhao, 92, 94
beauty, male and female, 104
betrayal, 110, 190;
    by literati, 111;
    in literature, 109, 132, 143–44, 147, 150
bianwen, 94, 147
body, female, 144, 162, 216;
    division from spirit, 133–34;
    erasure of, 90, 93;
    as factory of words, 184;
    fragmentation of, 90;
    inscription on, 117–18, 183;
    as metonymies of words, 182, 284, 190, 207
Bo Juyi, 79, 104, 106, 107, 148, 208
Book of Changes, 31–32, 39, 64
boudoir lament, 19, 110, 120, 158–59, 160, 161, 163–65, 169, 171, 174, 180, 182, 193, 197, 203, 204, 205, 206, 215;
    and absence, 164, 208;
    against, 209–10;
    boudoir woman, 186, 205, 206, 210, 212, 215;
    of courtesan, 202–03, 208;
    in ethical mode, 161;
    as love poems, 153, 159–60, 161, 170, 172;

    as lyrical convention, 151, 152, 175;
    as political allegory, 33, 152, 154, 169, 170, 174–75, 200, 201
Buddhism, 9, 10, 14–17, 106, 125, 131, 138;
    destruction of, 1, 4, 12;
    as female retreat, 16–17, 90, 95;
    influence on literature, 126, 27;
    Zen, 9, 15–16
Buddhist nun, 50, 51, 114, 122
buyu, 153

cannibalism, 89
categorization/instrumentalization of women, 109, 111, 115, 117
Chang'an, 3, 8, 10, 13, 25–26, 125, 131, 145, 215
chastity, 91, 215;
    against rape, 88–89;
    and loyalty, 89;
    of supernatural women, 136–37, 141
Chen Zi'ang, 64
chuanqi, 125–27, 130–31, 132, 133, 138, 139, 140, 143, 145, 148–49, 162, 166;
    as collective unconscious, 127, 133, 149;
    historical development, 125;
    "Huo Xiaoyu," 143–44, 149;
    "Lihun ji," 133;
    "Liu Yi zhuan," 137–38;
    "Li Wa zhuan," 145, 46, 149;
    "Li Zhangwu zhuan," 133–34;
    logic of, 134, 136, 138, 140, 144, 149;
    "Mingying zhuan," 141;
    "Pei Hang," 137;
    "Renshi zhuan," 136–37;

chuanqi (Continued)
  transference in, 134, 140;
  "Yingying zhuan," 146–50;
  "Zhou-Qin youji," 139–40
Chu Suiliang, 29, 34–36
civil service examinations, 5, 8, 9, 13–14,
    22, 110, 114, 115, 119, 138, 145,
    211;
  consequence of, 99, 216;
  obsession with, 12–13;
codes, for female bodies, 93
communities of women, 196, 197, 216
concubine, 94–97, 107–08, 115;
  concubinage, 96, 97, 98, 101, 107
Confucian calling, 30
Confucianism, 9, 15, 127, 130;
  fusion with Legalism, 28, 30
Confucian wives, 95, 96, 109;
  in literature, 162;
  symbolic position of, 159, 162
Confucius, 29, 42, 107, 139, 154
confusion of desires, 131–32
courtesan-literatus, 204, 205
courtesans, 109, 115–16, 145, 147, 163,
    184, 199;
  in *chuanqi*, 143–46;
  courtesanship, 109, 110;
  and language, 106, 109, 116–17, 118,
    120, 153;
  and literati, 14, 109–111, 114–16, 119,
    143, 210;
  official, 115, 182, 189;
  plight of, 199–200;
  as poets, 167, 182, 188, 198, 202, 203,
    211, 213;
  as professional women, 114, 120–21;
  relation with patrons, 116, 117, 120–21,
    201, 202
cross-dressing, 211;
  of desires, 121, 144;
  in writing, 170, 204–05

daughters:
  as exchange-gift, 45;
  filial, 50, 90;
  Yellow Emperor's, 45.
  See also princess

desexualization, of women, 93, 95, 97
desire, as transference, 49
dialectic:
  of the self, 16;
  of subject and object, 111;
  of suppression, 59
Di Renjie, 63–64, 72
discourse:
  history, 88–89;
  memoir, 95;
  poetry, 95, 119–20, 148, 181, 211;
  power of, 89, 95, 162, 174, 197;
  tombstone inscription, 94–95, 115, 120,
    182;
  and women, 95, 116, 117
divorce, 86, 94, 97, 107
Dong Zhongshu, 28, 31
Du Fu, 79, 157–58, 161
Du Mu, 79, 116–17
Dunhuang document, 84–86, 94
Du You, 108

ecriture feminine, 170, 193, 206
embroidery, 190–92
emperor. *See* Son of Heaven
Empress Wei, 40, 48, 54, 67, 70, 89, 216
Empress Wenxian, 69, 97–98
Ennin, 1–4, 9
entertainers, 115, 163, 167;
  imperial, 115, 121
erasure of history, 69–72, 180
eros, masculine, 174
erotics of editing, 180, 181, 182, 194
essentialism, 193
ethical codes:
  internalization of, 89, 91;
  pairings, 31;
  tightening of, 54–55, 89, 215–16
eunuchs, 26–28, 37–39, 43, 76, 156–57
exile, of women, 84, 96;
  from language, 68, 73, 80

Fang Xuanling, 41
fanzhen, 12
female consciousness, 162, 174, 187, 190,
    193, 197, 204, 206
female desires, 9, 19, 97, 99, 121, 135,

138, 144, 146, 148, 161, 164, 181, 182, 213, 216;
   of courtesans, 120–21, 145;
   and impropriety, 54;
   in writing, 206, 207
female persona, 151, 152, 155, 158, 161, 167, 169, 170, 171, 174, 175, 181, 186, 197
female personification, 167, 170, 174, 202
female subjectivity, 162, 182;
   split of, 10, 188, 193, 197, 211
female tradition, 179, 181, 194, 196, 197, 206;
   contamination of, 205;
   problematics of, 190, 193, 202
female virtue, deformity as, 90
feminine voice, usurpation of, 151, 152, 159, 160, 165, 167, 168, 170, 202, 205
fetishism, 108, 117, 119, 134, 180, 182, 183, 184, 189, 199
filial piety, over conjugal love, 107
foot-binding, 215
foreign influence, 8–9, 10–12;
   resistance to, 12–13
foreign policy, 12, 51
fox women, 131, 136–37, 144

gaze, male, 161, 188, 189, 193;
   See also women, conditioned
gender:
   confusion of, 172, 173–74;
   politics, 180, 200;
   stratification of, 170, 175, 204,217
gendered expression, 160, 161, 168, 171, 172, 203, 204, 208
ghosts, women as, 133–136, 144, 150, 164–65;
   psychology for, 135, 136
guilt, male, 134, 144, 149, 150

Han Fei, 30
Han Yu, 5–6, 9, 12, 106, 148
harem, hierarchy within, 87
heaven's mandate, 9, 29, 30
history, as site of struggle, 40–41
home, as battlefield, 95, 96, 99
homoeroticism, 195–96

ideologies, deployment of, 158
imperial phallus, 37–39, 46–47, 111, 130, 156–57, 158, 207;
   and impotence, 79
imperial verdict, 30
impotence, male, 140
inertia/waiting, and women, 19, 110, 120, 134, 162, 186, 194, 196

Japan, Heian, 50, 144, 147
jealousy: 10, 95, 96, 97–99, 105, 108, 143, 144, 215;
   codes against, 93, 95;
   male, 144;
   of princess, 48;
   as symptom, 98–99
jouissance, feminine, 121, 187, 197

knight-errant, female, 140

lack, the feminine as, 152, 159, 164, 166, 206, 212
language, and women, 179, 183, 184, 190, 199, 204, 210, 213
laughter, women's, 83–84, 94, 187
legal codes, 43, 86–88
Li Bo, 153–55, 156–57, 158–60
Li He, 152, 156, 163–66
Li Jing, 39
Li Longji, 47, 54, 66, 67, 70, 75, 76–77, 78, 79, 153
Li Qingzhao, 216
Li Shangyin, 37, 104, 106, 110, 152, 169–175, 185, 208
Li Shimin, 31, 33–36, 39, 41, 42, 46, 51, 59, 64, 65, 77, 105
   portrait of, 27
literati, 131, 204, 216;
   containment of, 5, 13;
   and courtesans, 105, 115–17, 146;
   dilemma of, 103, 104, 111;
   literati-feminine, 174, 180, 190, 193, 199, 204, 205, 206;
   rise of, 9, 14, 103, 104, 105, 111, 116, 148, 181, 199, 216;
   self-conceit of, 138, 140;
   use of words, 105–06, 109

literature, worship of, 14, 15, 22, 115–16, 183, 199, 216
little-man, the:
  and minister, 42–43;
  and woman, 43
Liu Gongquan, 36
Liu Yuxi, 117
Liu Zhiji, 41
Liu Zongyuan, 6, 12, 106, 192
Li X'ian, 67, 68, 70, 71, 75
Li Ye, 18, 188–89, 213
Li Yuan, 33, 59, 97
Li Zhi, 29, 31, 42, 47, 57, 59, 68, 69, 105
love, romantic, 107, 109–10, 217;
  absence of, 138, 152;
  expression of, 174, 175;
  men in, 169, 172, 208;
  poems, 108, 153, 160, 170;
  women in, 135, 144, 149
lust of the mind, 18, 140

madness:
  of Confucian wives, 98–99;
  of palace maids, 75
male chastity, 130
male concubine, 48, 64–66
male desires, 106, 109–111, 115, 120, 127, 133, 134, 135, 138, 140, 144, 149–50, 153, 158, 159, 160, 161–62, 163, 165, 167, 181, 197;
  problematic of, 106, 108, 217;
  tragic character of, 110
male subjectivity, 158;
  damaged, 99, 111;
  desire vs. decorum, 103, 104;
  and self control, 96
marginal women, 182, 198
marriage, 85–86, 107, 108, 137;
  conjugal relationship, 92–93, 96, 101, 107, 108, 152;
  social definition of, 95
masculinity/femininity, 185, 193, 204
masochism, 160
melancholia, 19, 144, 160, 161
metaphysics, for women, 92
mimicry, 197

minister:
  alienation of, 31, 39–40;
  as concubine, 34–37, 39, 42–43, 157, 158;
  in court session, 26;
  dilemma of, 28–29, 42;
  as heroes/victimized, 40;
  plight/shame of, 29–30, 36–37, 39–40;
  and Son of Heaven, 4–5, 28–29, 31–32, 37, 40, 42–43, 153, 157
minister-concubine complex, 33, 37–42, 152, 153, 155
modern China, 217–18
moon, 188;
  as feminine principle, 185;
  goddess, 86, 185, 187, 197;
  worship, 185–87, 194
motherhood, 88, 90–91
mourning, 144, 151, 160, 164, 167, 169, 172, 174, 175, 181, 186, 193

naming, of women, 91
narcissism, male, 140
nature, civilization against, 22
neo-Confucianism, 14, 215–16
Niu Yingzhen, 182–84, 192–94, 205, 213

object of desire, women as, 147, 155, 175, 186
Oedipus complex, 139
old clans, 8, 14, 103;
  daughters of, 10, 14, 104–05;
  marriage with, 111, 143

palace lament, 155–57
palace women, 26, 40, 73–76, 113, 139–40, 155–57, 182;
  in Buddhist convent, 50, 65;
  of King Wu, 83–84
passion, 146;
  feminine, 133, 135
passivity, and women, 159
patriline, 67
peasant women, 113
performers, women, 113–14
poetry, and power, 40–41
political allegory, of the feminine, 200–02

priestess-courtesan, 18, 182, 208, 209, 212, 213
princess, 113;
  Anle, 47–48, 67;
  desires of, 47–49;
  Jincheng, 51–52;
  as outsiders, 51;
  as pawns, 51–53;
  as priestess, 49–50;
  Taihe, 52–53;
  Taiping, 47, 67
professional women, 113–14

qing, 170, 171
Quan Tang shi, women in, 161
Quan Tang wen, 5, 42
Qu Yuan, 28, 129, 130, 154, 155;
  Lisao, 28, 33, 127, 153, 155

reader, women as, 174
representations of women, 10, 19, 149, 194–98
rhymed prose, 4–5, 129, 131, 138;
  "Dengtuzi haose fu," 130, 207;
  "Gaotang fu," 129;
  "Meiren fu," 130;
  "Xianqing fu," 131

sacrifice, female, 194, 210, 213
sage king, 130
se, 170
self-expression, of women, 203, 213
sexual alchemy, 101–03
sexuality, female repression of, 17, 97
sexual monopoly, male, 17
Shangguan Waner, 181
shrewish wife, 94
silence, and women, 147, 148, 149, 161, 175, 197
Sima Guang, 63, 72
Sima Qian, 7, 154
Sima Xiangru, 130
  and self-control, 43;
  as ultimate lover, 130, 154–55, 156–57;
  as victim, 26–28
Song Ruozhao, 181, 182, 183

Son of Heaven, 5, 9, 31–32, 155, 157, 179, 188;
  anxiety of, 25–29, 39;
suicide, female, 216
supernatural women, 18, 132, 133, 137, 138, 140, 166, 175;
  copulation with, 125, 129, 139;
  domestication of, 131, 165;
  dragon women, 137–38, 141;
  goddess Mt. Wu, 129
Su Xiaoxiao, 164–65, 205
symbolic other, women as, 127–29, 131, 139, 155, 164, 171

Taoism, religious, 8, 9, 14, 17, 19, 131, 138;
  against Buddhism, 9;
  alchemy, 17;
  priestess, 49–50, 114, 115, 121–22, 182, 188, 208;
  sexual yoga, 18–19, 101–13;
  and women, 18
Tao Qian, 131
trafficking, in women, 14, 45, 104, 116–17
training, of women, 83–84, 162
usurpation, by women, 185;
  of patriarchy, 187;
  of political order, 60–61;
  in writing, 207

virgin, as mourner, 90
voyeurism, 151, 160, 166–67, 170, 180, 210;
  voyeur, 199

Wang Qiang, 51, 139
Wang Wei, 106
Wei Zheng, 30, 34–35, 36, 39, 42
Wei Zhuang, 106
Wen Tingyun, 166–68, 208–09
witches, 114, 122
women:
  and abandonment, 19, 148, 151, 154, 157, 161, 181, 190, 194, 200–02, 206
  and alienation, 51, 86, 131, 147;
  as anonymous, 180;

women (*Continued*)
  as commodities, 117, 218;
  inner split, 211;
  and self-censorship, 181;
  and talent, 147, 181
women, conditioned, 186;
  by boudoir lament, 182, 186;
  through ethical canon, 91–93;
  by male gaze, 187–88, 190;
  by women's biographies, 88–91
women's handbooks, 92–94
women's position:
  in family, 91–92;
  in legal codes, 86–88;
  in literary anthology, 180;
  in official history, 88–90
women's status, 87;
  decline of, 14, 80, 99, 102, 104, 105,
    181, 215, 216
writing, and women, 147, 148, 151, 167,
    179, 180, 181, 184, 190, 196, 197,
    202, 206, 207, 216
Wu Zhao, 10, 12, 14, 29, 37, 40, 43, 54,
    57–59, 61–63, 66–67, 80;
  and accomplishment, 72;
  and cruelty, 59–61;
  as empress, 47, 48;
  erasure of, 67–68, 69–72;
  naming of, 70, 71;
  and passion, 64–66;

policies on women, 68–69, 97;
  use of Buddhism, 61–63

Xue Huaiyi, 61, 64–66
Xue Tao, 116, 182, 187, 189, 190, 197,
    199–202, 205–07, 208, 211, 213

Yang Guozhong, 77, 78
Yang Yuhuan, 69, 76–78, 139, 153,
    195;
  and An Lushan, 78;
  death of, 76–77;
  myth of, 78–80
Yan Liben, 36–37;
  painting by, 27
Yan Zhenqing, 36
  calligraphy by, 35
ying-yang, 18, 31–33, 64, 92, 101–103,
    209
Yuan Zhen, 107, 146, 149
yuefu, 152, 158, 181, 206
Yu Shinan, 36
Yu Xuanji, 18, 182, 194–95, 196, 197,
    205, 207–211, 212;
  death of, 184, 210, 212–13

zhiji, 109, 154, 204, 205, 211,
    212
Zhuo Wenjun, 181
ziye ge, 206

About the Author

Jowen Tung was born and raised in Taiwan. She then spent more than a decade in the United States, where she studied in Albany, Ithaca, and New York City, earning her Ph.D. at Columbia University. She now teaches in Hong Kong, dedicating her time to research on feminist cultural critique, trips to China, and creative writings.

Her books of poems and prose works in Chinese (including an extensive collection of fables) are her effort at contributing toward building a strong female tradition. At the present, she is working on her next book, which is essentially a critique on modern lives.